THE BROTHERS
COMPANION

THE STORY BEHIND THE CLASSIC **BBC tv** SERIAL

ROB COPE

ISBN: 978-1-716-25897-8

First published February 2021 by Meddling Monk Media, 251 High Lane, Burslem, Stoke On Trent, Staffordshire ST6 1BH.
meddlingmonk.co.uk   E mail: hammond.transport@virgin.net

Dedicated to Mum, Dad and Howard. With love.

CONTENTS

The Brothers cast circa 1974: (top row) Hilary Tindall, Richard Easton (middle row) Patrick O'Connell, Jennifer Wilson, Julia Goodman (bottom row) Jean Anderson, Gabrielle Drake, Robin Chadwick

INTRODUCTION: WELCOME TO THE 1970S

The 1970s should perhaps be subtitled "the decade that taste forgot". It is a decade full of contradictions. For the people of the not-so-United Kingdom it would mean strikes, out of control inflation, and a Northern Ireland pushed to the brink of civil war. On another flip of the coin it heralded a cultural expression which welcomed glam rock, disco and punk. What are we to make of a decade which seemingly decided that chocolate, cream and orange went together so well as to decorate our living rooms in a whirl of crazy patterns on curtains and wallpaper? In the month a brand new serial called *The Brothers* went before the cameras, the UK experienced the change over to a new currency system. Goodbye pounds, shillings and pence and hello decimalisation. The UK was on the verge of joining the "Common Market", we were aligning ourselves with our continental European neighbours in a big way with trade routes opening up and new opportunities for businesses both sides of the English Channel. However, the spectre of discontentment at home as the strength of the Unions made itself felt, threatened to derail our new found freedom for trade.

During the life of *The Brothers* on television, over a mere five years, our little island would experience the three-day week. Industrial action by miners had resulted in a Conservative government – led by Edward Heath – restricting commercial usage of electricity. It came shortly after an oil crisis which effectively slowed down much of Europe for several months. In Northern Ireland, "Bloody Sunday" in Derry was a low point of political unrest and activism by anti-coalition forces and the British Army. Added to a stock market crash which pushed inflation to unprecedented levels, socially and politically the early 1970s were not a pretty picture.

Is it any wonder that people wanted a bit of escapism? And the week that *The Brothers* was first broadcast, there was no shortage of entertainment on the three national television channels. Saturday nights were spearheaded by that most flamboyant of *Doctor Who's* Jon Pertwee reigning supreme on BBC 1 fighting The Sea Devils, Dick Emery was awful, but we liked him, donning a number of outrageous disguises with his long running comedy sketch series and of course *Match Of The Day* finished off the evening for sport addicts. The Sunday early evening 7.25pm slot which would later become associated with *The Brothers* success was occupied by Engelbert Humperdink in a variety series, his guests this week being The Goodies and Irish crooner Dana. As the week progressed we could find BBC1 giving us a diet of police dramas, both *Z Cars* (celebrating a tenth anniversary) and its spin-off *Softly, Softly: Task Force*. There were also repeats of *Star Trek* to be found for the sci-fi hungry. Galton and Simpson's masterpiece *Steptoe and Son* was now in full colour glory, as the Steptoe family gather for wake of a loved one in yet another classic episode. A glance at the TV Times for the week commencing 4th March 1972 – an Emergency edition in black and white due to power cuts brought about by strikes - confirms that nothing could topple Monday and Wednesday's visits to *Coronation Street* for ITV. Where soap legends Annie Walker, Bet Lynch, Elsie Tanner, Ena Sharples and the rest provided a working class cultural beacon which still resonates to this day. Perhaps not as culturally significant, but certainly with its own army of admirers, *Crossroads* was holding forth four times a week as Noele Gordon strived to get some order at the Crossroads Motel of the title. Among its other high profile offerings during this week were the bawdy comedy *On The Buses* and class drama *Upstairs, Downstairs*. It was into this television landscape that *The Brothers* was thrust by the BBC schedulers. For chart enthusiasts, the number one song on *Top Of The Pops* was Nilsson's plaintive "Without You".

Let's be clear about this. *The Brothers* is now a period piece. Just as much as its BBC contemporaries *Poldark* and *The Onedin Line* were about the 18th and 19th centuries. The tone of the drama, its attitudes and outlook are very much rooted in the early 1970s. There is very little currency given to multi-cultural casting. This is white middle-class territory with a healthy dose of the working man in order to appeal to a wider demographic. However, if you can bear to look past some of the fashions, it is also a programme of great story telling. *The Brothers* is very much a serial, the creators Gerard Glaister and Norman Crisp actively drawing you in, making you want to tune into what happens to the Hammond family week after week. Many people describe *The Brothers* as 'a soap' and indeed it could be viewed that way. Glaister and Crisp certainly knew how to combine elements of soap with drama production, creating their own take on serial television. The show managed to capture the mood of the time whilst ensuring a healthy dose of intrigue and conflict within the family haulage business setting of the series.

My own personal journey with Hammond Transport started with the repeats on the satellite channel UK Gold in the mid-1990s. After several viewings of poor VHS copies, I pestered Colin Baker and Jennifer Wilson for insider knowledge on the series, and bemoaned the lack of accurate information about the show publicly available. I knew then that if anyone was going to investigate its phenomenal 1970s popularity, it was going to have to be me. What you hold in your hands is the result of several years of on/off research and writing. Very few of *The Brothers* production files exist at the BBC's Written Archive Centre. So the memories of those who have contributed to this book stand as a testament to the making of the series. I hope the information included, and the memories shared, shed some light on the little bit of television history that is *The Brothers* and also act as a companion to the long awaited full DVD set that has now been released.

Rob Cope
January 2021

The author with Brian Peck and Jennifer Wilson
Cannes 2017

The original Hammond family at the start of recording in 1971:
Richard Easton, Jean Anderson, Glyn Owen, Robin Chadwick

BROTHERS IN ARMS: GERRY & NORMAN

The Brothers owes its genesis to two gentlemen. Both of whom were to become synonymous with popular television. Gerard Glaister and Norman James Crisp, using the professional moniker 'N.J.' Together they were responsible for some of the most popular television to air in the UK during the 1960s, 70s and 80s. Two giants of the genre.

Gerry Glaister with Jennifer Wilson

John Leslie Gerard Glaister – or Gerry as he was known to one and all - was born in Hong Kong on 21st December 1915 where his father was stationed as a Royal Navy surgeon during the first World War. He came from a family with a medical background, his grandfather held the chair in Forensic Medicine at Glasgow University. After schooling in Taunton, Gerry surprised the family by not following them into medicine and having showed great promise as an amateur actor he was accepted by RADA. Following graduation, he progressed to more experience around the thriving repertory countries to be found. His West End acting debut came playing Renaldo and Osric Hamlet at the Whitehall Theatre, in 1939. But this was on the eve of war, and with Hitler rampaging through Europe, Gerry applied for pilot training with the RAF. With only 11 hours of practice in an ancient biplane, he took up his first posting with a regiment in Norfolk. He flew his first mission in August 1940 in a Bristol Blenheim bomber heading for Brittany, Gerry could not get through to the target however and instead took his bomb load to the recently invaded Guernsey. Using cloud cover Gerry unleashed his deadly load on the island destroying a Nazi plane waiting on a runway. The ground defences were quick to return anti-aircraft fire but Glaister got the Blenheim back home despite having a large hole in one wing. It was the start of many courageous missions as a pilot which would take him to the Western Desert, Tobruk and Derna in Libya and the Italian campaign against the facist might of Benito Mussolini. On one mission to Libya his engine was hit and Gerry was forced to fly for two and a half hours at an altitude of just one hundred feet, finally landing with laess than one minute of fuel left. His tenacity was recognised when he joined the newly formed Photo Intelligence Squadron taking low level photographs of enemy positions in Hurricanes and

Spitfires. It was for services to military intelligence that he was awarded the Distinguished Flying Cross medal. After more than 100 missions, Gerry was posted back to England and worked as a flying instructor, and subsequently he joined the Air Ministry on intelligence duties based in Paris as Deputy Chief of Targets. At the conclusion of the Second World War, the by now 30 year old Glaister was posted to Egypt to service with the Joint Intelligence Staff. But throughout this time, the theatre remained in his blood and after two years in Egypt he chose to return to his home land, where he chose to sideline acting by running theatre companies in Luton and Aylesbury respectively. He was then offered the chance of running the Chesterfield Repertory Company in 1954 where he gave David McCallum and Nigel Davenport their first acting roles.

Whilst working in repertory Gerry had used his skills to write plays for his companies, and one of them – written with Gavin Holt – *Take Away The Lady* was adapted by BBC Television and broadcast on 26th April 1953. The Radio Times gave only the hint that "The action takes place in Johnny Fellowes' flat in Mayfair" as to its content. With the advent of ITV in 1955, the loss of talent from the BBC meant they were forced to expand their staffing and the following year Gerry applied for, and won, a place on the BBC TV Directors' Course. His talents and drive were immediately recognised and he was offered a one year contract as a director / producer. At that time staff were expected to multi task and perform the dual roles in production of what were mostly, at this time, one-off television plays. Gerry never took a permanent position as a staff producer or director, preferring to operate on year to year freelance contracts. This allowed him to keep the copyrights of any formats he subsequently created. As a staff producer at the BBC copyright would otherwise have automatically passed to his employers, it proved a canny move. With his producers hat on, Gerry dived into production of a range of television series for his new employers. *Widewake* (1957) saw a jewel thief released from prison intent of recovering his loot, *Big Guns* (1958) a series of stories set around London folk, and the early soap *Starr And Company* (1959) based around the unlikely premise of a family buoy making company. Sadly it wasn't as buoyant as the subject, lasting only a few months. But by then Gerry was off producing more one off plays in the BBC's *Sunday Night Theatre* strand. The thriller serial *The Widow Of Bath* (1959) and *The Men From Room 13* (1959), a series of crime stories, came under the egis of Glaister's producing talent. Followed by a drama documentary *Chasing The Dragon* (1960) about the Eastern drugs trade which took him back to his birthplace Hong Kong. Robert Hardy and Francis Matthews led the cast of *The Dark Island* (1962), a six part serial about an unexploded torpedo in the Hebrides. After directing a number of episodes of the highly popular new detective series *Maigret*, Gerry was back on familiar territory with *Moonstrike* (1963) set around espionage in central Europe during World War Two. It was after directing an adaptation of Robert Louis Stephenson's *Kidnapped* (1963) that Gerry moved onto *Doctor Finlay's Casebook*. The series was a massive success starring Bill Simpson as the eponymous Doctor Finlay, practitioner in a fictional Scottish town during the 1920s. Gerry directed a number of episodes before being asked to occupy the producers chair for this lauded serial. One of the writers on this serial was a man named Norman Crisp. The meeting of these two minds would fuel creative fires in them both.

Norman James Crisp was born in Southampton on 11th December 1923. Like Glaister he had served in the RAF between 1943 and 1947 although the two had never crossed paths. Upon his demob Norman reportedly went through a number of employments – a taxi company manager, Marks and Spencer management trainee and a typewriter salesman. But he had a yearning to be a writer, and had some short stories accepted by Reveille. He began supplying regular stories to the influential magazine John Bull and the American publication Saturday Evening Post, before approaching the medium of television with his scripts. His earliest produced work was in 1959. a half hour thriller set in the early hours at the offices of a provincial radio taxi service. It starred Andree Melly, Ballard Berkeley and Brian Wilde. The success of this play encouraged Norman to turn full time writer and his next play *The Dark Man* was also about the taxi business, but more specifically a black cab driver Robert Smith (played by Earl Cameron) facing discrimination at work. Crisp furiously turned out one off plays for the BBC and these included *A Kind Of Strength* (1961), *The Alderman* (1962), *The Man Who Opted Out* (1962), and *The Stepfather* (1962). He simultaneously supplied ITV with plays too: *The Two On The Beach*

(1961), *The Gentle Assassin* (1962) and *Danger Zone* (1963). By now Crisp's skill with plotting and character was established and he found himself in great demand. Not least for scripting the BBC's soap *Compact*, set in the offices of a woman's glossy magazine for which he wrote 29 episodes. "It was only after I sold three stories to the Evening Post for £2000 in a comparatively short space of time that I decided to become a full time writer," Norman told the press in 1974. "I turned my attention to television, and at that time I had no idea how to go about breaking into the media. I eventually wrote to the BBC with the outline of one play and they told me to write it and submit it for consideration. There was no mention of an ordered commission. That first play was a 30 minute slot called *People Of The Night*. This was about a radio taxi company and I obviously used my knowledge and experiences for the trade when I wrote the play. In those early years I made full use of my experiences but working for the series group in television you have to become an expert on many subjects which require a great deal of work. The subjects are wide spread from law, police work, doctors to espionage."

Crisp became a major contributor to *Dixon Of Dock Green*, the police serial starring Jack Warner which was a staple on the BBC for over 21 years. Between 1964 and 1975 Crisp furnished the show with 66 scripts of crime drama, an astonishing output. Meeting Gerry Glaister on *Doctor Finlay's Casebook* would provide Crisp with a creative partner who had the drive and the talent to match his own.

'

Norman 'N.J.' Crisp

Gerry and Norman worked together on several teleivison drama projects before finding their own particular niche. *The Revenue Men*, a series about customs officers, was produced by Glaister and for which Crisp wrote a handful of episodes. However, they collaborated fully on their next project which was to provide Glaister with the first of his co-created hits. *The Expert* which debuted on 5th July 1968 was focused on the work of forensic scientist Dr. John Hardy, played by Marius Goring. Glaister's family background undoubtedly contributed to his understanding of the subject (Gerry even employed his Uncle as a consultant to the series). It became pretty clear they had a hit on their hands. The opening episode was described in the Radio Times thus:

A forensic expert can become involved in crime in many ways. Often he will act for the police, but there are times when he can be called in by other interested parties. Dr. John Hardy is no exception and even when he has no particular liking for the people employing him, he will always ferret out the facts. When these facts do' not prove to be advantageous to his clients he can find himself in a difficult position. Three bullets, a dead man, and £50,000 in insurance - this is the background to tonight's episode. Troubles arise when Dr. Hardy discovers the Unknown Factor.

Naturally Norman Crisp provided the opening episodes, setting the template for subsequent writers to follow. The combination of John Hardy's demanding work and his personal life with his wife Dr. Jo Hardy (Ann Morrish) were the early beginnings of a format centring on these two aspects which would combine brilliantly in the coming years. Dudley Simpson wrote the theme music for the show which would eventually run for three series and 52 episodes (and revived for a further 10 episodes in 1976). With Crisp writing for various series and Glaister producing a further spy drama, *Codename,* they were scratching around for another format they could sell to the BBC. "We worked very closely on *The Expert* for the BBC," Crisp told TV Life. "I think we were both casting around for a new formula. Then we flipped through the Yellow Pages for inspiration and there it was – road haulage! Drama at board room level, and in the depots, drivers and management – and their women. The more we discussed the theme, the more the possibilities grew. Gerry suggested three brothers who had inherited their father's business." In another 1976 interview with the Liverpool Echo, Crisp expanded upon those early days. "We had both separately toyed with the idea of adapting a novel for television. The BBC do beautiful dramatisations but they're nearly all in period. We both preferred the idea of something modern. Then we asked each other – why bother with a book? Why not create something entirely new? First we worked out the characters and family relationships. Then we had to decide what sort of business it should be. Boat-building appealed at first. But it wasn't very exciting. Also, we would have to keep going to the coast for filming. That could be awkward. We sat in Gerry's flat and flicked through the Yellow Pages until the idea of a transport business struck us almost simultaneously. So you see, we didn't start out as Hammond Transport at all. That slotted into place later. Our original idea was a series of programmes about a tightly knit family business. We thought, if we were lucky, it might run to 30 or 40 episodes. But it's gone way beyond our wildest dreams. They've screened about 90 episodes already I believe and it's still going strong."

The germ of the idea was backed by the Head Of Drama, Shaun Sutton, who trusted Glaister and Crisp's track record to produce the goods. It was indeed a wild card. There were no detectives, or hospital settings or mucky streets up North. A haulage company on the face of it didn't inspire the setting for some heightened drama. But Gerry and Norman knew what they were about, how they could develop the characters and more importantly how to get it to the screen. It all started with a mistress. Gerry and Norman knew exactly who would play her and even named the character after her. The depot had just opened at Hammond Transport Services.

GETTING THE HAMMONDS ON THE ROAD

With *The Brothers* having been pitched and commissioned, there then followed the nose to the grindstone hard graft to get the show before the cameras. Norman Crisp was already committed to writing another series for the BBC, *Spy Trap*, so to lighten his load it was decided that respected script writer Eric Paice would pen half of the ten episodes. Prior to starting work on *The Brothers*, Paice had scripted two episodes of *The Expert* for Gerard Glaister. Paice had a long history of creating and scripting popular series and so was perfectly placed to deliver strong scripts for the new project. It was decided that Crisp would handle the writing duties on the first five episodes, and Paice would pen the remaining five. As the first scripts were delivered and the format of the show established, Glaister along with Ronnie Wilson, who would direct half the episodes in the series including the very first, turned their attentions to the casting. Wilson was a Canadian who had come to Britain as an actor in 1952, but subsequently found a calling as a television director for the BBC. He had worked for Glaister on several episodes of *The Expert*. Like Glaister and Crisp, he was up to his neck in *The Brothers* from the off. Getting the casting right is crucial to any series. Whilst a chemistry between actors can never be guaranteed, finding the right look and performance can make or break a show. Gerry Glaister and Norman Crisp had pretty much decided on the two leading ladies before the casting process started in earnest. For the family matriarch Mary Hammond, the duo looked no further than veteran actress Jean Anderson. Then 63 years old, Anderson had been at the forefront of British theatre and television for forty years. She had extensive experience in all aspects of her chosen profession from the jaunty music hall of the Players Theatre to a leading lady with the famous Gate Theatre in Dublin. Taking in numerous West End appearances and roles in classic movies such as *The Barretts of Wimpole Street*, *The Brave Don't Cry* and *A Town Called Alice*. There can be little doubt that her angular features and ability to play repression were perfect for the role of Mary.

Her nemesis in *The Brothers* was given to 38 year old Jennifer Wilson. Wilson had been something of a Shakespearean starlet at the beginning of her career, crystal clear diction and pretty looks made her a popular choice in the Bard's plays. As part of the celebrated Old Vic company she played many of Shakespeare's heroines which included a spell on Broadway in *Troilus and Cressida*. Jennifer was no stranger to television either having had an early success as Kate Nickelby in *Nicholas Nickelby* for the BBC. She had cemented this early sparkle with regular roles in the popular series of the day *Compact* and *Special Branch*.

Key castings were of course the eponymous Brothers. The production needed three actors who would embody distinct categories of individual. The working class elder brother, the career focussed sensible middle sibling and the youngest playboy graduate. For the no-nonsense straight talking Edward they found their man in 43 year old Glyn Owen. He had a strong background in theatre, having played the West End and New York, as well as a solid CV in television. He had been the popular Irish doctor Paddy O'Meara in *Emergency Ward 10* for four years and Norman Lindley in several episodes of *Coronation Street*, thus he was well remembered and liked by the viewing audience. But most crucially he was a powerful actor, and could handle the major bust ups in and out of the Hammond board room that the series would require.

For the role of Brian Hammond they turned to 38 year old Canadian Richard Easton. Easton had been brought to England on a scholarship to study drama in 1953 and quickly established himself as one of the finest stage actors of his generation. He found himself playing the classics opposite a succession of Knights and Dames of the theatre including John Gielgud, Alec Guinness, Ralph Richardson and Peggy Ashcroft. His television pedigree wasn't quite so strong, having appeared in guest roles in a number of series but without finding a regular role in anything. This was largely due to his stage commitments, but with *The Brothers*, the television audience would soon experience the fine acting talent of Easton. Gerard Glaister had used him in an episode of *The Expert* and remembered the tall and talented Easton when it came to casting *The Brothers*.

The trio of younger Hammonds were completed by someone who, by his own admission, had been struggling to find work. Robin Chadwick was a 32 year old New Zealander who had been studying accountancy before heading to the UK in 1964 to study for the stage at LAMDA. He found himself playing opposite Terence Stamp at the Bush Theatre and in *Saint Joan* at the Mermaid Theatre. Screen appearances to that point had included small roles in two Shakespearean extravaganzas, with Nicol Williamson in *Hamlet* and Charlton Heston in *Julius Ceasar*. He had also been seen as P.C. White in a series of *Waugh On Crime* plays for the BBC. Chadwick was up for the challenge of playing David Hammond, being a leading man in a prime time BBC drama was definitely a step up for him in terms of exposure and he grasped his chance to make an impression on the new show.

Robin Chadwick as PC White with Clive Swift as Inspector Waugh in *Waugh On Crime* **(BBC, 1970).**
Swift would later appear in *The Brothers* **as Griffith Trevelyan.**

A key role was Barbara, the illegitimate 17 year old daughter of Jennifer Kingsley. 20 years old Julia Goodman was the daughter of theatrical parents. She had managed a few worthy appearances on the small screen including *Up Pompeii*, *Z Cars* and *Owen M.D.* The ability to look younger was key to the casting process, but Julia also brought with her a strength to the scenes which would establish Barbara's inner trauma at finding out she had known her father all too briefly when her parentage is revealed.

The producer didn't have far to look for the role of Brian's wayward wife Ann. Hilary Tindall was married to Robin Lowe, literary agent for Norman Crisp. 33 years old at the time of filming the first episode, she proved perfect as the sultry schemer who pushed Brian to better himself and, when not getting her own way, could be an arch bitch. It was a role that was to make her both hated and loved in equal measure.

Much thought had been put into the supporting roles in order to make the show as realistic as possible. Three major positions that needed filling were discussed in a character breakdown document.

```
BILL RILEY
Probably goes all the way through the ten episodes.
Ep 1 - film only. Ep 2 - film and studio Ep 3 - film only
Aged 55. Drives. Senior lorry driver with the firm. Independent minded,
no fool. Has dignity, strength and a certain amount of stubbornness.
Representative of the men's point of view.


JILL
Ep 1 - studio only. Possibly Ep 3 - studio only.
Aged 21. Shapely blonde (though could be dark). Upper class. Preferably
tall, glamorous. Sense of comedy. One good studio scene in each episode
opposite Robin Chadwick.


PETER LOWMAN
Ep 2 - film and studio
Aged 19. Drives an open sports car. Middle class. Nice looking (though not
startlingly attractive). Regular boyfriend of Barbara. Normally sexy and
some (though limited) experience. A good supporting part.
```

The role of Bill Riley was handed to a massively experienced actor and playwright Derek Benfield. The 45 year old Yorkshire-man had already scripted episodes of *Z Cars* and *Dixon Of Dock Green* for the BBC. In addition he made his mark as a screen actor in *Coronation Street* and the cult children's serial *Timeslip* to name but two of many small screen appearances up to that point. His brash northern delivery was perfect for the no nonsense Bill Riley and he quickly became a favourite both on screen and off.

Auditions were held on Friday 14th January 1971 for the roles of Peter and Jill. Those seen for the role of Jill were: Rula Lenska, Gabrielle Drake and Fiona Kendall. Whilst in the frame for Peter were Gregory Phillips, Michael Osborne, Philip Trewinnard, Michael Wennink and John Tordoff. Despite a note that he had only done walk on work previously, Peter Trewinnard was considered the best candidate for Peter. Gabrielle Drake had rather more experience, having scored a big success as the purple haired Gay Ellis in Gerry Anderson's cult hit *U.F.O.* for ITV following nearly a decade of guest roles in many small screen series. They were both booked accordingly.

The principal cast were brought together for the very first time for a pre-filming rehearsal read through and 'general get together' on 29th January 1971 in conference room 7064 of Television Centre. Although all had attended costume fittings prior to this, this was the first time all the booked artists gathered together with producer and director. This was followed by a photo call in the basement of Television Centre from which the end title graphics would be created. It was a fairly jolly affair as mother met sons, and mistress met the widow for the first time. Location recording commenced on Monday 1st February with cameraman Elmer Cossey assigned to capture the action on 16mm film. A coach was laid on from Television Centre for all actors needed in these scenes which departed at 8.30am. Some 90 minutes later and the camera was turning on the very first scene of *The Brothers* which was the funeral of Robert Hammond. This was filmed at Teddington Cemetry, with extras required for additional mourners and pall bearers. Gabriel Woolf was cast as the Priest at the internment, with Brian's children in attendance played by Dominic Christian (Nigel) and Nicola Moloney (Carole). It was a dull and cold winters morning but everything seemed to go to schedule. The BBC had come to an arrangement with the Parks Department of the Richmond Borough Council that a fee of £20 per day would be charged by the department for use of the cemetery. The following day saw the production team descend on East Molesey in Surrey, just 5 miles from the cemetery. It was here that the producer and his team had found the locations for Mary's impressive residence: Ravenswood House (no. 39) on Palace Road. Just a mile away, in Upper Palace Road, 'Pineta' (no. 100) provided the more modest dwelling of Brian and Ann. Wednesday 3rd February saw the unit return to Teddington cemetery and onto Canbury Gardens in Kingston for additional scenes. For the major location of Hammond Transport's depot, the producers chose Ralph Hilton Transport Services at Lombard Wall, Greenwich SE7. This busy location was some 53 miles from the relatively quiet roads of East Molesey. In many ways Ralph Hilton was the inspiration for the show. He had started with one vehicle in 1954 and built up a formidable haulage company, which at the time *The Brothers* commenced production had grown to a fleet of 1,200 lorries housed at several depots throughout the UK. The Greenwich base of Hilton wasn't ideal, the coming and going of actual working lorries would disrupt the filming frequently, as would noise from the busy roads surrounding the depot. However it had the right look and feel to it. The BBC graphics boys devised logos for Hammond Transport and gave the depot a make-over when filming was required. Conveniently the lorries there were all emblazoned with 'H.T.S.' on the side however it was something of a mixed blessing. Gerry Glaister knew that having the Hilton lorries so recognisable would lead to accusations of unfair advertising from other hauliers, so the BBC graphics department disguised lorries in the Hammond livery for close up shots. The depot location was kept a secret from the public, the BBC were always careful never to give the secret away to enquiries about where the yard was to be found.

The mighty juggernaut that was *The Brothers* was off and running. Location filming and studio recording at Television Centre continued at a feverish pace until June, when all material was finally in the can. Everyone hoped that they had a hit on their hands. The feeling was among everyone involved that the scripts were excellent and that the cast and production crew had delivered. It had been a mammoth undertaking co-ordinating the rehearsals, extensive location shooting and the studio sessions, but with the kind of meticulous planning that goes into creating a television series, the story of the Hammond family was captured on videotape. Once the final edits had been agreed on between producer and director, it would be up to the BBC schedulers to decide when the British public would be introduced to Hammond Transport Services.

But shortly before the end of the recording sessions came word that the BBC wasn't going to take up the option on the actors contracts. Even before the episodes had gone to air, BBC management had deemed Hammond Transport not worthy of a further road test. After one, still to be broadcast, series the lorries of Hammond's had seemingly reached the end of the road. And it was a dead end.

BBC reference photos circa 1971 for Ralph Hilton
lorries needing Hammond Transport graphics

1971: Robin Chadwick, Glyn Owen, Richard Easton

SERIES ONE (1972)

The end of production on *The Brothers* in June 1971 was subdued. The cast and production team were informed by visting BBC hierarchy not to expect a further series to be commissioned. The feeling was within the Corporation was that it was a 'one series' kind of project and executives didn't have confidence there would be enough interest in it to merit further production outlay.

Everyone involved was resolute, if a little downbeat, but satisfied that they had all given their best to the show. As the summer became the autumn there was no sign of the BBC schedulers assigning a broadcast slot for the ten part series. Weeks turned into months. As 1971 gave way to 1972, and still there was no sign of it appearing on BBC1, onlookers could have been forgiven for thinking the BBC had shelved it indefinitely. Then out of the blue the show was suddenly given its chance. *The Brothers* would occupy a Friday evening slot commencing 10th March. It was a slot that had previously hosted the American import *Ironside*. Sandwiched between an episode of Carla Lane's Scouse sit-com *The Liver Birds* and the *9 O'Clock News*, it debuted to a fairly unsuspecting audience. The opposition came from the current affairs magazine *The Money Programme* on BBC 2 and more significantly would occupy the last section of the popular detective series *Jason King* (7.30pm-8.30pm) on ITV and run into the American import *The Jimmy Stewart Show* (8.30pm-9pm). The debut of the show was heralded with a feature in the BBC's listing mouthpiece Radio Times. Madeleine Kingsley (a fortuitous surname) talked to Glyn, Richard and Robin about playing the squabbling Hammond siblings. Glyn Owen told her "[Edward is] nothing like me. I dislike his streak of violence." Although what violent act he was referring to remains glossed over. Glyn did though bemoan Edward's lack of interest in women. "I am hoping for a sequel where Edward swans around the Cote d'Azur" he says. Meanwhile Richard Easton had his own take on Brian: "I liked him because he had a quality of incredible tenacity which I lack. Take the way he holds onto his very difficult wife Ann, who never stops screaming at him to earn more money. But Hilary Tindall, who plays Ann, is so beautiful and nice it makes Brian's adoration credible."

The Stage newspaper leapt in with a review of the first episode. James Towler noted that the series had high production values with its mixture of studio and location material, but was quick to note "But what I found rather harder to grasp was the fact that the wife, nor any of the family, had any idea what was going on. Surely, in a family business of all businesses, someone would have spilled the beans." Edward was described by Towler as "Quick tempered and impetuous" whilst Brian earned the label "distinctly wet". David though was classed as "Good managerial material once he gets over his birds and booze phase." He goes on to note "They struck me as somewhat stereotyped and could well have walked off the set of *Hadleigh* as could their elegant mother." The ITV series *Hadleigh*, about a wealthy landowner played by Gerald Harper, had featured a guest appearance by Richard Easton just two weeks previously. Praise was reserved for one cast member in particular, "The only person to invoke any real interest was Mrs. Kingsley who, it seemed, had been a Miss all the time. Jennifer Wilson is in her element in this kind of part. Indeed, I recall well her fine interpretation of a similar role in the classic *Man Of Our Times*. I suspect that her Mrs. Kingsley could well prove to be a major focal point as the serial is developed." Towler was in an optimistic mood as he ended his review by declaring "I am sure this serial is going to keep a lot of people indoors on Friday evenings during the next couple of months."

How right the perceptive Mr. Towler proved to be. It seemed the great British public cottoned on quickly to the Hammond family and their toils. Ratings were healthy and gathered momentum as the broadcasts progressed. The BBC mailbags were overflowing with questions and opinions at what the Hammond family were getting up to. Something was in the air. The BBC Audience Research report consolidated this, estimating the viewing audience as 17.1% of the United Kingdom's population. Of those that took part in the survey 58% found it 'entertaining', 70% 'easy to understand', 64% 'excellent plot' and 46% 'definitely out of the ordinary'. The report went on to deliver that generally it was felt to be a 'punchy start' and 'a worthy successor to *The Onedin Line*' which was a familiar fixture of the coveted Sunday evening drama slot and had debuted on the BBC the previous year. However there were reservations from some. 'A small minority were less enthusiastic, mainly because the episode was too slow-moving and even melodramatic for their taste.' It further stated 'Some viewers felt it was all over-acted very slightly'. However it concluded on a more positive note stating 'Jean Anderson and Glyn Owen won most praise, but Jennifer Wilson was also very good it was thought.'

Mary Hammond seemed to be the one character everyone had an opinion on. Mary had married Robert Hammond when they were both young, and he started out his haulage business with very little money. Things were tight and the eldest brother Edward was pressed into service as soon as he was old enough. Some years later Brian came along when the firm had found its feet, and finally David being the youngest saw only the trappings of success for the family business and he was indulged accordingly. Mary had two sides to her. She could be kind, thoughtful and a loyal friend. But if she thought it necessary she could equally be manipulative, intrusive and occasionally vindictive. Certainly as far as Jennifer Kingsley was concerned, there was no greater public enemy.

Although she played the stuffy and often devious matriarch Mary Hammond to the hilt in front of the cameras, Jean Anderson was a hugely popular figure in *The Brothers* extended family. She liked to laugh, liked a drink and liked a flutter on the horses even more. She became the real life maternal figure for the ensemble, and was often to be seen dishing out advice to her co-stars on personal and professional matters. She was the go-to woman. Having made her television debut in 1947, Jean brought twenty five years of screen experience to bear on the role of Mary. Recalling her early days in live television, Jean described them to the Birmingham Evening Mail: "A very good baptism. Nothing could ever frighten me again after living through some of those early plays." Remembering one particular engagement when she had to age from 70 to 30 and back again she said: "I took off my glasses and my shawl to drop forty years and just acted a different age. We did everything live. One performance of a play on Sunday. Another on Thursday – presumably for people who missed the first performance. To do a close up, they put your head into a sort of hood fixed to the camera. Changing scenes, as everything was live, was a matter of running through the cameras and cables, from one studio to the next, changing your clothes as you ran. It was very exciting though, being in on something that might catch on in a big way." Jean's favourite roles to this point were in two versions of *The Railway Children* in 1951 and 1957 respectively. "It's 20 years since the last version was shown," she told the reporter. "But I still get people talking to me about it remembering every little detail. Most actors don't like working with children, but they have always been lucky for me."

But of course it was Mary Hammond that was to be a lasting image in Jean's career. "A lot of women want to know where I buy my clothes. They aren't actually mine, but they are to my taste. I help choose them. I suppose there is some of me in Mary. Just two writers have been responsible for the whole series, and they work closely with the cast. Knowing us, they tend to take bits of us and add them to the characters. When I was offered the part I didn't know how successful it was going to be, but I had a hunch. Mainly because it was the best first script I had ever seen. There's an interesting happy cast to work with – that helps too." Jean's new found fame as Mary started to get her a lot of attention when she was out and about, she reports constantly being stopped and asked questions about the show. "They want to know what is going to happen next, will I let Edward marry Jennifer? The degree of public involvement is amazing. And it happens in the most surprising places. In the Highlands of Scotland I was practically mobbed, and on the Isle Of Man too. People seem to feel part of the Hammond family. It doesn't worry me. I enjoy talking to people. The only time it becomes a bit of a nuisance is when I am trying to do something in a hurry like shopping. I suppose I am one of the most recognisable characters with my grey hair and long nose!"

The grey hair and long nose were certainly put to good use when Jenny and Mary faced each other at a contrived meeting during the episode 'Confrontation'. The Audience Research gave the episode a 16.2% share of the UK population (one point up on ITV's rival offering). "These extremely favourable reactions, supported by warm comment, show that this new serial play has caught the interest of the vast majority of the sample audience, each episode leaving them eager for the next; indeed it has become increasingly absorbing now it had got 'into its stride' some said." Clearly the grip of the show was starting to be felt by the third episode. There was some comment in the report of a small number of those who took part feeling the characters too 'extreme or unpleasant'. But the majority found there was 'a wonderful tension between the characters which came over exceptionally well in this episode'. Once again Jean Anderson was singled out for praise, as was Hilary Tindall. It was noted also that the plotlines concerning the business were more gripping than the family personal squabbles by a small number of the panel. But overall the feeling in the report was overwhelmingly positive, a sure sign that the BBC might well have a hit on its hands, if it but knew it.

Mary's manipulation of her sons and her cunning in trying to thwart Jennifer's closeness to Edward was a major talking point for viewers, as they connected week on week with the flawed personal lives of the Hammonds whilst running an outwardly successful company. A major plot during this first series is the attempt by Sir John Borret, head of a large haulage conglomerate, to acquire the Hammond concern for a song with foreknowledge of a strike situation. Borret is a ruthless business enforcer, who uses his personal secretary Sally Woolf as a plaything. He orders Sally to "cultivate" David Hammond. Thus she becomes the first temptation of the series for the youngest brother. Borret is played by veteran character actor Hamilton Dyce, who would die on 8th January 1972 aged just 59, just a few weeks before the episodes went to air. His unscrupulous secretary Sally was given to Australian actress Annette Andre who had scored a considerable hit as Jeanie Hopkirk in the cult ITV hit *Randall & Hopkirk (Deceased)*. Borret knows that a strike is looming and Hammonds will not have anywhere to store the business he has off-loaded onto them and thus have to default on their contract. He aims to sweep in and swallow up the smaller company, adding the Hammond group and all its customer base to his own, and in the process ridding himself of the family name and their independence. It is a trick he has tried on unsuspecting competitors before. Edward is suspicious from the start but his fellow Directors out-vote him. Borret's game is afoot.

The sixth episode 'Turning Point' held a healthy 19.6% share of the Friday night audience against ITV's slightly higher 20.3% against the latter half of *Jason King* and Shirley Maclaine in her sit-com vehicle *Shirley's World*. It might have been a turning point in other ways as the official JICTAR ratings (the company responsible for ratings information supplied to television) recorded a mighty 12.65 million tuning into the episode. Comments were favourable with the Audience Research report too. "If possible, more engrossing every week." The report went on to say "The characters and relationships were firmly established and the various themes so far introduced – office politics, marital problems and conflicts between the generations – were all represented and blended this week in 'a particularly meaty episode'. There was also praise for the cast too. "Almost without exception, reporting viewers thought the characters very well cast and convincingly portrayed, often seeming so right that the actors in question 'might have been hand-knitted for the part.' Glyn Owen won most praise, but Jennifer Wilson was also well liked and there was a special word of commendation for Hilary Tindall in the unsympathetic part of Ann Hammond." Clearly the series, as the new kid on the block, was making waves with its audience.

As the heat is on with the dock strike The Stage was monitoring the series closely again as it reached the episode 'Crisis': "In episode eight the business is increasingly in financial trouble, aggravated by a dock strike" observed Graham Clarke, "Each of *The Brothers* reacts to this in a characteristic way, but the strength of this series has been in the treatment of comparatively minor personalities, such as the way in which the firm's foreman Bill Riley, loyally helps the bosses in a bit of strike-breaking but, as a union member, hates himself for doing it." Clarke is by and large impressed at the depiction of the working ethic. "Unlike some series, where nobody ever seems to be doing any recognisable work, this story does show business being done, but has managed to avoid its technical dullness or confusion, and emphasis has always been on personalities. If the plot in 'Crisis' showed signs of converging on the conventionally trite, then this can be excused on the grounds of the need to appeal to uncritical viewers." A need to appeal to uncritical viewers? Well they certainly were vocal when it came to some matters.

The location filming around Greenwich, East Moseley and other locations pepped up the earthy drama. David Hammond was required to woo both Jill Williams and Sally Wolfe with a cruise down the river. Robin later confessed that the steering on this, and earlier the lorries, was not his forte. He told Weekend Magazine: "I've caused havoc in *The Brothers*, I think the writers are wary of me now. The theme of the series is the road transport business – and I'm unlucky with anything that has a motor. In one early episode I was supposed to be directing a lorry out of the family firm's yard, It ended up smashing into another vehicle parked nearby. As if that wasn't embarrassing enough, another episode demanded I drove a speedboat along a river with all the bravado of a young man about town. I played the part too well. There was a smart cabin cruiser quite thoughtlessly, I thought, moored nearby. What do I do? I ram into it and cause chaos."

As the series started to reach the end of its run, and with a reaction from the audience far exceeding anything that had been expected, voices in the BBC Drama Department started to wonder if there were any plans to bring it back. The answer was, of course, no. Gerry Glaister smugly informed his BBC superiors that they themselves had poured water on the flames of any further run. With what looked like a major hit on their hands, the BBC didn't want to let it slip through their fingers all too easily. Glaister was instructed to start the process of getting scripts written and the cast reunited, Hammond Transport would be hitting the road again. But it had been almost a year since the final scenes had been recorded. The cast had been released from any further contractual obligations and set loose on the open market. Glaister started negotiations with the aim of reuniting them for another outing. The Hammond brothers would be back bickering again - but for one of them, change was in the air.

Putting on a brave face:
Jean Anderson and Jennifer Wilson

ANNETTE ANDRE REMEMBERS

I think I got the role of Sally Woolf through the director Philip Dudley, we had worked together several times before and he liked what I did, and we got on well. I wasn't playing too many characters like her at the time, it was a meaty role, she was quite bitchy. I really enjoyed it. It gave me another step on the ladder, I'd played similar roles before but mostly in theatre. I was really sorry in fact that they didn't carry me through to the next series. A lot of my scenes were with Robin Chadwick, and we became very good friends. I well remember the scene where he is painting my toe nails. We worked together in the theatre after The Brothers. I did The Collector, a quite well known play at the time by John Fowles. I did it first at the King's Head Theatre. It was all about a man who kidnaps a woman and keeps her in the basement and treats her like a butterfly he can pin on the wall. We did a season and it went very well, we repeated it at the Bush Theatre. We were the very first production at the brand new Bush Theatre, which was exciting. The actor I originally played opposite was very erratic, a bit strange. He started drinking heavily. Shu Chadwick, Robin's wife, was the stage manager although Robin hadn't met her at this point. Shu started to get worried on my behalf about the actor's behaviour. One night he threw me on the bed in the play, and he did it with such ferocity that I banged my head and momentarily blacked out. It was a scary thing. I somehow got through the scene, but this guy had bruised me before during the play. Shu said to me 'This can't go on' and she said 'we have to try and convince the management to get somebody else to play the role.' They brought in Robin Chadwick to replace him I'm glad to say, and that is how he met his wife Shu.

At one point we lived in upstate New York and Robin and Shu lived in Pennsylvania. My husband and I went to stay with them, it was lovely and they came to visit us. Nobody thought way back then we'd ever be talking about these shows fifty years on. They were just jobs, we did them and moved onto the next one. I toured in the theatre with Kate O'Mara and Robin in a Brian Clemens thriller called Shock! Kate was a feisty lady but I liked her and we got on really well. It was so sad that she died. I worked with Jean Anderson a couple of times. She was rather stately but a nice warm lady. I wasn't in The Brothers very long, but it's amazing people still talk about it to this day.

SERIES TWO (1973)

The success of Series One had taken everyone by surprise, not least the BBC management themselves. Having indicated to the Producer and cast that they should not expect a further commission of the series, they were now faced with an about-turn. Viewers were demanding to know what happened next in the saga of the Hammond brothers.

As soon as budgets were set and scripts then commissioned, the wheels swung into motion in order to reunite the cast for a second outing. This was assumed to be a matter of course, but Gerry Glaister suddenly found a major obstacle in the form of eldest brother Ted. Glyn Owen wanted a pay rise. The cast had all been offered a modest rise to entice them back on board but Owen and his agent decided that he was central to everything going on in the show, and his fee should reflect that. "We thought we wouldn't be too greedy or push it too much," Glyn explained to ITV in 2002. "So we just asked for a 25 per cent rise, and they said 'No no no'. And so we said 'We'll go then, that's it'." Glyn was already the highest paid member of the cast. To give him another 25 per cent would have been pushing his fee far above that of any other cast member. It was felt that he was effectively blackmailing the pay masters as pre-production geared up towards Series Two. Richard Easton commented, "Glyn had persuaded himself that he was the star. Because he was the eldest son and because it was the plot. It's this thing that happens to actors. It's the plot, that he thought he should have been left the business. He [Glyn] asked for an awful lot of money." The management at the BBC knew that if they caved in to Glyn's demands, the entire cast would have their agents making similar proposals. It had to be stamped on. With Owen and his agent sticking to their demands, it was felt there was only one option - to re-cast the role of Ted Hammond. It was a bold move, Glyn Owen had undoubtedly been a major contributor to the success of the first run of episodes. They needed to look for an actor who was as powerful and yet could handle the gentler material when required. Gerard Glaister found just what he wanted in Dublin born Patrick O'Connell. 39 year old Paddy, as he was known to friends and colleagues, had gathered for himself a reputation for bold acting on stage. He further impressed with the lead role of tough talking Detective Inspector Gamble in the ITV drama *Fraud Squad* (1969-70). Paddy had just the right amount of edginess in his acting that the fiery, outspoken Ted Hammond needed. He was swiftly engaged as Owen's successor. It meant that the middle-class English brothers were now played by an Irishman, a Canadian and a Kiwi! *Stand By For A New Big Brother* ran a headline in The Sun. Patrick commented to the reporter "It is a bit difficult taking over from someone else in such a well established series. But they are great people to work with, and I became quite dependent on them until I had found my feet."

Production started in September 1972, and changes to the cast were not the only changes in the air. The previous series had been recorded at the BBC's flagship base Television Centre in London. But the fight for studio space was becoming a problem. Anticipating this, a Midlands option had been built by the BBC and opened in 1971. Pebble Mill Studios in Birmingham would become synonymous with daytime broadcasting through the long running *Pebble Mill At One* magazine programme which began in 1972 and ran through until the mid-eighties. However, Studio A at the new facility boasted the latest high tech lighting and recording equipment which made an attractive alternative to Wood Lane. *The Brothers* decamped to the Midlands. Location filming would still take place in Greenwich and East Molesey, with rehearsals continuing at the Acton Hilton. Then the cast would take the train to Birmingham for a couple of days studio rehearsals and recordings every fortnight. Most of the cast were London based and found this an irritant to begin with, but the routine was quickly established and Pebble Mill became the permanent home to *The Brothers*. A new title sequence was commissioned to reflect the fact that the show was moving away from the ramifications of Robert Hammond's will and onto the operation and development of Hammond Transport Services. Shot on 16mm film, this showed a stretch of motorway with traffic flowing both during the day and at night. It would become the iconic opening to the show over the next four years.

Once again the scripting honours were divided between Norman Crisp and Eric Paice. Glaister and Crisp agreed that some new characters needed introducing into the mix to pep up storylines. Chief among these would be a new antagonist, Harry Carter of Carter Express Deliveries. The role of Carter was given to Mark McManus. Now principally remembered by viewers as the hard bitten Inspector Jim Taggart, he was born the son of a Hamilton miner but had emigrated to Australia in 1963 where he had discovered acting. Returning to Britain in 1971 he resumed his acting career with the Royal Shakespeare Company. McManus had appeared for one episode in Glaister's *Colditz* where he was spotted as an actor with some television potential. This led directly to his being cast as Harry Carter. Having spent the best part of a decade Down Under, McManus was perfectly placed to bring the Aussie brashness to Carter as the entrepreneur strove to make his mark on Hammond Transport. Also joining the cast were the voluptuous Gillian McCutcheon as photographer Julie Lane and dashing 33 years old Jonathan Newth, who as lothario and artist Nicholas Fox would become the older crush of Barbara Kingsley. Anna Fox would also join the cast as a schoolteacher and possible love interest for Brian, Pamela Graham. When the opening episode of the second series debuted on Sunday 14th January 1973 (sandwiched between the hymn request show *The Choice Is Yours* and a showing of the John Wayne movie *Stagecoach*) it was not heralded by any repeats to recap the storylines from some eight months previously. This was a pattern that the BBC would follow. During its television lifetime, no repeats of *The Brothers* were scheduled on BBC television. But viewers memories were strong and it was welcomed back heartily by the loyal audience. Some 10 million viewers now chose to switch to BBC1 on a Sunday evening. It had the school comedy series *The Fenn Street Gang* in opposition, but *The Brothers* held its own as it sought to attract back the vociferous viewers from the previous year. Oddly the Radio Times made no mention of Patrick O'Connell's arrival preferring to lead with a piece about Jean Anderson. "I'd be the last to suggest that Mary Hammond is the perfect example of how a mother should deal with her children," she told the magazine. "Mary is one of those mothers who is very possessive without being aware of it. She has no life of her own, and can't help trying to organise her children. She's completely outrageous about it, and at the same time she can sincerely justify all her dreadful deeds to herself," Jean explained. It seems fame in *The Brothers* was something of a double edged sword for her. "People seem to become very involved in the series. I spend a lot of my time defending myself on buses, in the street or on trains. I get remarks like 'You're just like my mother-in-law' and once I had a man come up to me and say, aggressively, 'I'll ring your neck I will…'"

The BBC Audience Research into the opening of the new series gave it a 13.5% share of the United Kingdom population (ITV's offerings at the same time gave it a much healthier 26.8% share.) The report noted that "… the series was welcomed back by many who enjoyed the previous story and anticipated its continuation with great pleasure.". However there were criticisms from those who took part in the research. It was thought "… the series had not quite the same impact as before, according to some disappointed reporting viewers; the plot seemed slower moving and lacked zest and excitement it was said." It seemed the Hammonds themselves were getting on some nerves: "Here and there were remarks to the effect that the family bickering was tiresome, the mother unbelievably dominant over the family, some scenes over emotional and the whole lacking in humour." It is certainly true that humour was hardly ever a factor in *The Brothers* scripts, and this sometimes perhaps gave it a certain intense element. But drama often benefits from constant tension build up. Catch 22. The lack of repeats was also touched upon, "One or two new to the series felt a résumé beforehand would have helped." On the tricky subject of the re-casting the report started its assessment in sobering fashion "… a number definitely regretted (some bitterly so) this change, missing Glyn Owen who had seemed so right as the 'tough, dynamic, slightly aggressive but down-to-earth eldest brother'. However light was on the horizon when it went on to say "But others gradually overcame their disappointment when they discovered that Patrick O'Connell had 'fitted in well' and proved a plausible Edward'…" There was a brief mention of a minor member of the cast "A handful thought that Marion unsuitably portrayed. No firm would ever employ an office secretary 'so dim and untidy'." It seems the irreverent attitude of Marion in the depot and its comedic possibilities in Grazebrook's scatty performance passed the BBC's audience researchers by, sadly her character was phased out during the series.

Having an actor of the calibre of Patrick O'Connell on board helped enormously with what could easily have – in lesser hands - been seen as a poor substitute for Glyn Owen. Patrick, as an actor, has a certain edgy quality about him which ideally suited no nonsense Edward. Audiences are slow to accept change but mercifully for *The Brothers*, the change over of a lead actor was less traumatic than it could have been. Such was the audience interest in the lives and loves of the Hammonds that within a few weeks Patrick's take on Edward ceased to be an issue for the loyal viewers. They were already willing him to get together with Jennifer. And they wrote in large numbers to tell the BBC so. Born to an army officer and his wife in Dublin, Paddy was given away at birth and from the age of three was set to be raised by his adoptive mother Dorothy Thomas in Washwood Heath, Birmingham. At the age of five his natural father placed him in a Dublin orphanage and Dorothy fought for several years and was eventually allowed to take him back. Leaving school at 15, he worked for a time in Lewis' department store publicity department. During his National Service in Cambridge, Patrick also spent his time attending art and drama lessons. "But I also joined an amateur dramatic group and that gave my acting the edge on my painting ambition," Patrick remembered. "When I finished with the RAF I went into drama school and won a scholarship to the Royal Academy of Dramatic Art. Becoming an actor was the happiest decision of my life, because I met my wife [actress Patricia Hope] whilst on an Arts Council tour of Wales and the North in 1957. We were both appearing in a production of *Look Back In Anger*. Patricia, as well as acting in the play, was wardrobe mistress. As well as acting, I was also the electrician. Doing both jobs meant long hours working together from seven in the morning 'til midnight. I remember thinking that as we got on so well together all that time surely we could do so for the remainder of the 24 hours. I proposed and we were married at Marylebone Register Office, London in 1959." Paddy's talent was eventually recognised by the Royal Shakespeare Company and the Royal Court Theatre where he earned his stripes as an actor. He played Macduff to Paul Schofield's Macbeth in the much lauded Peter Hall production of 1968 and was indeed accepted as a classical actor of some great future. O'Connell though was well aware of the pitfalls of having high critical acclaim with a struggling bank balance. He told the Birmingham Evening Mail in 1974: "I prefer the stage to television because you have a live audience to tell you how the performance is going. The stage is a much harder business. In television you can always go back and do it again." He further reasoned "Only a handful of actors can make a successful career on the stage alone. Small theatres cannot afford to pay you enough to make a good living and live in London at the same time."

Getting the part of Edward Hammond was something of a lucky break for Paddy. "Actor Glyn Owen had the part then, but when the series came round for a second time he had too many commitments and the producer had to look around for another actor. I was spotted, they say, doing a *Softly Softly* episode for which I was a police examiner dealing with Barlow's promotion prospects, and got the part." An essentially private man, Patrick was sometimes puzzled at the attentions of *The Brothers* fan base. "The surprising thing is how many letters I get saying how wonderful my TV mother is. A retired colonel from Bournemouth once wrote to complain about the way I held my knife in an incorrect manner. He said that with a mother like mine, it could never be. I much prefer the part my real mother plays to the one my fictitious mother plays." Patrick went on to tell readers of The Sun his views on Edward. "I think he is weak and a bit boring," he told the newspaper. "Edward can't even run his love life without reference to his mother, I couldn't bear a mother like that. Sometimes I wish he would stand up to her a bit more often." It was a sentiment millions seemingly agreed with. O'Connell seemed constantly amazed at how much viewers liked the characters. "They are always quarrelling and plotting against each other. People think they are so nice. Yet the implications in the show are incredible." He then addressed the question of confusing characters for the actors who played them. "The love affairs are strictly screen romances. That is one reason we get on so well. We don't have those emotional ties that can split up a company. We are all good friends and nobody is having an affair." He also tackled the issue why there is never any bad language from the tough talking characters. "It comes on after *Songs Of Praise*, so we can't really swear. I once said 'bloody' and they cut it out." The article finished with O'Connell stating his desire for the quiet life "I'm in a play with Richard O'Sullivan [the star of ITV's flat sharing sitcom *Man About The House*] in Oxford at the moment. He is recognised wherever he goes and when someone stops him in the street, I just stand aside."

Whilst the cast may not have been having affairs according to O'Connell, their on screen characters definitely were. David is lured into the arms of man eating Julie Lane. Very must the scarlet woman in the show, Gillian McCutcheon revels in her role as a morally bankrupt femme fatale. 25 years old at the time of getting her role as Julie, previous experience had included roles in *Z Cars* and *Dixon Of Dock Green* along with the role of Martha in a BBC adaptation of *A Little Princess*. This was McCutcheon's first opportunity to make her mark in a high profile series as a regular and she does so with some panache. With long flowing blonde locks, and a sultry not to mention brusque demeanour, she is perfect as 'the other woman' who stands between our perceived happiness for David and Jill. It was a game of cat and mouse which would be played out throughout the next two series.

Gabrielle Drake's return to the show as a regular was a boon for everyone, both on screen and off. Gabrielle was born in India but moved to Warwickshire at an early age. "Where we lived, near to Birmingham and Stratford meant we could see the pantomime at Christmas and Shakespeare all the year," she told the Birmingham Evening Mail. Gabby achieved her ambition to play pantomime in Wolverhampton in a production that incredibly used real live lions. "The lions terrified me" she told the reporter "I used to stand in the wings quaking. They have to be treated with a healthy respect." On the subject of her character Jill, she noted "There has to be one nice woman in the series. It's much easier to play a controversial character you can get your teeth into." On the subject of the series popularity, Gabrielle offered her own take on why it had become so immensely popular. "It contains so many different elements. People always enjoy a story about family. It has the sex element and the business side. I think people in the Midlands enjoy that side of the programme. It is accurate in portraying the problems that confront a small business and the loyalties and conflicts that surround this." Jennifer Kingsley has cooled her relationship with Edward, who has sought refuge in the arms of his former fiancé Nancy Lincoln, however daughter Barbara is maturing rapidly. She accompanies her art tutor Nicholas Fox to Paris but finds that she is merely his plaything, and her hopes of an intense romance are unfounded. Fox is what might be termed these days as a 'player' and his suave manner would be unleashed further in forthcoming episodes, to more devastating impact for one of *The Brothers*.

Gabrielle Drake as Jill Williams

SARAH GRAZEBROOK REMEMBERS

I'd been working in Rep and I thought it was time to get into television. So I wrote to every one I'd ever heard of and nobody replied. One of the few that did was Gerry Glaister. He offered to see me, which I did, and we had a chat. Needless to say nothing came of it. So then I thought ' Well if they won't come to me, I'd better go to them.' So I got a job in the coffee bar at Television Centre where I reckoned I'd see everyone who was anyone. In fact I got sent out to the Spur which is where they did the weather forecast from. When I finished work I used to brush my hair and go around the fifth floor of TV Centre, which is where all the drama was based, knocking on peoples doors saying 'Can I be in this?' Most of them said 'Certainly not'. However one day whilst I was working I was taking a tray of Danish pastries somewhere or other, and got into a lift with Gerry Glaister. 'What are you doing here? ' he said. So and I told him and we started to talk – and talk and talk. We just commandeered the lift whilst we chatted, much to the annoyance of other people I expect. He ended up saying 'Leave it with me' and spoke to one of his directors, Viktors Retilis. At that time they were doing The Expert. They changed one of the parts so I could play it, a sickly girl. Just a spit and a cough but that didn't matter really. I thought no more of it. Then six months later my agent rang up and said 'Gerry Glaister is doing a new series called The Brothers and he wants you to be in it.' I got excited because I thought it was Dostoevsky's The Brothers Karamazov because I'd always wanted to do a BBC2 serial. But of course it wasn't, it was Marion who had a line and half in every episode. They originally wrote it at forty-five minutes per episode which they filmed. Then they found out the slot was actually a fifty minute slot, so they had to write these extra scenes. But because the plot was so convoluted it was hard to feed extra lines into that, so they got me or someone else on the end of the phone doing some small talk just to pad it out. So it began to build up this non-existent character a little. Then when the second series came along I got a bit cocky and said 'Well I'll do half of it and see how it goes' because I was doing something else as well at the time. They eventually got rid of me because I was badly behaved. It was when we got up to Birmingham and recording at Pebble Mill. We used to catch the late train back to London, but before that we used to go out to dinner. I got very drunk on one occasion and found myself sitting opposite the writer Eric Paice. He said ' So what do you think of your part?' and I said politely that it was fine. Then he said, 'Go on, what do you REALLY think?' So I told him it was a bit rubbish. The next thing I heard was that the way they felt the plot was developing there was not space for Marion in it. I was not that bothered at the time because I wanted to do other things. Now it would be completely different. I didn't get typecast but ultimately I was. I met Richard Easton in a supermarket about three years later and he said gleefully 'I'm having a nervous breakdown in episode four. I can't wait!' He'd grown a bit sick of it.

Marion's stroppiness came out of rehearsing scenes with Glyn Owen who used to screech his lines at me. He didn't think I would react but I did. We tempered it down a lot for the recording but in rehearsal it was like a scene from Virginia Woolf, with me snapping back at him. The cast were very nice to me, it was only the second thing I'd ever done on the telly and they were very experienced. Glyn and I obviously had this mock battle going on. Robin Chadwick was terribly sweet and kind, and so was Richard Easton. Both lovely. Hilary Tindall was magnificent in the part but it followed her wherever she went, although I didn't have any scenes with her. They seemed to spend most of the budget on her wardrobe, whilst I had one green blouse the same colour as the filing cabinet, so I was virtually invisible from the neck down. I do remember the meeting we had, because the BBC had the option to take up our contracts for a second series by episode eight of the first one.There was a terribly solemn meeting and I think it was Paul Fox who came down and said 'As much as we love it, we are not going to take up the option.' Of course when it came out about six months later weirdly enough people loved it, so they had to negotiate new contracts. I went up by £3 an episode! Glyn Owen held out too long, and they got rid of him and Paddy O'Connell came in as a result. It was so lovely to be in something with Jean Anderson. She wouldn't exactly give you advice but would tell you things which helped your performance, and you thought 'Oh yes, that is so right'. It was a wonderful training ground.

My writing career started when I had children and I got a bit sick of traipsing around doing not very much in distant places. I never stopped acting, I just didn't pursue it in the same way. You only have to be out of it a fortnight and everyone thinks you are dead, so I kind of faded from the scene. I have always written, I used to get a lot of auditions by writing quite good letters, but when I was stuck at home with small children I started writing about being stuck at home with small children, and it went from there. One of my books, A Cameo Role, is very loosely based on The Brothers. It is about a woman who gets a small part in a long running saga. I then recorded it as a talking book and found out there were thirty four different characters in it, not only the actors in the piece but the characters they played in the soap opera, so it was perhaps the most challenging thing I have ever done.

Mr and Mrs Johnny Trent
(Malcolm Stoddard and Julia Goodman)

By the ninth episode 'Storm Birds' in March 1973, the BBC Audience Researchers were getting some very positive feedback. Slightly up on the opening episode with a 13.9% audience share, it effectively meant that the show was retaining its core audience. "This episode was well up to standard in what is clearly proving a very popular serial." The report noted. "Dealing mainly with the strike that was crippling Hammond Transport – it was, viewers thought, topical and convincing, showing the problems of both management and workers in their attempts to reach a compromise, while at the same time advancing the other, more personal, strands of the story." It did though record some disenchantment with the way the series was progressing, stating that drama centred around industrial strife which was prevalent at the time "hardly the subject for entertainment". It seemed the many plot strands were also something a small proportion of viewers were struggling with. "There were also a few complaints of too much switching from one theme to another and a feeling that so many side issues were being introduced that Hammond Transport Limited might soon start to fade out entirely." One viewer labelled it "Nothing but trouble and misery so far!" One can only hope that he or she never clapped eyes on *EastEnders* a decade or so later… But it was not all doom and gloom for the report. "Clearly, though, the vast majority of viewers were 'hooked'. 'The only series I never miss'" Harry Carter had a few critics "Isolated viewers said that Mark McManus' Australian accent was overdone in the part of Harry Carter or that they still preferred the original Edward." Overall the realistic performances were praised, mentioning particularly "…the men picketing the depot… and rocking the van of a driver attempting to leave." Certainly these storylines were reflecting the growing social unrest in 1973. On 1st July the Trades Union Congress' called for a one day strike across manufacturing industries; the rail, car and steel sectors were badly affected. *The Brothers* effectively had no choice but reflect the developments in the UK with the Trade Unions, and indeed it made for good drama to do so. The 1973 oil crisis which saw crude oil leap from US $3 a barrel to US $12 would have badly affected Hammond Transport too as it did the whole of the country, by the time it ended in April 1974 global trade had been shaken badly by the scarcity of fuel for vehicles. Frequent mention is made in the scripts of a possible Nationalisation of the freight transport industry. It had been a subject under discussion by successive Governments for a few years, and nobody knew which way the wind would blow. Thankfully the haulage companies were never subject to such a takeover, but the fear of what might happen if it did is an undercurrent in the programme and very topical. Within the series confines, Kenneth Watson as Union representative Bill Turner would be a recurring character who would return in Series Five. His down to earth, tough talking negotiator is a perfectly pitched performance as the series strove to demonstrate the tricky and demanding line walked by the Hammond management in keeping their workers happy. It was a line many companies were walking with increasing frustration, and their workforce were equally frustrated at wages and conditions. A combustible combination which marked a troubled socio-political climate, the full effects of which were to be felt throughout the decade.

Brian Hammond was weathering the storm of his separation from Ann, he is attracted to Carole's school teacher Pamela Graham, a dependable spinster who is perhaps much more suited to Brian's temperament than fiery Ann. However, boredom at her parents has Ann making a play for Brian again. Using her text book of womanly wiles, she slowly edges out Pamela and back into the heart and the home of her husband. Easton and Tindall are dynamite together on screen and having them sharing the marital home once more would undoubtedly bring more of the emotional fireworks that had provided so many highlights.

With Jill's inheritance backing the company (much to David's disapproval) the series ended in a blaze of glory on the 8th April 1973 with the episode 'No Hard Feelings' written by Norman Crisp and directed by Ronald Wilson. Pitted against Reg Varney's very final episode as Stan Butler in *On The Buses* (it would continue without him) and the first section of the Gregory Peck Biblical epic *David and Bathsheba*, the show did well to average a 17.2% of the population against ITV's 24.1%. The BBC Audience Research comprised of its usual conflicting responses. "An excellent ending of thirteen weeks' entertainment; it left me looking forward to another series; there are so many new strings to be tied up," enthused one reviewer. However others found it 'Too neatly rounded off'. Detractors also accused it of 'getting stale' and 'veering too much towards soap opera'. The report ended very upbeat thankfully: "According to the general run of comment, however, the whole series had been most entertaining, and the story should certainly be continued, some adding they could not wait to see the series back again." A satisfactory end of term report for sure. Even as the credits rolled, plans were already firmly in place to return to Hammond Transport, and 1974 would bring a bumper crop of episodes as the production geared up to run a full six months of the year on screen.

Hilary Tindall as Ann Hammond

IN CONVERSATION WITH
ROBIN CHADWICK

RC: How did you come to leave your native New Zealand and what were your career ambitions?

Robin Chadwick: I always wanted to be an actor. I had no other expressed idea of what I wanted to do, but I lived in a country that had only sporadic "professional" acting companies. I wanted to be an actor, although I did not know much about what that entailed. I loved reading: I read all Shakespeare's plays. I saw a few plays – my parents wanted to be actors, but their times (the depression, the war) did not allow for it. So I left school, got a job as an audit clerk and went to university classes at night and on weekends. I became Treasurer of the University Drama Society and one night an actor was ill. It was N.F. Simpson's *A Resounding Tinkle*; it could be read (a sermon). So I did it, and then auditioned for every amateur repertory group in Auckland. *Five Finger Exercise*, *Luther*, Shylock in *The Merchant of Venice*, *Where's Charley?* Along the way, I gave up the accounting work and became a "postie", a mailman. I finished work by 11am having run my round and concentrated on theatre. And for all my efforts, I would have gone nowhere if not for the people who helped me. Among them, Gil Cornwall, my first coach, and particularly Edna Harris who gave me direction and belief. And thanks to the New Zealand Arts Council which awarded me a two year bursary to study overseas; I won the drama competition the same year that (Dame) Kiri Te Kanawa won for music. I worked 5 years as an audit clerk and as a postman to earn the fare to England, but the bursary was the key. I went to LAMDA (London Academy of Music and Dramatic Art) for two years.

RC: How did you come to play David Hammond in *The Brothers?*

My first professional job was at Cheltenham Repertory. Then the Little Theatre at Bristol Old Vic, and a year at the then brand new Northcott Theatre, Exeter. While there, I commuted to London to do a TV play with Sheila Hancock and Robert Stephens. Other television work came in, such as a small part in Eric Porter's *Cyrano de*

Bergerac, Colonel Fitzwilliam in *Pride and Prejudice* (not the famous one), and a Sunday night "religious' comedy program for ITV called *Beyond Belief* – and it was. But *The Brothers* came about, I believe, through the recommendation of Innes Lloyd, the producer of *Thirty Minute Theatre*. I had portrayed a young, bumbling Constable in *Something To Hide*, a three part story of a dead body found in a house. Charles Gray was the "brilliant" detective whose brilliance was illuminated by my incompetence. Filmed and broadcast live, it was a great success for *Thirty Minute Theatre*; they wanted to do more but Charles Gray did not, so another actor was engaged to play that part. Unfortunately, the actor was having a breakdown, and we were having to do twenty or thirty takes for each scene. I saw my role as standing ready to do as many takes as needed. I was learning all the time, so why complain? But Innes Lloyd thanked me for not adding to the problems. Anyway, the series was cancelled. Later, I did the series with Clive Swift as the detective. But Innes Lloyd remembered me and recommended me to Gerry Glaister. Or that is what I believe, and I have always thanked Innes in my mind. A lovely man.

RC: Were you nervous at being one of the leading men in the series?

Nervous? No, it was work and who knew how it would go? Well, I was always nervous beginning every job, just not especially for *The Brothers*. As for learning from the other actors? Always. Was it the down to earth professionalism of Glyn, and Richard, and Jean that laid the foundation for the series' success? Glyn was loud and unpredictable but professional. Richard quiet and calm, exuding a quality that could have, SHOULD have, made him a star. His Tony award was no surprise to me. And Jean was a star – but never anything other than one of the company, but always special.

RC: What were your initial impressions of your fellow cast? Was there anyone in the regular ensemble you had worked with before? Did you feel that the show would become a hit during the making of that first series?

In Gabrielle Drake, I was very lucky. She was beautiful, talented and very easy to work with. When she left the series, for me a lot left with her. Jennifer Wilson, Julia Goodman, Gillian McCutcheon, Derek Benfield, Maggie Ashcroft and Hilary Tindall – I suppose other series are as successful at putting together a group of actors who 'get on', work like a family – but it was certainly true of this company of actors. I had not worked with any of them before and never thought beyond the scene, the episode, the family. And when I was married in 1974, I used them to 'dress' my side of the church: Jean as my stand-in mother, Richard as best man. It truly felt like a family occasion.

RC: The BBC delayed its broadcast until almost a year later, were you despondent that they didn't put it out straight away?

We were shown Series One or some of it (perhaps only the first episode) and it seemed to me as good as anything I had seen of its genre. I cannot remember any disappointment at its apparent rejection by the BBC. I was young, and I went back to my day job – cleaning lavatories at the Wigmore Hall Studios. Then a friend asked for help getting the Bush Theatre, Shepherds Bush, open. So I went there – and met my wife. An American in England on a tourist visa, she had answered an advertisement in Time Out 'to convert a room over a pub into a theatre'. She went along to the initial meeting, stayed and became stage manager of the first production, a stage adaptation of John Fowles' *The Collector*. So if you ask if I was despondent about the prospects of *The Brothers*? I do not think so – I was in love. Yesterday, we celebrated our 43rd Wedding Anniversary! Meeting her at The Bush was the best thing that ever happened to me.

RC: Do you remember how Ted described David in the first episode? How did you see the character? What were his good and bad attributes?

"A first class lay about with a second class degree." I could wish to be described otherwise and often disagreed with story lines, but I saw my job as getting on with it and getting it done. I found it stimulating to work out at the depot – more like theatre – we always had an audience. Working with Gabrielle was lovely, as a new husband in life, I felt less enthused by the affair with Julie Lane, but Gillian was great.

RC: Obviously the fashions of the 1970s have not dated well, but the outfits were very trendy for the time. Did you have a hand in saying what David would wear?

My memory is that my clothes budget for a series was £60.00. I think I wore much of my own wardrobe.

RC: Were there any particularly memorable moments when making *The Brothers* that spring to mind?

Only the first scene at the grave. Very cold, snowflakes, wind-whipped, and nervousness, consequent upon the situation, made it – in my mind – the coldest day ever.

RC: How did the public react to you in the street, particularly when you were two timing Jill. Did they greet you as Robin the actor or as David the playboy?

The public reaction was always pleasing, but I wished they had called me by my name rather than the character. Only in Scotland was I Robin Chadwick who *played* David Hammond.

RC: How do you think the show changed when established leads Hilary Tindall and Julie Goodman left, and were replaced by Colin Baker and Kate O'Mara. Pretty sensational new additions, along with new producers.

Any long-running series relies on new actors to bring not only new story lines, but a fresh air and acting attack to the set. I do not think the series would have lasted as long without Colin and Kate and Mike Pratt. Even smaller roles were memorable; I think with a smile of the episodes with Carleton Hobbs - "Hobbo"- whose voice was part of my New Zealand childhood via BBC radio, playing Sherlock Holmes. Did he first awake my desire to act? So thanks to everyone who contributed to the success of the series, especially to the staff and studio crews in both London and Birmingham. They were amazing. I would ask for and get a camera script; look at the scenes I was in, ask if there was any way I could make their shots easier – lead a camera, etc. Always I felt that what they saw through the lens was who the audience would see. As for producers, the show was always Gerry's. I did not get close to Gerry, but admired him. The story lines I did not enjoy emerged under Ken Riddington. I was not a fan. Derek Benfield was the warm heart of the series. I loved his portrayal of the yard foreman, Bill Riley. R.I.P. Derek and Jean and Maggie and Hilary.

RC: Why do you think *The Brothers* captured the imagination of such a wide audience across the world?

I cannot account for it. I did not really like it. It was a job I tried to do as well as I could, and I said yes when approached to do another series, the one that did not happen. But, yes, I think it changed my acting 'path'. I wanted to be a stage actor. I wrote to the Royal Shakespeare Company but was not given the courtesy of a reply. The BBC seemed loathe to audition me. So when I realised my wife was missing her family and America, it was amazingly easy to say "we will go." I have worked steadily and worked all over this great country, and formed a great respect for many Americans. Would I have liked to work with the RSC or the Old Vic? Yes, but what I have done, and what I have, makes me happy. Proud? I hope not. I did not do it on my own.

RC: Where does *The Brothers* sit in your life?

Squarely and firmly as a foundation stone. If *The Brothers* were to be done again (and it could), it would be so different. I would watch it.

SERIES THREE (1974)

It had been nine months since viewers had tasted wedding fever at the picturesque nuptials of David and Jill. Production had been re-started on the series in May 1973, it was business as usual with location filming in East Molesey and Greenwich to the fore, rehearsals at the Acton Hilton and two days recording at Pebble Mill studios in Birmingham each fortnight. *The Brothers* roared back onto BBC 1 on Sunday 3rd February 1974. The Radio Times gave it a rather low key welcome with a short piece on the work load of producer Gerry Glaister. The article tantalisingly made mention of a feature film based on the series to be made at Pinewood. "The public like to see things they are familiar with" was his only comment. The growing popularity of colour television meant that cinema audiences were dwindling as their trump card of full colour was now replicated in living rooms across the land. The British cinema industry turned to television, with a succession of films based on popular comedies such as *Steptoe & Son* and *For The Love Of Ada*. Overtures had certainly been made regarding a feature film of *The Brothers* but ultimately it would come to nought. Comedy was a safer bet in the troubling socio-economic climate of the mid- 1970s.

Glaister had actually vacated the producers chair for the third series in favour of Ken Riddington. Leicester-born Ken had started his life in showbusiness as an actor before becoming a stage manager at the Adelphi Theatre in 1950 and onto the Palladium and Palace Theatre's as a company manager. Joining the BBC as a floor manager, Ken's first leap as producer came with *The Brothers* although Gerry Glaister would keep an eye on things as Executive Producer whilst simultaneously producing his wartime drama *Colditz* and setting up his next project *Oil Strike North*. It was now the custom for Norman Crisp and Eric Paice to divide the writing honours for the thirteen episode series between them. The regulars all returned supplemented by Jonathan Newth and Gillian McCutcheon once again. A new script editor came onboard in the shape of Simon Masters, a promising writer himself who would go onto script episodes of Emmerdale and Dallas. The themes of Series 3 seemed to be temptation. Julie Lane was back to bating the now married David and Nicholas Fox sets out to seduce Ann Hammond which Ann returns with an all-consuming obsession for the marketing guru. In the wider business world, Hammond's take their first steps towards expanding their European market in cahoots with Christian Van Der Moewe. The first shock to the loyal audience though was the arrival of Barbara from travelling replete with a new husband in tow. It set the scene with a series that had plenty to offer in the intrigue department with Jennifer shocked and disappointed whilst Ted is quickly suspicious and wants to know if Trent knew Barbara was an heiress when he married her. The BBC's Audience Research department were on the case needing to know if the return of *The Brothers* had met with approval. It registered a steady 16.8% population share against ITV's commanding 21.3% with Jim Dale hosting *Sunday Night At The London Palladium*. "A new series has opened up promisingly...half the sample registering complete satisfaction" the report began. "Those familiar with the story of the Hammonds and their family haulage business said that the gap since the last episode had been successfully bridged, the characters effectively re-introduced, their personal relationships brought out very well." Praise indeed with one of those sampled claiming "Almost as good as *The Onedin Line*." However it wasn't all wine and roses. Some felt the plot followed "a predictable course" with plot elements described as "sluggish". Elsewhere "too much glamour, not enough real business being transacted". And one, in opposition to his fellow panel member offered it as a "poor replacement for *The Onedin Line*". Going to prove you can't please all of the people all of the time. But the report noted too that those giving criticism felt that the should would improve now "the thread has been re-established" and offered optimism for forthcoming episodes. "...more punch and realism – less bickering" were cited as improvements on the previous series. It noted too that the cast all gave convincing performances with the women particularly being singled out. It seems Ann's party dress was the biggest bone of contention among the cast contributions. "Over lavish, not in the best taste" came the verdict of the anonymous cross section. Shots of the business premises however were praised "adding an atmosphere of realism some had not felt before." In summary the research concluded that 91% of those polled watched all of the programme, 5% came in during the middle whilst 2% "tried a bit" and another 2% switched off before the end. Overall this was considered to be a pleasing start to the latest series with events destined to hot up over the coming weeks as the plots were played out to an increasingly addicted core audience.

Over the next few episodes Norman Crisp unravels the Hammond family in a succession of events that bring the cracks to the surface. Johnny Trent's boutique is a failure, it is losing money and raking up debts. Barbara eventually has to step in and inform the apparently oblivious Johnny that they are in serious financial trouble. Nicholas Fox continues his pursuit of Ann who is weakening and becoming irritable and all consumed by thoughts of Nicholas. As the show reached the mid-series mark, the BBC's Audience Research was on the case again. With an 18.66% share of the population (against ITV's 22.9% with Victor Borge topping the bill on *Sunday Night At The London Palladium*) the Hammond star was clearly on the ascendant. The episode "Trade Wind" by Eric Paice involved more of the Ann-Nicholas-Brian-Pamela dance at a dinner party. And Barbara seeks to cover Johnny's loans from an unexpected source, Mary Hammond. Meanwhile Mary takes it upon herself to confront Julie about her actions, the encounter doesn't end well. "Although there was a feeling the story sagged a little this week, there was a wider agreement that the series keeps improving" noted the report. "Clearly many viewers have found a compelling interest in the everyday private and business interests of the Hammond family, experiencing a strong feeling of involvement with the characters – 'every one seems true to life' – 'the cunning permutations of their private lives never fail to hold the interest'." It was no surprise that there were the usual criticisms that there was too little of the haulage side of the story, that was now a constant with most of the reports coming into the research department. 'It began with a series about haulage and it's route now leads to soap opera' was a typical comment from one of the less satisfied of the panel. However, it was clear that the majority of those whom the BBC researched were still very taken with the series. Its hold over the core audience was growing despite one or two grumbles Incidentally this episode sees future *Howards' Way* regular Jan Harvey turn up in a 'don't blink or you'll miss it' role, as one of Jill's modelling chums Briony.

One very pleasing aspect for the BBC were the overseas sales for the programme. Many European countries had purchased the series and it was, rather surprisingly, going down a storm. In particular the Netherlands where it was known as *De Gebroeders Hammond* ("The Brothers Hammond") and in Sweden as *Arvingarna* ("heirs"). So much so, that N.J. Crisp and members of the cast were invited onto local television shows to discuss the latest intrigues of *The Brothers* plotting. Back at home a succession of mass market paperback novelisations of the series scripts had been written by Janice James (in reality Gerry Glaister's wife) for Sphere Books. Initially retailing at a mighty 35p, they sold in their thousands and were translated for the Dutch and Swedish speaking markets. The BBC didn't quite know what to make of the unprecedented enthusiasm for the series they initially thought would not go beyond ten episodes. But it was certainly making BBC Enterprises money, so they did not fight it and just issued the licences for the novels and translations, happy with what they were bringing back into the corporation coffers.

The cast were enjoying their new found fame greatly. Most of them had enjoyed success in one medium or another during their careers but the level of interest and enthusiasm for *The Brothers* was un-paralleled. Wherever they went, people wanted to discuss the show and more importantly what was in store for their characters. Derek Benfield was certainly more than happy with his lot. In Series Three we learn a little about Bill's background, just after he is demobbed from the army he ends up in trouble with the police for breaking and entering with some pals. It comes back to haunt him during the episodes 'Hijack' and 'Riley' when his criminal record puts him firmly under suspicion. His valuable load is hijacked by a well co-ordinated gang. Benfield later commented to the Radio Times that the day after the hijacking was shown on TV he turned up at the Hilton Transport depot for filming and heard an announcement: "Will all drivers return to their vehicles...Bill Riley has arrived!" He would later comment that the hijack episodes were among his favourites from the series.

Benfield's no-nonsense playing of Riley had made him a favourite with viewers, whilst they peaked in at the elevated middle class fussiness of the Hammonds with relish, they could readily connect with Bill and his working class ethics. Bill is a man who says what he thinks in any given situation, he doesn't sugar coat the truth as he sees it and everyone respects him for it. Derek Benfield is perfect casting for the loveable curmudgeon, and it is massively to his credit that a part that was originally conceived as a supporting role grew to a series lead under Benfield's masterful playing.

Born in Bradford during 1926, Derek Benfield found himself doing some forces radio drama during the hostilities of World War 2 which resulted in him training for the stage at RADA. Whilst there he received the Gertrude Lawrence Award for his performance in the play *French Without Tears* from Miss Lawrence herself! His stage debut came with comedies for Brian Rix at Ilkley and Bridlington, after which Derek learned his craft as many of the established repertory companies flourishing around theatres in the UK. His television debut came with the science fiction series *Return To The Lost Planet* in 1955 and he never looked back as far as television was concerned, it became a staple of his career for the next fifty years. Stints in *Coronation Street* and the children's television serial *Timeslip* had made his face a familiar one, but appearing as Bill Riley brought a new level to his public appreciation. "Like Birmingham, the BBC here is a friendly place that impresses people accustomed to the hard professionalism of life in showbusiness," he told the Birmingham Mail. "Maybe it's the sheer size and range of activities that makes the London set-up seem impersonal by comparison. Here it's cosier and far more friendly. There's an atmosphere that encourages players to break through individual barriers so that all enjoy a closer acquaintance and friendship." On his alter ego Bill, Derek observed "I enjoy playing Bill Riley for I like to think I share some of his honest-to-God standards. It's quite a challenge to sustain the awareness of the gulf, social and intellectual, between him and the family whose members have enjoyed so many more advantages. There is, too, much interest in the character of any man who has 'got on'. It's there wherever I go. We went to a big London transport yard to see what goes on. Now, when I meet some of the drivers they pull my leg about our screen lorries. But they are very helpful whenever I want a bit of guidance – and I can drive a heavy goods vehicle." Derek told The Sun "We have had a few good laughs making the series. Richard Easton is really very wicked." Derek had a few hairy moments behind the wheels of a lorry during the filming of the show. He told TV Life: "...my first days filming when I had to back a lorry around a corner with a whole fleet of stationary lorries next to me. I was told by a professional driver that the whole thing was 'in lock' and all I had to do was start it and turn the wheel. It wasn't 'in lock' and the nearest lorry took a battering." Of his double life as a script writer and actor, he had this to say "I spend so much of my time sitting in a lorry or behind a type writer I've got to play something incredibly active – like squash."

Meanwhile the series continued on a-Paice, in the episode "Echoes". Julie Lane continues to play her games with David leaving Jill the casualty. We do have some relief with filming on the south coast of Ted and Jenny having a pleasure trip in a boat owned by a business friend of Ted's Alex Dyter. For the second time this series we find a future *Howards' Way* stalwart in the shape of Stephen Yardley as Dyter. Yardley would have to wait eleven years for a chance to take centre stage in a Gerry Glaister drama which he did spectacularly as Ken Masters.

Just when it might be thought there is a cooling between Jenny and Mary, the subject of Mary's secretive loan to Barbara rears its ugly head. Jenny intends to pay Mary back at all costs on behalf of Barbara. She won't be beholden to the elder Hammond. It results in Jenny putting up her shares in Hammond Transport to the highest bidder. Brian and David see this as an opportunity to put themselves in the driving seat as Managing Director of the company and start efforts to raise the cash to buy Jenny's holding. A trip to the Bank Manager isn't very fruitful for Jenny, ironic as the said Bank Manager is played by Jennifer Wilson's real life husband Brian Peck. The dynamic between *The Brothers* changes completely during these episodes, Brian and David are actively plotting to vote Ted out as Managing Director. They are both shown to be power hungry, ambitious to get ahead, even if brother Ted's head is on the chopping block. With Ted away in Europe on a recce to see if an alliance with a Dutch haulage firm headed by Christian Van Der Moewe would be a good move, the plotting becomes thicker and more devious. But just as it looks as if Ted has been out manoeuvred in his absence, when he learns of Jenny's reasons for putting her shares up for sale, he brings his own cheque book to the table averting a nasty take-over of the Hammond Board by his siblings. Naturally Ted has a few choice words for them in the aftermath. By the penultimate episode of Series Three 'Perchance To Dream' Ann is now quite obsessed to the point of exhaustion with Nicholas. She tries to fly to Brussels to be with him. Trying to balance her life Ann visits her daughter Carol (we are now on our second Carol of the show, Charlotta Martinus) at her boarding school. No joy to be found there, with Carol showing little real affection for her mother. It is all too much for Ann. Without Nicholas or it would seem the need of her children, Brian finds Ann on the bed at the end of the episode having taken an overdose. Hilary Tindall is superlative in her depiction of Ann's breakdown, her ability to play neurotic is tangible in every scene during this storyline. Tindall's on screen presence as Ann searches for something to hold on to in her life reaches new heights and makes for a fitting cliffhanger for the penultimate episode of the series.

As the series concluded in May 1974 with the episode 'Return To Nowhere' we viewers are left wondering what is to come. Ann is in hospital with Brian wondering what has driven her to this course of action. His pursuit of power has blinded him to the developing relationship between Nicholas and Ann, of which he still has no knowledge. Julie has finally been out trumped by David who has made his choice, his wife Jill comes first. Naturally viewers were thrilled. Gabrielle Drake's Jill is such a sweetheart, how could David ever even consider having a bit on the side with the deceitful Julie? Whilst taking a break together Ted and Jennifer decide they simply cannot live without each other, they need to marry. Rushing home to tell Mary they find her lying on the conservatory floor. She has had a heart attack. Whether she is dead or not isn't clear as the credits roll. This triumphant cliff hanger was greeted with shock and frustration for the Sunday night audience. It was the end of the series. They needed to know whether Mary was going to live. It remained debatable whether *The Brothers* replacement in the schedules , *The Onedin Line,* was going to lessen their frustration.

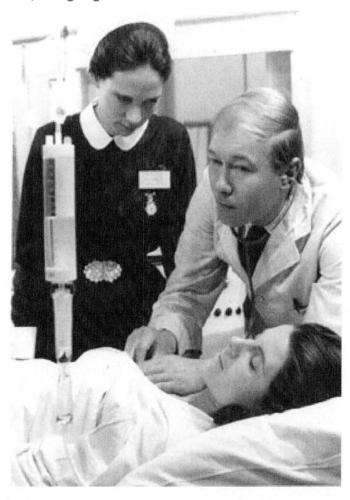

Hilary Minster and Hilary Tindall in 'Return To Nowhere'

IN CONVERSATION WITH
JULIA GOODMAN

RC: I believe you were born into a theatrical family?

Julia Goodman: My mother was a co-founder of Theatre Workshop with Joan Littlewood, she went up to join them in Manchester when she was 19. My mother was in the Land Army but before that she was singing and was about to go off to have film tests with Ray Milland. But then World War Two started so she had to go home, and into the Land Army. She got a telegram from Joan saying 'I'm starting up a theatre company and I'd like you to join it. I'll send you a telegram after the war.' She was a very beautiful working class girl and a great singer in Chichester. Sure enough she did get the telegram and decided to go. She had a year or two up in Manchester, in a lorry going all over the place putting on the most amazing plays to Welsh miners among others. Later on I met and worked with some of the people who had been in that Theatre Workshop such as Harry H. Corbett. My father was a painter, from a long line artists and theatre impresarios. So yes I came into a very creative environment. With my father's family who were artists, painters and theatricals, they were also ran businesses. That was a very unusual mix which has come right through the family. My son is the same. For a long time we were totally poor, living on farms or anywhere we could get a roof over heads. With my Mum milking forty cows before breakfast just to keep us in accommodation. My Dad taught painting and painted, and not a lot else actually. My Mum did most of the hard work. When we moved to Chichester, Dad was involved with Laurence Olivier and the Festival Theatre. His graphic design businesses started to flourish a bit more and we started to live a different life.

RC: Was it inevitable that you went into the theatre then?

An interesting question. When I was six my Mum was doing *Henry V* and I roped myself into it. So I think you can say from a very early age I had this sense that I wanted to be on the stage. I started in amateur dramatics the Chichester Players which Brenda Bleythn was in and various other people. I was 15 and I had just been made a prefect at my school in Bognor Regis, two girls had been caught smoking. I got the whole school together, and I remember this sea of faces hanging on my every word as I gave them a lecture on the evils of smoking. We were all at it so it was completely hypocritical, but I suddenly felt this extraordinary feeling that this was what I was born to do, not so much acting but me performing in front of an audience. Being able to have an influence on how they felt. The work I do now with Personal Presentation, my company, is all about having the confidence to speak in public and that was the origin of it really. I was an usherette at the Chichester Festival Theatre with a couple of girlfriends. Our boyfriends were Michael Gambon, Michael Byrne, Michael York, Tom Courtney, Albert Finney. We were all groupies to their circle. We had a wonderful time. That really focused my feeling about being an actor. We were able to see the best stage actors in the world: Laurence Olivier, Sybil Thorndyke, Michael Redgrave – all the greats. You saw the best every night. So your standards were always that high. Recognising that great acting and great performing was another factor in starting my own business, because I knew what you had to get out of people was the authentic truth. Helping people who are not actors discover the truth in themselves and able to project it in front of other people is my life's work really. David Wood, Howard Brenton, myself, Malcolm Stoddard, Michael Elphick – we were all kids at Chichester and we had our own theatre company called The Attic Theatre Company which is where we started our theatrical life.

RC: I notice one of your earliest forays into television was with an uncredited role opposite Frankie Howerd in *Up Pompeii!*

I did the pilot. In my early days I worked with a lot of comics which really taught me about the art of comedy and timing. As well as Frankie there was Michael Crawford, Dick Emery, Ronnie Corbett, Leslie Phillips... loads of them. In those days you did live television in front of an audience so there were no second chances. They are mostly bastards to work for. Totally self focused. Very introvert and self-serving. So when you actually work with them they are are nightmare. You don't get anything from them. No performance at all. If they see you getting a laugh which might distract from the spotlight on them, they will clamp you down. I learned never to show very much in rehearsal. I was cast as Ophelia opposite Douglas Hodge as Hamlet, in an episode of Sorry! with Ronnie Corbett. I said to him, 'Don't show too much of what you want to do in rehearsal or it'll get cut'. Douglas said, 'Oh I know what I'm doing...' OK, fine. But then he found his part was getting smaller and smaller. Ronnie used to say to me "You are a canny girl aren't you?" I told him I learned from the best. Anyway, Frankie was difficult as everybody knows. I was called Cilla in the pilot and I had a feed line. I ended up fluffing it, and Frankie went ballistic. This whole thing of coming out and doing it live in front of an audience, and suddenly being faced with Frankie's full on performance for the first time threw me. Where did that come from? We'd never seen it in rehearsal. The energy and power of his performance completely took me by surprise. So I learned a lot from Frankie. He didn't like young girls particularly, only the young boys!

RC: Can you remember how *The Brothers* entered your life?

Yes, I can. I was with the agent Michael Ladkin who told me he had got me an interview. I had just met my first husband Geoffrey, and we were arranging to go to the cinema. I thought it was a pain that I was having to go to an interview, and it was all a bit last minute. So I duly went to the BBC and there was the director Ronnie Wilson and Norman Crisp. I had this dress on which I'd got from my Mum's little boutique shop in Chichester. It was rather sweet with a little white lace collar. I was actually 21 at the time, so my agent might have told me the part was a much younger girl. Anyway, all I was bothered about was getting to the cinema so I sat there being a bit sulky. Little did I know it was just what they wanted and I got the part. It is a very key thing I always tell would-be actors, be yourself. You are never going to win the battle in an interview of trying to be someone that you are not. The most powerful thing is just be yourself. Sometimes it's right and you will have chemistry with the casting person, and sometimes it's not. I had no idea, none of us did, of what was going to happen subsequently with that show.

RC: Would it be fair to say *The Brothers* was your first television lead role?

Well yes. When we did that first series we didn't think it would be coming back, so off we all went to do other jobs. I was doing the spy drama *The Lotus Eaters* and suddenly they wanted us all back together again. We were all taken by surprise.

RC: Was there a hierarchy on the programme, and were you ever treated like Barbara and not Julia?

When it was revealed that Glyn wasn't coming back – which was ridiculous when you consider all that he wanted was £400 an episode instead of £300 or something - the BBC called his bluff. But anyway all the actors' fees came out into the open. Hilary Tindall was incensed. I wasn't because I was a junior member of the cast. I was getting my £150 or something. But Hilary wasn't getting much more than me, and she was ten years older and had a major role. I was always the difficult one in the sense that I stood up when I thought things weren't right. So they were never able to treat me like the junior member of the cast. I wouldn't allow them to do it. I had major ructions with Gerry Glaister. There was one time there was a real row about how to pronounce the Tuilerie Garden in Paris. This went on for a week. I threatened to leave over it. Anyway they put pressure on me to say this word which I knew was the wrong delivery, and I said on the take "Tuuuuu-lery" in a very feisty way. So there was no Barbara-like introvert off camera.

RC: What were your cornerstones for playing Barbara Kingsley?

My sister. She was 16 at the time. I studied her, looked at her mannerisms and how she dressed. I consciously took on her persona, not in personality but her age. The best thing was going out with our costume designer Barbara Kronig to do the shopping, and having to buy all these clothes which I wouldn't have been seen dead in otherwise. I really got into it, I loved playing this character which wasn't me. An introverted, sensitive, moody girl. I don't think I fully understood the depth with which Norman Crisp had written the role if I am honest, because I was still quite young myself. I played what Norman wrote, and I did what I thought was right. Purely instinctive and intuitive. But based on my sister's generation.

RC: Did you find a rapport playing opposite Jennifer Wilson as your mother?

I made it my business to get on with Jenny. She was very obsessed with the make-up and the hair. I had seen her in a show before and she had been brilliant. So I knew she was a good actor. As an aside to the power of *The Brothers* at that time. Three very successful business people who are my clients, very well known figures whom I can't name obviously, were 16 or so at the time. They found their way to my company later on in life to do some work with them, and all three said it was that series which changed their life. Extraordinary. I wish I could tell you who they were. You would be very surprised. I only found this out when they came to me some twenty-five years later wanting to use my skills. It was such a popular and powerful show.

RC: I'd like to ask you about your specific memories of some of the cast. Starting with the original Edward, Glyn Owen.

Glyn was wonderful, born to play the part. He should never have been sacked. He had his issues, drink being one of them. But he was never less than professional when he was working. I think it was a very big blow when they let him go. He was so right for the part, slightly street wise. I liked how Paddy played him but it wasn't how Norman wrote it. Glyn and I remained friends on and off. The last time I saw him was at the *After They Were Famous* reunion for ITV and he died not long afterwards sadly.

RC: Jean Anderson

Jean was ambigious in her personality, she was playing a very uptight role but had a naughty twinkle about her much of the time. She was fun. An under-rated actress because of her looks I think, she had a rather haughty look about her which then lent itself to lots of those type of roles. She was our social secretary. I'm not quite sure whether she really approved of me entirely, but I think she saw something of herself in me. A bit of a rebel.

RC: Patrick O'Connell

Paddy had quite a lot of demons. I was doing a show at the Orange Tree Theatre in Richmond when a message came through that Paddy had gone AWOL. Gone off to Amsterdam, because what he really wanted to be was a painter. I think the acting profession never sat with him terribly well and he had ambitions in other directions. He did well playing Edward, because he is a good actor, but I never felt he was entirely comfortable in the role.

RC: Robin Chadwick

When I knew Robin he was a young actor, and he drove me mad in rehearsal because he was so self-consciously a show-off. When we did the ITV documentary, he was quite different. Very sweet and affectionate. But we didn't really hit it off during that time we were making the show. I suppose we were opposites really. David Hammond was important to one of my business clients because of the scene where David is learning about the company and he suddenly says "Do you mean lorries come back with empty loads?" and sees an opportunity to increase the revenue of Hammond Transport. My very influential client was watching as a 15 year old and realised at that moment, watching that scene, that is what he wanted to do with his life. Restructure companies to make them more efficient. So life imitated art.

RC: Richard Easton

Lovely Richard. He came to my wedding. A fabulous actor. The best actor in *The Brothers*. I had a special relationship with him, I was his little sister on set and off. But like a lot of people who are gay, there is a wariness and distance which didn't allow you to get too close emotionally. He would not get involved in any emotional discussions, which is sad because he was a very passionate and intelligent actor. Hugely under-rated.

RC: Hilary Tindall

Hilary and I had great fun together. When we were up at Pebble Mill, we'd get in a cab and go out to find the remotest, weirdest Chinese restaurant in Birmingham. She was always the epitome of style and elegance. I was deeply envious, and she inspired me to dress better. Her children – Kate and Julian – were bridesmaid and pageboy at my first wedding.

RC: Derek Benfield

Derek used to live just down the road in Barnes, where I have a flat to this day. There was an edge to him, which I was a little wary of if I am honest. He worked a lot with Margaret Ashcroft and they were very close. We got on fine though, and we worked together well for the few scenes we had together.

RC: Gabrielle Drake

She was the opposite of me. Tall, slim, sophisticated. She sort of adopted me because of the way I am, and I think she quite admired my personality. We hung around together, and I was on her *This Is Your Life* with Jennifer.

I remember standing in the wings before the broadcast started and Eamonn Andrews had sweat pouring off him, he was so nervous. Total fear in his eyes. Then when he walked out he was such a smooth operator. Gabby was very supportive during the years I was with the actor Peter Woodward, trying to manage my relationship and bring up two children.

RC: Mark McManus

Mark came in as a young Aussie actor. Hilary fell madly in love with him, I'm never quite sure whether they had an affair or not. He was just great fun, open and innocent. He didn't drink back then. To see his slow decline was just tragic. I met him at an airport many years later and he was totally out of it. He was a total drunk. He had such promise and talent. Very sad. Maybe what he wanted out of his acting life didn't happen. One of the things you find with some actors is that we (and I include myself in this) are much greater actors than the series allow you to be. Trapped in the format. I had the perspicacity to get out. You have to look into your soul as to what you really want. A lot of the time the money gets you, and from then on it is not about your art. Then it is destructive.

RC: Jonathan Newth

I knew Jonathan before *The Brothers*. All I remember of him is that Jonathan and his wife came to the very first party I hosted for the cast and she threw a glass of red wine all over me. Accidentally of course! That whole storyline of Nicholas Fox having an affair with Barbara never really went anywhere. I didn't see the point of it.

RC: Malcolm Stoddard

My younger sister went out with Malcolm for a bit, so our families knew each other. I nearly died when he was cast as my husband because he had been my younger sister's boyfriend in real life.

RC: Colin Baker

I had a very few scenes with Colin. I knew him and Liza outside of *The Brothers*. Merroney became such an important figure within the show. We didn't have those sort of Merroney people in business until the 1970s. *The Brothers* was embryonic for so many changes in business and society. But like all pioneering things, you are in a lonely place because it takes time for people to catch up.

RC: Kate O'Mara

Kate joined the show, and I was fascinated by her. When I was a drama student at the Central School Of Speech and Drama we went out to see a play in the West End and I saw Kate for the first time playing a gypsy. She turned up on *The Brothers* years later and I am intrigued by her, and she is intrigued by me. She had arrived during the period I had left the show and had already made her mark as Jane Maxwell. I really got to know her during that period I was in the final series. I had met Peter Woodward during a production of Fanny By *Gaslight*, and we eventually after a couple of years decided we would like to start a theatre company together performing the classics but without directors. Everybody who came into the company did everything. We would have a detached eye on the productions and build the show from the ground up. It was a fascinating process and was the start of my business career. Being involved in every aspect of the theatre world showed me I could do many more things with my life. I didn't realise I could produce, direct and run a business. It was hugely pivotal for me. Anyway, Peter said he would like to ask Kate if she would join us in our new venture. So we had talks with her, the three of us founded The British Actors' Theatre Company. Kate was an amazing woman. She could act, direct, paint scenery, sell programmes – you name it and she was doing it. She also had a string of disastrous relationships, which I would constantly be on the other end of. I would often have phone call with

Kate which would go on for three hours. We shared our shit. I remember once we were up in Birmingham with one of the Shakespeare plays, a millionaire up there who was a fan of us both had given us his whole house to stay in. One morning I wanted us to go out for a walk to clear our heads, she was putting up excuses saying she would have to put on her lashes, her wig, her make up... Anyway, I kept on and on and I got her as far as the front door without all the slap before she dashed back in screaming "I can't do it". My daughter went out with her son Dickon for a while. She had another son who she gave up for adoption, who tracked her down but she didn't want anything to do with him. He later committed suicide, so both her children ended up killing themselves. Very sad. She was an appalling mother, although she loved Dickon to death. Kate was emotionally driven by being in relationships that were wrong for her, the men either didn't want her or she didn't want them. She was constantly let down by her choices of men. Quite self destructive in that way. But I loved her. The last time I saw her was at Patrick Garland's memorial service at Chichester in 2013. Kate walked in and she was white haired. I had never seen it like that before, she had stopped colouring it. She was there with her friend Patricia Shakesby. I tapped her on the shoulder, and she turned around and flung her arms around me. "I'm in denial" she kept saying. She just couldn't get her head around Dickon's death. I didn't know what to say. Kate had moved down to stay with Patrick's wife Alexandra Bastedo but within weeks Dickon was dead and not long after Kate was dead too. She lived a life of extraordinary complexity. She had had a very difficult relationship with her father. We weren't close for the last few years of her life, however we had some extraordinary times together over the years.

RC: Were you surprised to get the call from ITV in 2002 wanting a reunion of *The Brothers* **cast?**

Oh yes indeed. At the time, I was running a business which was three times the size it is now. About fifteen or twenty people in an office co-ordinating everything. It was a genuine thrill to meet up with everyone again. We staged all that stuff of us arriving at the dinner. It was a shame that not everyone was there. I wish I'd been involved in those tours abroad, I would have loved it. All that Beatle-mania style adulation. People often ask me how I found my brush with fame. It was very different back then. If you were on television once a week you were famous, it was nothing to do with your art. It was purely the fact that you were in peoples living rooms at a time when there was only three channels. But having said that, the period when I was in *The Brothers* and then *The Lotus Eaters* I was recognised all the time, life was extraordinary. I couldn't go anywhere without someone clocking my face and wanting to talk to me. The weird thing fame does is that you begin to see the world through a different lens. Everybody is nice to you, everybody likes you. They can't do enough for you. You start feeling rather wonderful. You can do no wrong. Then it all stops. You realise that you have just experienced fame. I remember coming back from the Acton Hilton on the tube when Barbara had just gone off to Canada in the show. A guy gingerly came up to me and said "I thought you were in Canada". I had to explain to him that Barbara was, but Julia was still in London. It was a very heady, interesting and fascinating time. It made me realise I didn't want it or need it. I have a whole different life and vocation which has been incredibly successful. I love now being recognised from the work I do with life skills. It nice to be behind the scenes. You don't have to worry about being on show or how you look. I was glad to experience a bit of fame though.

RC: Was *The Brothers* **part of a golden age of television?**

I think there is a tendency to look back. I think that nostalgic thing is a way of making us being able to get hold of a time we perceive to be good, especially if we are not in that place now. But certainly there was some fantastic stuff being produced in the 1970s. A blossoming of so many talents who had found their way onto television. I am very proud of being a part of *The Brothers*, it opened so many doors for me. When I started Personal Presentation, I could walk into any CEO's office and they would welcome me because I was Barbara from *The Brothers*. That still goes on today interestingly enough. It did though take me off track from the kind of actress I wanted to be for a while, but that's by the by.

SERIES FOUR (1974)

With an insatiable public demand for *The Brothers* developing both at home and abroad, a further fourteen part series debuted on BBC1 on Sunday 1st September, which would accumulate into a massive twenty-six episodes broadcast during 1974. Six months of the year with Sunday evenings given over to *The Brothers*. No wonder viewers were becoming addicted. The Radio Times celebrated its return with a one page feature in which viewers commented on the characters and the actors who played them gave their response. 'Edward is such a dull dog and so weak, he doesn't seem to see that his mother is a scheming old bitch' one viewer commented. "I have no interest in business and certainly do not experience Edward's emotional timidity with women. But he is in an extraordinary situation," Patrick O'Connell responded. Another viewer wrote 'Jennifer Kingsley is the most wonderful person. In character, loyalty and intelligence, she stands head and shoulders above the Hammonds'. Basking in this high praise Jennifer Wilson replied "She is no saint – she just does what she thinks is right. Actually the part was written especially for me. I do have a daughter myself and some of the scenes are uncannily like real life."

Producer Ken Riddington meanwhile was speaking to TV Life about the continuing popularity of the show. "It's definitely a good time," he said of the 7.25pm broadcast slot. And he answered queries from real truck drivers concerning the lack of adventures out on the road. "Road adventures need more film effort than we can afford, and we insist on location shooting," Ken admitted. "There's no question of using moving back projection to give the effect of the road going past the lorry window. That's just not on."

The fourth series would see the first scripts not to be penned by either Crisp or Paice. Five of the episodes are written by John Pennington, a writer whose pedigree included *Coronation Street, Dr. Finlay's Casebook, General Hospital* and the Crisp - Glaister show *The Expert*.

The loss of Julia Goodman as Barbara, who had moved on to pastures new, was keenly felt. But as ever Riddington had new blood in the wings. Much mention had been made of Bill Riley's wife Gwen in previous episodes, and finally here she was in the flesh played by 38 year old Margaret Ashcroft. Maggie, as she was known to her friends and colleagues, was at the time dividing her allegiance between *The Brothers* and playing solicitor Margaret Castleton in ITV's legal drama *The Main Chance.* "Some time ago I seemed to get a lot of roles as a working class Mum" she told The Sun. "Because of the part I play people think I must know all about the small print on legal documents. Even real solicitors seem to think so. At the Law Society, three of them came up to me and asked me where I practised." The niece of theatrical great Dame Peggy Ashcroft, she fitted the role of Gwen Riley like a glove. Maggie often told interviewers that she and Derek Benfield first met in the cold light of a 7am coach en route to shooting on *The Brothers* and by 8am had shot their first scene together. It was an instant chemistry and the two actors became great friends. From a dramatic point of view, her burgeoning friendship with Mary and devotion to her husband Bill enabled both characters a friendly shoulder with which to discuss the latest plot points, and also fleshed out the Riley's home life enabling viewers to see the working class situation that juxtaposed nicely the middle class comfort of the Hammond's themselves. Hammond Transport Services moved a step nearer to being floated as a public limited company, and guiding them this road is one Martin Farrell, played by Murray Hayne. 43 years old at the time of getting the role, Hayne had been born in India where his father had been a missionary and was sent to boarding school in England. After a spell in the Navy he landed up at drama school but not before he experienced a variety of employments to make ends meet. He was a time an encyclopaedia salesman. "I enjoyed that," he told the Birmingham Mail. "It brought me into contact with all sorts of people. I was good at it, perhaps because it required a certain amount of acting skill. Then one night I was talking to this man with not a lot of money and six kids, giving him my pitch. I suddenly looked at myself and thought what am I doing? If he reads a hundred pages of this lot he'll be lucky. He was on the point of committing himself, my commission was in sight, and I ripped up the prospectus and told him to forget it and save his money. He must have thought I was mad. Next morning I resigned." Hayne is a self-confessed private man, being recognised for his television roles comes with a price. "People ask me the most incredible questions," he said. "There comes a point when I have to tell them politely to mind their own business. I am not anti-social, I like people, but basically I am a listener." Speaking to The Sun, Hayne commented on his character Farrell: "He is 100 per cent fella. Nobody is as good as he is. And he is very much a loner, not like me." He did admit surprise at the amount of fan mail he received from women viewers. "One even got my home telephone number and almost propositioned me over the phone!"

We return to the action with an Norman Crisp penned episode, 'Emergency'. Edward and Jennifer having returned from a holiday ready to tell Mary of their plans to finally marry only to find her collapsed with a heart attack. The four month gap between series had led many a viewer to wonder if it was a dead Mary that had been glimpsed face down among the pot plants. But you can't keep an old schemer like Mary Hammond down for long, and she is soon lapping up the sympathy and guilt of her sons from a hospital bed with Gwen Riley subsequently roped in as a home help. Pitched opposite the Leslie Crowther sit-com vehicle *My Good Woman* and a showing of the 'Star Movie' from 1957 *Fire Down Below,* it was a ratings victory for *The Brothers* which achieved 19.6% share against ITV's 17.9%. The Stage newspaper waded in with their verdict. "Familiarity breeds contempt," wrote Geoffrey Wren. "The series formula is nearly analogous to a friendship, patiently forged and enriched by long acquaintance, a luxury denied to viewers coming afresh to the series. Credulity must first be established, though Radio Times offers a potted guide to the neophyte." Following a lengthy summing up of various plot strands, Wren comments "An exploratory opus and the director Roderick Graham paced his production sensibly to allow the respective of relationships to be absorbed. There were however too many telephone conversations and the writing was occasionally sketchy. Excellent performances from Jean Anderson, dignified and shrewd; Patrick O'Connell fate-bound, tortured by conflicting emotions; Jennifer Wilson, seemingly feminine yet ambitious and calculating; Hilary Tindall, a sophisticated intelligent and resourceful temptress; and finally Richard Easton and Robin Chadwick as the other brothers." He concludes the episode "A spicy potion of power, intrigue and sex, the full flavour of which will emerge in the forthcoming weeks, ensuring attentive viewing from devotees." Not a rave, but neither was Wren's review scathing. Would the BBC's own Audience Research match this sitting on the fence? "There was some feeling that this first episode was slightly disappointing," it began. Ouch. It further went on to report that the panel felt that the episode "spent most of its time picking up threads from a previous series." With no repeated showings during the off screen period, it has to be conceded that some repeated plot points were necessary, however… As usual the criticisms of too much screen time spent on the personal aspect and not enough on the business implications were evident. "It seems to be settling for the usual round of intrigue, matrimonial tangles and drinking. One didn't see one truck!" Another panel member put it even more bluntly, "It needs to get back to the transport business." Even the look of the show came in for some criticism. "The same rooms, offices, hospital beds seen so often before." The cast gloried in some high praise thankfully, "[it is] difficult at times to realise it is not real". "One lived every minute with them" said another.

The plight of Mary Hammond's illness had been keenly felt all over Europe. Jean Anderson informed the national press: "I went to Holland to appear on the Dutch equivalent of the David Frost Show. Before they introduced me they showed the studio audience and the viewers that episode where I finished up lying on the conservatory floor after having a heart attack. They had a similar set in the studio and when the scene finished, I was lying on the floor just as I had in the scene. A gauze went up and the chat show host said 'You can get up now.' There was a deathly hush – and then a gasp from the audience. It was quite dramatic. At that time in the series, when I had my heart attack, I was approached in a London station by a well dressed young man wearing a bowler hat. He said 'it's so nice to see you looking fit. My mother works in the London clinic and they're very concerned about our condition.'" Viewers it seemed were more wrapped up than ever in the continuing

Hammond saga. *The Brothers* had by now established itself as a firm fixture of the Sunday evening schedules, and its loyal audience were savouring every moment. Brian Hammond is seemingly still oblivious over the next few episodes to his wife's out of character socialising, as her obsession with Nicholas Fox kicks in again. He is too busy scheming to get Hammond Transport floated on the stock exchange. It even extends to subterfuge to get Martin Farrell on the board. But Edward is a smarter cookie than they realise, he restores the status quo by inviting Bill Riley to the board too. Eventually, though domestic matters have to be faced. A parking ticket and a telegram spell it out for Brian that Nicholas and his wife are indeed having an affair. The episode 'Partings' finds Ann leaving Brian, and the famous slap (more of a push really) which sends Ann sprawling onto the armchair. This brief moment of domestic violence is quite tame compared to the kind of excess that pervades television today, but was shocking enough to provide a strong reaction from the viewers. It has to be said that more than a few were very much on Brian's side, given the treatment he had received from Ann.

A key story arc which runs through this fourth series is floating Hammond Transport as a public company on the stock exchange. Two characters who are introduced in respect of this storyline would be important to the future of the show. The first the Chairman of the Bank, Sir Neville Henniswode played by veteran star of radio, theatre and film Carleton Hobbs. Hobbs was once Sherlock Holmes on radio and had built a career which was the envy of many of his peers. The second arrival is even more significant, Sir Neville's protégée, a brilliant banking executive named Paul Merroney. Colin Baker's low key arrival in five of the episodes, whilst expertly played, only hint at the major impact the character was to have the following year. In the episode 'Hit And Miss' (a John Pennington script) the Hammond brothers are summond to Sir Neville's country estate for a shooting party. It is surprising any of them can hear Sir Neville's wise words amid all the banging. The viewers were certainly taking notice. "*The Brothers* clearly continued to provide very enjoyable viewing for most of the sample audience," the internal Audience Research Report on the episode began. However there were as always in these reports words of criticism. Ann's ongoing affair was pronounced "a bit of a bore" with "not a laugh or smile in sight" levelled at the show as a whole. However it was generally accepted in the report that the majority of viewers were still happy with the interweaving of the boardroom and domestic storylines. "If one member of the cast impressed above the others," it went on to say "it was Derek Benfield as Bill Riley" although it also noted that all the actors were well cast and had contributed greatly to the overall enjoyment. Viewers of this episode particularly enjoyed the clay-pigeon shoot. It concluded that more outdoor filming would be welcomed in future series. Having had a 23.4% share of the audience, it was slightly outflanked by ITV's 26.4% share in the form of a half hour David Jason comedy vehicle *The Top Secret Life Of Edgar Briggs* which was then followed by the premiere of *The Planet Of The Apes*, a TV spin off of the successful Hollywood films.

A sub plot which arrives and disappears just as quickly occurs in the episode 'The Race', as *The Brothers* production team have a day out at the Oulton Park race track in Cheshire. David is driving a Formula Ford car sponsored by Hammonds and we get some nice shots of the paddock and cars zooming around the track. The whole enterprise is quickly dropped after a showcase episode, which does at least give us some respite from the depot and the boardroom bickering. The winner of the race is named over the tannoy as Tudor George, co-incidentally the name of the costume supervisor on the series! The subject of labour relations continued to be a focal point of *The Brothers*. With the quest to go public the men working for Hammond's pitched their claim for improved wages if the company was being put on a potentially international footing. With possible strike action in the air, an atmosphere of unrest pervades the depot and *The Brothers* want to know who is stirring them up. Could it be Riley? As ever the outspoken foreman cops the flack. These management versus labour battles couldn't have been more topical for the Union strong mid-1970s.

Brian Hammond had his own worries aside from his relationship with Ann. He accidentally knocks down a little girl in his car. Naturally an already emotionally vulnerable Brian is beside himself with guilt. Richard Easton had proved a powerhouse during the course of *The Brothers* thus far, bringing a determined practicality to the Hammond's schemes, which proved a solid base rock by which to operate the company, even if his marriage couldn't be guided as successfully. By this point an actor of massive stage experience in the classics, it was still something of a novelty for Easton to have a recurring television role in a top rated series. Speaking to The Sun, Easton confirmed his feelings towards his on screen character Brian. "I quite liked him at the beginning of the series. He has one quality that I admire and don't have myself. That is patience. But now he has become so silly and negative. His attitude to Nicholas Fox for example. I would rather punch him on the nose than refuse to talk to him". He takes issues with Mary Hammond's austere dwelling too. "I do hate that house. It really is frightful. You could never live in it." Like many of the cast the fame the role attracted came with some surprising recognition. "It has had the most astonishing effect," claimed Richard. "People have recognised me from in the streets of Marrakesh, and on the beach in Cyprus. They are generally very nice to me. There is not very much you can hate about Brian – unlike Ann. Although people know you are not the real character, it is a sort of game to pretend you are. Hilary, who plays Ann, and I are very good friends. Though when I first met her I thought 'How am I going to cope with this?' She had this terribly sophisticated county image, and I really thought of her as the bitchy Ann. She is not at all like that. Whereas Jenny Wilson, who plays Jennifer Kingsley, is a much tougher person than her on screen character. The seven main characters tend to be a bit cliquey and a bit suspicious of newcomers to the series. But we don't have time for temperament. If one of us tries it on a bit, one of the others will soon slap him down. There is none of the sort of backstage nastiness that has been known in other long running series. It has been fun to make. People from all walks of life seem to like the programme. I was at a reception once where the Bishop Of Durham left early. He said he wanted to get home to watch *The Brothers*." Evidently he wasn't the only one rushing home from church to catch the latest goings on with the Hammonds.

Being sweetness and light is something that Richard's co-star in the series Hilary Tindall did not have to worry about. Hilary earned herself the tag "The bitch of *The Brothers*" due to her manipulative nature and her treatment of her husband Brian. "Playing bitchy roles never did Bette Davis any harm," Hilary told the press. She also revealed to the Daily Mail that women in Ann's age bracket – 25 to 35 – actually approve. "If she's having an affair it makes it all right. They feel less guilty about their own. It's a tremendous responsibility in a way. Some women criticise usually on the grounds that Ann handled the affair badly. She let Brian find out. In *The Brothers* I send my lover a telegram from Brussels. Brian gets it on the bill and questions it. That's how he finds out. I believe Ann really wanted him to know. She wants to get a reaction from him." Reflecting on the public reaction to Ann, Hilary confessed "I get the feeling that people are sitting back and daring me to go further. Young women are all for it. Older women accept it and are interested from a distance. Men are more disapproving but they can't help approving the spirit of the girl. One man told me he loathes women who are too sweet. He likes women to be bitchy. Since playing Ann I find that men fall into two groups in their attitude to me. Some are afraid of someone they think of as sexually challenging, the others take the attitude: OK chaps we're all right for tonight. When it comes down to it, women take the lead anyway. Leave men, especially Englishmen to their own resources and they wouldn't get past first base. Englishmen are rather afraid of sex. Women make the first move. Lots of young men fancy me. I can only assume that they want to be initiated by an older woman – it's a rather Continental idea. I had a letter from a young boy of 17 who said: I know I am only young but Brian doesn't know how lucky he is. Richard Easton who plays Brian gets letters blaming him for not appreciating me, but other people criticise him for not kicking me out. This series ends with Brian filing for divorce and Ann is upset because she is left without anyone. Ann's lover – an advertising executive – doesn't want to know." Reflecting on four series with *The Brothers*, Hilary said "When I took the part of Ann I decided to play it without compromise. I wouldn't play for sympathy. She was written as a baddy, so I played her as a baddy. And though eventually a lot of people liked and envied her – I quite like her myself – others really hate her. Walking around our local supermarket with a wire basket, a middle-aged man followed me right through the shop. When we got outside he said 'Well, you are charming I must say.' Men look at me in a different way because of Ann. One man I've known for years and years said that despite himself, he now thinks of me differently. He said 'I always used to think of you as a nice girl.' Once in a discussion about whether wives should be allowed to have affairs when everyone expects the husband to be unfaithful if he is away for a time, I said that what was all right for one must be all right for the other. But the man rounded on me and said: 'You are saying that only because of Ann Hammond.' We still have this double standard." Hilary came to acting after being encouraged by television legend Violet Carson, *Coronation Street's* fearsome Ena Sharples. Carson spotted Hilary in an amateur talent show and suggested that she try for a professional career. "So I wrote to BBC Manchester and said I would like to take part in plays on Children's Hour. I did one or two and then decided to go to RADA." From there she graduated to repertory companies in Bristol, Leatherhead and Windsor. Landing a part in a West End production of William Douglas Home's *Aunt Edwina* was a turning point "I thought I'd really arrived" remembered Hilary "but the play did not run for very long."

Hilary had made the decision to leave *The Brothers* at the end of the fourth series whilst the series was reaching a zenith in its popularity. She feared being typecast. As an actor, Hilary had been besieged with offers from the theatre with roles that she very much wanted to explore. Something had to give. As one of the key dramatic lynchpins, clearly losing Hilary Tindall would be a big loss to everyone. Ann Hammond had been one of the characters that had really caused a reaction from viewers, whether they approved or disapproved of her behaviour, she had been a reason to switch on every week. The mail bag to both Hilary and the BBC in general confirmed that most people had an opinion on her one way or another. "One gets lazy, too used to security and having the money coming in steadily", Hilary said of her departure. "This can be dangerous. I knew I needed to move on."

Ann plays her deck and is found with a losing hand. She has humiliated Brian, Nicholas Fox who was drawn to a sharp and mercurial woman is now bored of her, and she has failed to develop a bond with her own children. She is alone. Defeat and divorce are in the air as Ann walks through the door for the final time. Goodbye Ann Hammond. You have been a supernova.

Viewers had a shock on the 24th November waiting for the series penultimate episode, it was delayed by one week because of the Royal Variety Performance dominating the BBC1 viewing that evening. It seemed that a combination of Perry Como and Noele Gordon was more important than Hammond Transport Services quest to go public. However, by Sunday 1st December everything was back on track. Ted has made a serious faux par at a meeting of prospective investors and for the first time in the series his position as Chairman is under real threat. It proves to have long lasting consequences, Hammond's does indeed go public and is found to be under performing. Market confidence is required and that comes at huge cost to Ted. Norman Crisp ends the series in his usual dramatic style with Martin Farrell appointed as Chairman of the Board. For the first time in its history Hammond Transport Services doesn't have a Hammond in charge. The mysterious case of the changing Carol Hammond is further deepened by having two child actors play the role, Charlotta Martinus (daughter of television director Derek Martinus) appeared as Carol in the episode 'Public Concern' as she had done in the third series, but by the final episode Carol was now Annabelle Lanyon (later to star opposite Tom Cruise in the movie *Legend*). A further regeneration was to come. We are on our second Nigel too, a young Joshua Le Touzel who went on to make a name for himself in many prominent television and stage productions.

The Audience Research Report offered an end of term assessment from a section of the viewership. 'The Crucial Vote' written by Crisp had a 23.3% share of the available audience against a 3.7% share from BBC 2 (documentary series *The World About Us*) and 30.3% over on ITV (*Planet Of The Apes*). The report opined "This was a splendid last episode most felt. The boardroom coup made for an exciting end to the present series; involving all the main characters in a dramatic collision of personalities; at the same time it left viewers 'all agog' how the company and individual characters would fare under a new dispensation. Many said they would wait for the next series with considerable interest." It did however also note: "...some viewers were less enthusiastic – occasionally finding domestic events, in particular Brian's failed marriage, less interesting than the transport company. The series was generally enjoyed and many viewers seemed loathe to miss a single episode." Having opened the fourth series on a 19.6% share of the audience, clearly the armchair viewers were enjoying what they saw, ending the run of episodes on a 23.3% share. The series was clearly in rude health. Changes were indeed a foot at Hammond Transport, but so too were changes looming within the show as four new regulars would shake-up the cosy on screen Hammond family set up. Would the viewers welcome the new faces on screen? Time would tell. They had a mere four month (yet still anxious) wait before *The Brothers* was back on prime-time BBC1.

THE BROTHERS   PATRICK O'CONNELL   BBC tv

THE BROTHERS   JENNIFER WILSON   BBC tv

IN CONVERSATION WITH
JONATHAN NEWTH

RC: How were you approached to play Nicholas Fox?

Jonathan Newth: I think I had been in a show either produced by Gerry Glaister or Ken Riddington. Or perhaps a director I had recently worked with at the BBC suggested me to one of them. In those days, as an actor, you got onto the carousel of BBC popular drama, and if you didn't cock it up, you could be quite regularly employed. Fortunately that happened to me.

RC: Did you know any of the cast before you went into the show?

I had worked with Richard Easton about ten years previously. One of my first theatre jobs was in a lavish production of *The School For Scandal* at the Haymarket Theatre in London and then subsequently on to Broadway. It was directed by and starred Sir John Gielgud and a cast which read like a Who's Who of theatre aristocracy of the time: Ralph Richardson, Geraldine McEwan, Gwen Frangcon Davies. I was playing two very small parts and understudying Richard, who was excellent as the apparently ne'er-do-well Charles Surface. I liked him enormously, he was witty, engaging and is a very good actor. He went on to a highly successful career on both sides of the Atlantic.

RC: Did you like playing Nicholas Fox?

It's generally more fun and easier to play baddies. Making decent people interesting is harder. From What I recall Nicholas Fox was more of an amoral chancer than a complete bastard.

RC: You had many of your scenes with the late Hilary Tindall as Ann Hammond. What are your memories of her?

Hilary was easy to work with , entirely professional and 'unstarry' in my experience.

RC: Do you recall any specific scenes with her?

I recall the swimming pool sequence. I remember this because wherever it was a grassy slope which led up to the pool. The director decided it would make an interesting shot if Hilary and I appeared running over the crest of the slope and dived simultaneously into the pool   Well, the nature of filming is repetition. So after a number of takes the grass was getting very wet and therefore slippery. The inevitable happened. Take Five – Action! We come bounding romantically across the green sward and I fall flat on my face. Very alluring. And of course much merriment from the crew.

RC: Were you recognised when you were in the street whilst playing Nicholas?

Yes I was. It goes with the territory of appearing in a popular series. Quite often the recognition would take the form of "Are you who I think you are?" My reply was always "Tell me who you think I am and I'll tell you if I am him." A lot of viewers like 'bad boys' especially where there is a frisson of elicit sex.

RC: You did three series and left. Why did you leave?

It was my decision. It was pretty clear there was going to be little further character or plot development.

RC: You worked under two producers on the show, Glaister and Riddington. Any memories?

I remember very little of Gerry. Ken I remember well because he also produced *Tenko* [Jonathan was Major Clifford Jefferson in the show]. He was a very able producer and though I had a falling out with him over a couple of *Tenko* scripts, I had a good working relationship with Ken.

RC: Why do you think *The Brothers* captured the imagination of so many viewers?

Family sagas have always been (still are) a rich vein for TV, and you had the interesting dynamic of three brothers manoeuvring for power overseen by a dominant matriarch. And maybe a transport firm offered a backdrop that most people could relate to.

RC: Do you think *The Brothers* was made in a golden era for television and if so why was it a golden era?

Well that is the one that really should form the basis of a dissertation. There are so many social, economic, technological and political strands to this question. Television drama has always been expensive but I think there was a greater willingness to take risks both artistically and financially. There was more cross referencing between theatre and television in terms of writing and directing. Television was still a relatively young medium with fewer channels, innovative experiment allowed for the 'right to fail' whereas today everything is cost-ed down to the last penny. I cut my teeth during that time and I'm well aware that my bi-focals may have a rosy hue and that there was an awful lot of dross among the quality. All that said, I think the general level of excellence in performance on television is probably higher today than back then.

The Hammond boardroom went through
a design make-over in 1975 to
accomodate the larger cast (below)

Feathers ruffled: new arrivals to shake up the Hammond
family. Above: Colin Baker and Carole Mowlam
Below: Kate O'Mara

SERIES FIVE (1975)

Edward's shock departure from the Managing Director's chair had kept *The Brothers* loyal audience of reported 10½ million viewers on tenterhooks for a full four months. Letters of outrage arrived at the BBC adamant that Edward should be re-instated at once. The week following the broadcast of the final episode of the fourth series in December 1974, rehearsing was once again underway for the next set of thirteen episodes. The juggernaut was truly rolling without any sign of stopping. After having brought in a third writer on the previous series, the writing duties reverted to having Crisp and Paice divide the load between them on the show.

Producer Ken Riddington was forced to ring the changes when actor Murray Hayne decided he did not want to return as Martin Farrell. It left the production team with a bit of a hole. A new chairman had been appointed as far as Hammond Transport was concerned. The obvious choice was to recruit from within the ranks and so Colin Baker's city whizz kid Paul Merroney was quickly promoted and destined for the Managing Director's chair. We had seen Merroney being knowledgeable and curtly efficient during the previous series, but now we were to see the bite with the bark. Riddington and his new script editor Douglas Watkinson ensured that Merroney was the cold fish who would shake the incestuous Hammond Board to its core. He was all about profit and expansion, and he certainly wasn't going to let no familial infighting get in his way. In many ways this series can be counted as the start of a new phase for the show. The original premise is pushed aside for bolder schemes as Hammond goes into Europe in a big way. Merroney is as sharp as a kukri and he brings with him a personal secretary in the shape of Clare Miller. 39 year old Carole Mowlam, who had starred as Pat Grove in the BBC serial *The Grove Family* in the mid-1950s, was tasked with playing the complex Clare who was clearly carrying a torch for her boss. Over the course of the next two years she would be used by him both professionally and personally, often pressured into putting aside her own morals to spy and manipulate on Merroney's behalf. It was a way of filling the large gap left by the departures of Hilary Tindall and Gabrielle Drake.

Whilst the missing Ann Hammond could be easily explained away with a divorce, given the fractious way the Brian and Ann had parted at the end of the previous series, Riddington and Crisp decided on a more dramatic end for Jill. The first episode 'Life Goes On' was designed to feature some small talk of Jill, leaving the viewer wondering where she was, then in the last seconds of the episode David reveals to viewers that Jill is dead. It is Crisp's writing at its best. And it would have been a genuine shock to viewers except that the BBC played a home goal, as The Sun reported the day before transmission. "What should have been *The Brothers* best kept secret is well and truly out," ran the opening tag. "And the series producer is furious. Because it is all through a muddle at the BBC. One of the stars of this long-running series, David Hammond's wife Jill, will be 'killed off' when it returns on Sunday. The news should have hit the programme's faithful fans like a thunderbolt at the climax of this weekend's episode. Instead the BBC are stuck with a damp squib. Because they have already told millions of viewers what is going to happen. And who it will happen to. The BBC's own trailers for the return of *The Brothers* have told viewers that since we last met the Hammond family, Jill has been killed in a car crash." Producer Ken Riddington is then quoted as saying "This is quite extraordinary, I am very angry indeed." What a palarva. In fact Gabrielle Drake was alive and well, then appearing in Andrew Lloyd Webber and Alan Ayckbourn's West End musical *Jeeves*. However this was of no consolation to either Riddington or the grief stricken David Hammond on screen. It appeared that whilst carrying David's baby, there had been a car accident and Jill and the unborn baby had tragically been the victims. For viewers who had invested in four years-worth of personal crises, this was one of the most touching of them all. Naturally the Audience Research department swung into gear wanting to know what their cross section of viewers thought. It had held a 19.7% share of the audience against ITV's 25.4% with a showing of the 1965 movie *Von Ryan's Express*. Although there was some very positive feedback about the episode in general, it went onto to say "A number of the remainder [of the panel] were 'annoyed' and 'disappointed' at Jill's death and the way the news of it was 'so casually slipped in' at the end." A pity these people didn't watch the BBC1 trailers, they would have been well prepared. "There was praise all round for the 'usual high standard of acting' (although the absence of Hilary Tindall and Gabrielle Drake 'left a gap which will be hard to fill.' The cast were entirely suited to their roles and totally believable: 'they appear real-life people', especially this week Robin Chadwick as David: 'His grief was so real, I could have wept for him'." In this episode the role of Sir Neville Henniswode who had been previously played by Carleton Hobbs, was played by another actor, 74 year old Llewellyn Rees. Hobbs had not been available and so it was decided to re-cast the part, however Hobbs did resume the role for the sixth season.

Richard Easton had only committed himself to six episodes of this fifth series, and took a sabbatical to explore other roles. The emotional isolation Brian Hammond felt from his divorce and the pressure of being Hammond's Managing Director was taking a heavier toll than anyone realised, and Brian has a nervous breakdown. Easton's skill as an actor meant that these scenes were utterly raw, and visceral. They were easily among the best scenes of the entire series from a dramatic point of view. However, it did yet again create a vacuum. Luckily along with Baker and Mowlam, another major player was about to enter the arena. Once again The Sun was on it like a car bonnet. The 22nd March edition boasted 'Brothers Face Up To A Tough New Bird' as its sexist headline. "The Hammond Brothers are heading for trouble again. When the series returns next month, Edward, Brian and David will be pitting their wits against a very shrewd cookie. She is Jane Maxwell, the latest in a long line of women to play havoc with the Hammond brothers' lives." Kate O'Mara was on her way into the show. 34 year old Kate was already a stage and screen veteran. From stage Shakespeare to Hammer horror, she had proved a sexy leading lady who could act the socks off many of her colleagues. Explaining her arrival in the show, Kate told the reporter "She is not so much a bitch as a very tough businesswoman. She sees men not only as her equals, but frequently as her inferiors. She knows what she wants and she usually gets it. She likes to call the tune. It's a smashing part. Something I can really get my teeth into. I usually play strong, sexy ladies who put their all into being a man-eater. Jane is different. She has a different sort of strength." When asked which of the Hammond brothers she would be falling for, Kate tactfully said "I don't even know myself. I haven't seen the scripts for the later episodes yet." Clearly someone was going to be targeted by Queen Vamp. Jane Maxwell is the owner of the struggling Flair Freight airline and initial sparks fly as Merroney spots an ideal opportunity for adding a bargain purchase to the Hammond portfolio. Jane comes with her ex-husband in tow. Pilot Don Stacey played by Mike Pratt. 45 year old Pratt was a song writer, musician and actor. He had co-written the hit 'Handful of Songs' for Tommy Steele in 1957. By far his most familiar guise was as Jeff Randall dealing with his dead partner Marty Hopkirk in 26 episodes of ITV's *Randall & Hopkirk (Deceased)* which had become a cult hit. Pratt brought a little laid back hippy philosophy to the permanently uptight Hammonds, and also a fondness for the bottle. Yes, everybody's dream combination – an alcoholic pilot. It was very clear that Merroney and Maxwell would cross swords, and they do from the very first moment Maxwell storms into her airfield office demanding to know what Merroney is doing in there. It was television dynamite. The friction even spilled over into the actors' billing on the show, with Baker and O'Mara finally agreeing on alternate turns to receive preferential treatment in the series closing credits.

The production used the airport at Lydd, near Ashford in Kent, as the Flair Freight operating centre. There was plenty of scope for footage of freight planes taking off and opportunities to film inside them whilst they were grounded. In interviews later in her life O'Mara revealed that she was in a bad mood on the day of the audition with producer Ken Riddington for the role, she was going through a divorce and just couldn't be bothered to do a reading for him. Her stroppy demeanour on that day secured her the role of Jane Maxwell because unwittingly she was behaving just the way they saw the character. Riddington and Head of Series and Serials Bill Slater were convinced they had found their new leading lady. Certainly the balance of the show had altered considerably during the fifth series. The insular world of the Hammond's now had to cater for a ruthless ambition driven Chairman, a slightly obsessional personal secretary and a shrew-in-high-heels new Director of the Board. In truth though, at this point the series needed to change if it was to keep the loyal viewers hooked. There is only so many storylines around three brothers, a former mistress and a scheming mother. These elements were all weaved into the new format, but certainly Paul Merroney was now in the driving seat as far as plots and dramatic conflict were concerned. Changes to location filming were also to the fore. Ralph Hilton Transport's Greenwich depot was now elbowed in favour of another location some 44 miles away in Burgh Heath near Epsom. Kinloch Provision Merchants had warehouses and offices that were situated in a quiet area in comparison to the city madness near Greenwich. There was a lot less intrusive noise and more room to manoeuvre for the production team as they set up their shots. Kinloch's were responsible for transporting the Wavy Line discount food range, and sometimes the Wavy Line logo was glimpsed on lorries in shot. It was unavoidable. The production team explained away this change by having Paul Merroney unilaterally purchase the property of an adjoining printers and completely re-design the depot for easier access of the lorry fleet. The set designer complimented this with new studio office sets, including an octagon shaped conference table. With an upmarket beige interior, dominated by photos of the fleet, it was a far cry from the stark brick walls of the previous depot Boardroom. Another clear sign that the Merroney era had arrived.

The episode 'Tiger By The Tail' has one of those 'only in the 1970s' moments when the tale of Little Black Sambo is recounted. The book published in 1899 had long since courted some controversy for its stereotypical depiction of racial origin. It is amazing to think the writers and producers of *The Brothers* thought nothing of summing up the plot details, which in itself are not controversial, whilst openly using the title character name. Were *The Brothers* to be repeated today, this is one of the few edits that would have to be made.

This fifth run finally addressed the on – off relationship of Edward and Jennifer. In the storyline Merroney had engineered that they both had to fly off to Switzerland on business, and even arranged for them to stay over on holiday. With the constant letters being received regarding the subject, Ken Riddington and Norman Crisp decided it was time they put the viewing audience out of their misery. Not before some location work in Aviemore, Scotland, gave the production team scenes of Edward and Jennifer playfully mastering the ski slopes of Switzerland, which cemented the couples resolve to tie the knot. The wedding episode in question, 'Special Licence' directed by Australian Lennie Mayne, was seen on 4th May 1975. It was considered important enough to merit a Radio Times cover featuring the bride and groom, the only time in *The Brothers* history that the coveted listings magazine devoted their cover to the show.

The episode got a massive 23.5% share of the available audience, its ITV rival sitcom *Doctor On The Go* starring Robin Nedwell managed an 18.8% share. Clearly this was a big Sunday night event for viewers who had stayed loyal through the high and lows of the Hammond lovebirds. The Audience Research report noted that the wedding had been "Much needed light relief". "Delightful, exciting and completely credible" reported one delighted panel member. It did note though that one in four were no more than "moderately impressed" feeling that the build to up to the episode left its execution as "just a very ordinary episode... consisting mainly of the usual petty quarrels". The continuing thread of Brian's breakdown offered more opportunities for comment. "Brian's breakdown is incredible and doesn't seem to tie up with the character previously portrayed," sniped one member. And according to one or two, the show was becoming "Just another soap opera... a middle class *Coronation Street*." Once again there was universal praise for Jean Anderson, and so too Richard Easton with the difficult job of bringing Brian's deterioration to the screen. "Superb" was the overall verdict whilst there was concern too that he might be gradually phased out. One viewer observed that "Edward seems to be more at home with his work colleagues than his wife." Generally, despite the misgivings of a few, the episode was very well received, with most taking part noting that the cast were "A splendid team". Jennifer's wedding outfit was commended upon and the parting comment of the report quoted a viewer as saying: "I can never fault this series. In particular this episode, the Registry Office wedding was very true to life, and the reception so well arranged." It summed up the tone of the nation on that Sunday night.

Understandably the wedding brought with it a massive response to the BBC. "It brought a mixed bag of mail," Patrick O'Connell confided to the Weekly News. "Many congratulated us and wished us happiness together. Several disapproved. They thought I was a terrible, nasty person to treat my mother so." Of the filming of the ceremony itself, O'Connell was daunted by the scenes. "I was more nervous than at my own wedding. Everything seemed so real. The scene was filmed at a register office near Twickenham about 9.30 in the morning. As well as the BBC cameras we had five photographers taking shots of the happy couple. There were about a dozen or so onlookers thinking they were watching a real wedding, and that made it seem even more genuine. Everything went smoothly because we had rehearsed the scene many times. I remember one occasion when I was rehearsing the wedding day kiss with Jenny in the studio, I didn't know that Jenny's husband, Brian Peck, was watching. I had Jenny in my arms when there was a commotion and Brian came storming on the set acting the outraged husband – but it was all in joke of course. He's a good joker. We all had a good laugh." Not quite everyone was as keen on the wedding episode. O'Connell's two daughters were not thrilled to see the happy couple. "My children hate to see me kissing Jenny on television. Frances, especially, was most upset to see me marrying another woman. She sometimes forgets it is just a play. I am getting some funny looks from her when I go home in the evenings." The trip to Aviemore – doubling for Switzerland – brought more stress for Patrick it seems. "I shuddered when I learned Jenny and I were to be filmed skiing, for I'd never been skiing before. I'm so bad the crew had to stand me up on the skis. I was warned never to cross my skis – which I promptly did and fell over. We had expert skiers doing the long shots but Jenny and I did the close up shots on skis. It was dead easy when the scene called for me to take a fall while skiing. I didn't have to pretend. I was put up on my skis and given a push start. Off I went down the slope, to tumble over in grand style. Even the stunt men reckoned they couldn't have done a better job."

The South Wales Echo opted to print a feature on local boy made good. Bridgend born Tudor George was the 25 year old Costume Designer on the show, and gave the paper an insight into how the look of the characters was formed. "There's a surprising amount to it," Tudor said. "The personality of the characters is established now, but we have to keep supplying them with new gear in each of the series, and have to keep up with the fashions of the day. David Hammond has to be kept looking sharp, and judging by last Sundays episode Paul Merroney, the merchant bank executive, will be running him a close second." Tudor described Edward as a "Solid dependable type. Doesn't particularly care about his clothes but has to keep well dressed for business reasons." Brian however is "Quite a nice dresser, but has never changed very much." He admitted to one mistake made for Jenny Kingsley, "I put her in a skirt, a beige one with a pattern around the hem that someone else had worn earlier in the series. I realised but hoped no-one would spot it. Sure enough though, someone did."

The article went on to describe the costume budget for the series as "surprisingly modest". Tudor explained his job involved borrowing from stock, going around jumble sales looking for particular items and sometimes buying clothes, which are put in stock soon after. Occasionally it seemed actors would wear their own clothes, but there was no BBC payment for this.

From a political correctness point of view, there was a particularly problematic piece of casting in the episode 'Jennifer's Baby'. In it, the Hammond's encounter a Sheik Abu. It is suggested he is a bit of a con man, but the real problem lies in the portrayal. For the second time in this series, we come to a moment that would perhaps not pass muster in today's very sensitive media marketplace. Not that Cyril Shaps performance can be faulted, but he was required to 'brown up' in the way that Michael Bates was also doing at the time in *It Ain't Half Hot Mum*. He is also seen to be particularly randy, trying to persuade Clare Miller to socialise with him, his ulterior motives not very hidden. From todays perspective when there are so many excellent actors around of all ethnicities for casting directors to choose from, seeing a character who is so obviously placed for comic effect in such a manner jars with the rest of the excellent dramatic happenings of the episode. Luckily director Vere Lorrimer manages to keep things on a tasteful track. It's just a pity that a series with so little involvement from non-caucasian actors should stoop to such a ploy when one is called for. But we once again have to put on our 1970s head (as Worzel Gummidge might have it) and realise how far attitudes and sensibilities have changed.

The final episode 'War Path' went out on 29th June and it provoked an attack from Margaret Forwood of The Sun: *Brothers! They're The Laugh Of The Week.* She sharpened her claws to take a swipe at the series which she asserted was becoming a bit too big for its boots. She begrudgingly acknowledged its undoubted popularity "But, like so many series it has since become too dramatic for its own good. Just look at the unbelievable line up. There is the mother, forever meddling in her sons' affairs and doing a good imitation of Snow White's wicked stepmother. Then there is the long absent Brian who finally returns for the farewell episode. At the beginning of the present series he was cracking up, crying, yelling and gazing into space with a strange smile on his face. But there is a limit to this sort of thing. Even in *The Brothers*. So Brian was dispatched to a mental home. Then there's David. His wife Jill was whisked out of the programme in between series, the victim of a fatal car crash. So there have been endless shots of David coming over peculiar every time he sees a car. Elder brother Edward and the long-suffering Jennifer – she was his father's mistress – have meanwhile been behaving like love sick teenagers ever since the show began. Even though they are both on the wrong side of 40." Like any success, *The Brothers* had become a victim of that success and bitchy critics were now quite happy to chop them down. It was all at odds with the BBC's own Audience Research and the mounds of letters from home and abroad that flooded into Television Centre. The ratings were constantly high and viewer reaction vociferous. The cast were by now making regular trips to mainland Europe to promote the show. The BBC's own internal magazine Ariel raised the subject: "*The Brothers* has become one of [BBC]Enterprises most successful exports to Sweden and Finland and when the fourth series began on Swedish screens recently there was hardly a magazine or paper not carrying news of the fact. The Finns sent a reporter and photographer from one of their top magazines to interview the production team and the stars of the series. A Swedish TV journal went one better by flying over three of *The Brothers* team for personal appearances. Hilary Tindall plus husband Robin Lowe and co-creator Norman Crisp went first to Gothenburg to appear on the early evening TV programme 'Sweden's Magazine' (seen by roughly half the population). After that they were feted in Stockholm as guests of TV Expressen." Scenes of mobbing were not uncommon in the Netherlands and Sweden at this time as the stars were flown over by television companies and magazines to promote the show. The fifth series proved to be the last with Ken Riddington at the helm, and also the last series where the writing duties were evenly divided between Crisp and Paice. Change was afoot behind the scenes.

IN CONVERSATION WITH
COLIN BAKER

RC: Presumably you had been aware of *The Brothers* **before you were actually cast in it?**

Colin Baker: Yes indeed, I used to watch it. Loved it. It was one of those shows that I thought 'that would be fun to be in.' I got a phone call from the Producer, Ken Riddington, to my home. I'd worked with him on *War & Peace*, and before that *Roads To Freedom* when he was a production manager. Ken cued me once in the very first television I ever did. I was playing a rapist in *Roads To Freedom*. There was a bed in the middle of a big empty space with me and Alison Fiske in it, there was another scene going on at the other side of the studios and the cameras were cutting backwards and forwards. The only way he could cue me was to lie under the bed and prod my unclad posterior to make me start humping! So that was the first time I met Ken. That was in 1970. I worked with him again on *War & Peace* and interestingly the assistant floor manager was Graeme Harper who I went on to work with in *Doctor Who*. So I knew Ken of old, we got on well. He phoned me up in 1973 and said "We have got a two scene part in an episode of *The Brothers* and I would love it if you would say you would do it. It's all business speak. I know you trained as a lawyer so I know you can do it." So it was basically doing him a favour to go in and do it for him. So I readily agreed and he rang my agent and did the deal. It was around about the same time that Murray Hayne was in it, and either he decided to leave or his contract wasn't renewed. They liked what I had done as Paul Merroney, so purely by chance with Murray Hayne leaving they decided to write my part up. So they contracted me for more episodes, and the rest is history.

RC: Was it explained to you at the beginning it would be a recurring – and eventually – regular role and that you would in effect be the antagonist of the show?

Nope. I always liken Paul Merroney to a proto-type J.R. Ewing except that J.R. broke the law. Paul Merroney never did. He used the law and he was never really interested in lining his own pocket either. He was the kind of guy who when given a job wants to do it better than anybody else. He cared about the company of which he became chairman, and in some senses more than the three Hammond brothers did. They generally cared about themselves and their lives. He certainly didn't care about upsetting other people. He didn't particularly want to upset them, but if he did then it wasn't that big a deal to him. Except perhaps Brian Hammond, whom he was genuinely fond of. This was mirrored by my own personal fondness for Richard Easton who played him. So it kind of evolved. And I realise now in retrospect that if the producers had realised what that part was going to turn out to be, there would have been at least ten other people whose agents would have been battling to get them into the show. So it was pure luck that I happened to know Ken Riddington and it started with me doing him a favour. I would probably never have got it if there had been a big casting search for Paul Merroney as a major character.

RC: Watching it again, what surprised me is how quickly Paul Merroney became central to virtually every story line from the beginning of Series Five onwards. It was a big change for the show. Did you feel as resistance from the regular cast when you went in to the show full time?

Interesting, because I was never told my character was going to be such a major character in the piece. The scripts started coming in and I realised that Merroney was going to be a force within the show. One or two cast members did start to show a little concern. I think Robin Chadwick had his nose put out of joint, as the youngest of *The Brothers*. He did actually say that he was surprised that Merroney was doing this or that in the show, as his own character might well have been in the business of doing similar things as regards plot development. He wasn't actually unfriendly to me, but he did include me in conversations that he was surprised that maybe my role was eclipsing his a little. Jennifer Wilson also voiced a similar viewpoint, asking if it was necessary for Merroney to have the plot narrative as much as he had. And I have every sympathy for them both. If you have been in a series for years, then somebody new comes in and gets the lions share of juicy scenes you may well think your star is being eclipsed slightly. I don't blame them for feeling that way. I might well feel the same under the circumstances. I remember at the end of the fifth series, my first as a full time cast member, the producer came in saying 'Can all of the regulars meet in the green room so we can talk about plans for the next series...' I got up to go and someone said "Oh it's just the regulars Colin". Then bless him, Richard Easton chimed in with "Don't be ridiculous, Colin is a regular." That kind of revealed how they were not wanting to accept the awful truth that I was quite central to it by then.

Maggie Ashcroft, Derek Benfield, Carole Mowlam, sometimes Richard Easton and myself always used to go up the night before recording at Pebble Mill and stay in a different country hotel. We'd all have dinner together on a bit of a jolly away from home. We always arranged it so we could get back for the hot food after a rehearsal or recording session. We ended up at the Abberley Arms pub in Birmingham a lot I seem to recall. Jean and Jenny by contrast used to stay at the Albany Hotel.

RC: There was quite extensive location filming in *The Brothers*, do you have any specific memories of being out and about?

I never did much at the depot as I recall. My location filming tended to be in cars outside banks and also at Lydd airfield where Jane Maxwell's planes were based. I don't think I had as much location work as some of the others I don't think. We did go to Holland though when the negotiations with Van Der Merwe were happening in the show. We flew over to Holland with Joby Blanshard who was playing Van Der Merwe and his daughter was played by Carmen du Sautoy and there was a thought that she might have been a regular girlfriend for Paul at one time. We did that several times I remember, a couple of nights stay each time. I got on extremely well with Joby. One day someone said something to me and he turned to me and said "That's exactly the wrong thing to say to you isn't it? If there is anyone I've ever met who is counter suggestive it's you. If anyone suggests you do something then that is the last thing you are going to do."

How right he was! He made me laugh. It helps to have people you respect telling you the awful truth. That was an interesting storyline. I did like the stuff with Kate O'Mara. We had exactly the same relationship in reverse a decade later when she appeared as The Rani in one of my *Doctor Who* stories. It was great that as Jane Maxwell she was a passionate person who tried to undermine me whenever she could, she had a real go at Merroney sometimes. We had some very frosty scenes together. Some of those Boardroom scenes were ten minutes long, which you wouldn't get today. The set was circular with pictures of lorries around it which slid out so a camera could poke through to get an alternative shot. The cameramen were rehearsed like dancers, the cameras choreographed so they poked through at exactly the right moment. The scenes were mostly played out as in the theatre, without stopping wherever possible, so the pictures had to be pulled back and the camera be in its spot at exactly the right moment. There were five cameras.

RC: There was a lot of business and banking dialogue. Was it difficult to learn?

No not really. I have always been quite lucky in that respect. It is more difficult delivering scenes which are general chit chat because there is nothing to anchor to. When it's very specific dialogue it goes in quicker. We used to rehearse each episode for a week so dialogue is naturally absorbed anyway. It would be rehearsed in sequence for five days, then the producer and the technicians would come and watch you run through it like a play, the entire thing. Then you would be given any notes either technical or about performance. When you get to the studios you then record it out of order, but until that point it is all in sequence. So it is then easy just to pick out chunks and perform them for the camera depending on which sets they needed to use. We would record from 7.30pm to 10pm on the second day at Pebble Mill so we had to get on with it. There is barely any rehearsal time these days, but we had the luxury back then of five days at the 'Acton Hilton' and then a day and a half in studio, rehearsing before the camera, before the red light went on to record. Not too long ago I actually recorded a scene for the BBC's *Doctors* with Christopher Timothy and the scene was us chatting as we walked along a river bank. The camera was on the other side of the river bank tracking us. They said, 'Can you just do the walk and say your lines so we can see how it looks?' So Chris and I went through the rehearsal as we thought, then we said "Are you ready to do it for real?" And they told us they had just recorded our rehearsal and they would use that as it was fine!

I remember at one point the cast who had been in *The Brothers* from the beginning used to get nostalgic for their original directors. One of them was Philip Dudley. "Oh it's such a shame Philip isn't on the production, things aren't what they used to be and we should get him back, he was terrific" sort of thing. He then came back in series 5 or 6. Philip said to the original cast "I've been watching the whole thing and it has gone down the pan. All you older cast are coasting, just trotting out what you have always done. The new ones are fine but the rest of you need to buck your ideas up." He gave them hell! From wanting him back, it quickly turned to them wanting him out because he was properly directing them and picking them up on their performances.

RC: You had some terrific guest actors on *The Brothers* over the course of its run.

Yes indeed. Clive Swift was one, and of course Richard Hurndall who went on to play the first Doctor in 'The Five Doctors' episode of *Doctor Who*. Plus of course the legend that was Carleton Hobbs. He played Sir Neville before Llewellyn Rees came in for an episode I think. Carleton was a God in the profession. Ask any drama student ever, and they were all desperate to win the Carleton Hobbs Award. Richard Easton was one of the people who had made me want to act years before. I saw Richard playing Richard II at the Wimbledon Theatre in the 1960s and he was sensational in the role.

RC: Can you give me any specific memories that come to mind of the cast, lets start with Jean Anderson

If there was a female word for The Guv'nor, she was the one to whom everybody deferred. If we were being naughty she would say 'Now now, stop that please'. And it could be anyone, she didn't pick on people. She was a quiet matriarch of the show. She spent most of her time with the Racing Post and would always be nipping off to put a bet on with her bookmaker. She was very good at it too, she knew her horses. She was a bit of class amongst us, I've not got a bad word to say about her.

RC: Patrick O'Connell

Paddy should not have been in *The Brothers*, it didn't help him. I saw Paddy at the Royal Shakespeare Company doing brilliant stuff. He found *The Brothers* a bit of a struggle, and I think perhaps he would have loved to have moved on but either couldn't or wouldn't. Possibly money, I don't know. At every studio recording without exception at 7.30pm as they were piping the theme music through before the cameras started recording, he and I used to gallop around the studio patting our backsides like two people riding horses. He liked to do that and because I liked Paddy, I joined him. We were a couple of big kids really. Towards the end he struggled with line learning, but I was very fond of him. If he had a confidante on that set at the time, it was myself I think. I loved Paddy.

RC: Richard Easton

I adored Richard. He was a superb actor. During the very first episode I did, there was a scene in a restaurant which we rehearsed several times. Richard bet me a fiver I would cock up the line. It was something like "I think you are overlooking the fact that it is part of our job to find new ways of providing a service that by sheer weight of numbers can no longer be provided on a personal basis." So there was a fiver riding on it and I buggered it up. Richard was looking at me as I said it making me self-conscious. He made me laugh. If I hadn't liked him so much I would have hated him for putting me off, but I loved Richard. He was someone I could talk to. If there was a line or a direction I wasn't sure of – and I was 30 when I started *The Brothers* and he would have been 40 - I would ask his opinion and he would always be right. He never joined in the bitching, he and Jean were above all that. They were very sane and balanced folk. Richard used to hold games evenings at his home in Earl's Terrace in London, which is a beautifully terraced set of regency houses He had a first floor flat. These games evenings – card games, board games – he would have the most magnificent guest list. I was invited around on a couple of occasions so I would be sitting there playing whatever game had been ordained that night and opposite me would be the likes of Judi Dench, Michael Williams, Frank Hauser who used to run the theatre in Oxford and Ian McKellen. To say I was the least well known in that room was a definite understatement. I was delighted to say I won one of the games, I got very competitive that night so I was accepted into the clan. I was with a girlfriend at that time – which was Kate O'Mara's fault as she introduced me to her – who was not into that kind of thing, and Richard knew that so stopped inviting me. Particularly because Richard's performance as Richard II had ignited my acting ambitions – along with David Warner's Hamlet – I always valued his opinion greatly. Later on Richard used to go and perform in Sweden as I did, and he did *There's A Girl In My Soup* with my wife Marion. So I kept in touch with Richard for a long time after *The Brothers*.

RC: Jennifer Wilson

Although Jennifer didn't perhaps welcome Paul Merroney with open arms, she was a nice lady. We worked together in the theatre too, a tour of *September Tide* sometime in between making *The Brothers*. We did play a joke on her that I remember very well. During all that storyline about wanting to adopt the baby. Paddy and I hatched a plot, and everyone was in on it. We arranged it that just at the beginning of the evening shoot this scene would be shot first. We had a pretty big pram or cot on set, I can't quite remember, and they had me squeeze into it with a baby grow, big bonnet and thumb in my mouth. When Jennifer pulled back the curtain it was me, she was so shocked she screamed! That was quite a funny moment. Enough people were in the loop to make the japes acceptable.

RC: Derek Benfield

I loved Derek. Long after finishing *The Brothers* I used to go around to Derek and Sue's with Marion and have dinner, then they would come to us. That went on for years. Derek has written more comedy plays I should think than Alan Ayckbourn. They are still done all over the world, producing income for Sue which is lovely. We used to call him The Baron because he came from Bingley so he was 'Baron Bingley'. His other nickname was Ruby as you may well know. There was a misprint in the script once 'Ruby' instead of 'Riley'. Much later on I worked with him on a *Doctor Who* audio story.

RC: Margaret Ashcroft

Maggie was lovely, quite camp and I love camp people. She was very different from her character. She would turn up at my house years later on a bike ride with a young actress she was friendly with, and we'd go for a drink. I did a summer season with her years later and we had a brilliant time. She had a bad stroke which was very sad, and now she's gone. But she was part of our social circle. She could be hysterically funny about certain cast members!

RC: Kate O'Mara

I have worked with Kate a lot over the years really. On my very second job I did some plays at Guildford. We were doing *Shakespeare, Cabbages & Kings* at youth clubs and various venues around the area. But we got a few pence extra for understudying whatever play was on at the main house, the Yvonne Arnaud Theatre. Stephen Barry was one of my best friends, and was an assistant director at the Arnaud. We were supposed to have understudy rehearsals but we never got time. But then I was suddenly grabbed on a Saturday lunchtime by the stage manager of the theatre directly after a performance for a group of disinterested young people, and told I was 'on' that afternoon in the play *The Holly and The Ivy*. This was at 1.30pm and the curtain went up at 2.30pm! We had never rehearsed it. Amazingly, I had learnt it. But I had never rehearsed any moves or indeed met the cast who were in it. I was bundled into the theatre, had a costume thrown on me, dashed into the wings where the play had already begun. I wasn't on until about the fourth scene. My first line was I think "Hello aunty". So I confidently strode on and said the line to the actress I assumed would be the aunty character. She looked at me with wide eyes and nodded to another lady behind me. And so this madness began. I remember clearly doing a line and then one of the actresses, Agnes Laughlan I think it was, said out loud in front of the audience "Oh the other one doesn't get a laugh with that!" I was quite pleased actually that I got a laugh and the person whom I was understudying didn't. I got through that show and Kate O'Mara who was in the cast told me afterwards that everyone on the stage for that show was terrified. Apart from me it seems. I was on a win/win. The fact that I knew the lines and could even get through it albeit gingerly, meant that I had done the job they paid me for. I just wandered around the stage to wherever felt appropriate to be honest. Kate said it was extraordinary. I sailed through it unconcerned, doing what I pleased, where as they were all terrified because they didn't know where I was going to be from one line to the next. Mercifully the guy whose part it was returned for the evening performance.

So that was my first time with Kate. Then the next occasion was a year later on the television series *Don Quick* where people were money on a planet. Ian Hendry was basically Don Quixote in space. We were playing people in silver jump suits in jail who were being used as money. So if you wanted to buy something it would basically cost you something like seven people. I only had one line in the whole thing. Quentin Lawrence was the director and I boldly asked him if I could change my line. He said "No, say the line that is written". The line was "We are revolting". I wanted to change it to "We are rebelling" but he wouldn't have it. So when it was shown I can imagine the viewers responded in unison with a pantomime like "Yes you are". I was once driving down a street in London and I saw Kate walking down the pavement. So I tooted. She ignored me. I tooted again but she wouldn't look. So I drove ahead and jumped out. She recoiled in horror, before realising it was me. "Oh thank goodness it's you" she said. We embraced warmly. Then of course she was The Rani in *Doctor Who* so Kate is dotted through my career at pivotal points. She was the quintessential professional. She was stunning, a very good actress and never coasted anything. She put her own house at risk financially, she lost money putting on a production of *Antony & Cleopatra* because she wanted to do a good production of it.

RC: Carole Mowlam

Carole lived not far from me, so I used to have lunch with her and her son. Along with our script editor Douglas Watkinson. She was smart and again very professional. She played a lovely character in Clare Miller.

RC: Mike Pratt

A couple of the cast went to see Mike just before he died in hospital. He said to them "Ironic isn't it? I've kicked the booze, I've kicked the drugs, I'm clean and it's the fags that have killed me." It made me give up smoking, he told me to give it up because it's a mugs game. So I thought I would make his death a little less pointless and heed his wise advice, and I'm now glad I did. He might have saved my life, I suffer from asthma now. It would have been much worse if I'd carried on smoking umpteen fags a day. Mike was like an old ravaged rocker, who'd seen it all and done it all and come out the other side. He wasn't arty farty in any way. He was brilliant in *Randall & Hopkirk*. That face of his told a story, there was a life there.

RC: Hilary Tindall

Hilary Tindall I liked a lot. We crossed over briefly in the same episodes and she was a terrific lady. Very waspish, but great fun. We got on really well over those few episodes.

RC: Liza Goddard

The first time I met Liza – apart from in the street once with my girlfriend at the time Angela Down who had been in *Take Three Girls* with her – was dressed in a wedding dress at the altar when we pre-filmed the wedding scene. She had just had a baby. She was sweet and vulnerable. I metaphorically picked her up on my white horse and cantered off with her. We got married six weeks later. That was the mistake I think. We didn't know each other. I wasn't what she was really looking for. So that's fair enough. She was very good as April, perfect casting. It was quite nice for that character who was indomitable in his arena, which was business and the Hammonds. The one thing Paul Merroney couldn't legislate for was his own life. He got it all wrong. Despite his command of banking and business, he blew it very quickly where his own personal life was concerned. So this made for a much more interesting character. Interestingly, Terence Frisby who played April's brother was very keen on Liza himself. I had to fight him off for her.

RC: What about the huge following in Europe?

I once went to open a shop somewhere in Holland. It was the equivalent of Times Square being full. All I could see was a sea of people. The same when we went to Israel. We went to visit the Wailing Wall, the

the Holy site. The people who were praying at the wall and putting pieces of paper in with their prayers on, dropped everything and ran towards us because "Aharim" (The Inheritors) were there. It was huge. We went to a party, Moshe Dayan the Prime Minister rang up. I think Jennifer spoke to him. He told her that if the Arabs had attacked not on Yom Kippur but on a Wednesday night when *The Brothers* was on they'd have had more chance of catching them unawares. A charming story. It was so popular there.

RC: Why do you think audiences abroad took to *The Brothers* specifically as oppose to say Poldark or The Onedin Line and other shows of the time?

Matriarchal societies is my guess. Israel is certainly a matriarchal society. Maybe because someone, somewhere, in that country was persuaded to buy the series. The family is quite important in Sweden and Holland too. We made the Christmas album as well. All in one day I might add. It was a terrific seller and we have all got Gold discs for it. Who would have thought that eh?

I met someone a little while ago who used to work at the BBC and she said to me "Do you know why *The Brothers* disappeared?" Naturally I was curious. She explained "I worked in the finance department of BBC1. We had a yearly budget which was then allocated to various projects. They simply forgot to include *The Brothers*. The budget had all been agreed and rubber stamped at senior management level when someone said 'Hang on, what about *The Brothers*?' and it was simply too late by then." That is the story she told me. Also Bill Sellars had left the show to set up *All Creatures Great & Small* so there was nobody in the producers chair batting our corner really. I was always surprised nobody has done a sequel or an update of it, because it was so huge back in the 1970s.

For twenty years after *The Brothers*, the seventies fashions prevented it from being acceptable for repeat showings until now. But now it is so far in the past we can look at it as a costume drama. What Robin was wearing sometimes looks a little ridiculous viewed from todays perspective.

Bill Sellars during his first year on the programme was a producer in a suit. Very BBC. He had a wife and his BBC suit. We finished that series, we assembled for the read through of the next series. This guy came in and someone said 'Who's that?' and someone else said "It looks like Bill Sellars in a wig". And it was Bill in a wig. He had a wig, draped himself in scarves, had left his wife and outed himself. Nobody said a word. About the wig or the complete change of personality. How British.

I loved Mary Ridge and I think she liked me as well. I don't think the others like her so much, but for me she was great. There was Rodney Graham who stopped rehearsal so that I could finish the last three pages of *Lord Of The Rings*. I was reading it and it got to my scene, so I protested that I'd only got three pages to go. So he said "All right we'll break for lunch then!"

RC: Looking at *The Brothers* from this perspective, how do you view it all now?

I was chuffed that *The Brothers* has found its way onto DVD. It is something I am proud of. I was lucky to get it, the planets were in the right aspect for me to a) get a great part and have it last for three years and b) to be part of something of quality. I am certainly not embarrassed by it and I can watch it because it is now like watching someone else in the role. The scenes hold up, the character was interesting. Just as a carpenter can look at a cupboard he has made and say it's good work, I can look at *The Brothers* and think the same. I believe I did do good work in that. The fact that I still want to know what happened to the character means that I have an attachment to it. So in a sense it sits alongside The Doctor as the two major landmarks of my career.

IN CONVERSATION WITH
DOUGLAS WATKINSON

Douglas Watkinson was Script Editor on *The Brothers* during 1975 and 1976 and also wrote the episode "A Clean Break". He went onto enjoy enormous success with Lovejoy, Midsomer Murders, Boon and Howards' Way to name but a few. He is also a successful novelist.

RC: How did you come to get the job as Script Editor on *The Brothers*?

Douglas Watkinson: I was a script editor before that on *Z Cars*. I was up and down at the BBC, and people knew what I could do as a writer. I'd also had a few things produced that I'd written myself. We were doing forty episodes a year of *Z Cars*. The guy who was in charge of *The Brothers* back then, Ken Riddington, and Gerry Glaister who was our combined mentor wanted me, to do it. It was just before I went freelance as a writer myself, I was on the verge of leaving that. But I did come back to do *Howards' Way* later however. So they just came to the *Z Cars* office and asked me. They needed someone, and at that time the BBC were churning out hours and hours of weekly drama.

RC: With those unfamiliar with a Script Editor's responsibilities on a programme, can you go over what the job entails?

The main thing is to get the long term storyline worked out, then the serial elements you then allot to the writers. So that needs careful handling. When I was working on *Lovejoy*, we didn't have a Script Editor, we just used to get together around a table on a particular day and decide what we were going to do mutually. We then knew where it was going. We made sure we didn't cross over into each others territory. And that really was my job on *The Brothers*. Making sure that nobody was repeating somebody else. With *The Brothers* it was all quick fire stuff, so it's bound to be a bit messy. You have to make sure it is the right length, nobody is saying something that was said two weeks before, nobody was contradicting what was said the previous year. Or indeed straying into pastures that hadn't been discussed. Then there was the BBC fifth floor – the Bush House mob – who would read every script and pick up every vagary, they had to be dealt with too. I remember at one stage the series drifted on and we got to a point where we didn't really know where to go next. We had created so many loose ends that needed tying up. And I remember Norman Crisp saying "I don't know what to do next. I don't know how to bring it all together." I was the one who wrote the script that saved it from disappearing into thin air. I wrote this script – quite a boring one actually – that brought all the loose ends together so we could kind of start again. It was an enjoyable job and I liked it a great deal.

RC: Did you find that there was much re-writing on *The Brothers* scripts required?

No not at all, very little. Without being rude about it, it's fairly basic stuff. If you knew what you were doing as a writer, you couldn't really go wrong with it. What you mainly needed to do was try and keep it alive. Eric Paice was a very witty man. I'll tell you a funny story actually. I was sitting in the office at the BBC, and a hand written letter arrived for the Producer. He opened it, read it and pushed it across the desk to me. "What do you think of this?" he said. It was a handwritten letter from Mary Whitehouse. Self appointed head of the Viewers & Listeners Association. In this letter she went on to say how delighted she was to be writing this letter praising a series that was basically clean and unsullied and so suitable for family audiences. That it had no bad language, no sex, no nastiness in it at all. "May I congratulate you..." and all that shit. Well, the very day before I had been at a production meeting with Ken Riddington, and the writers decided who should be destroyed emotionally, who should be destroyed physically, who should be destroyed economically, who should get off with who... We had been plotting and planning the most horrible set of circumstances for the characters. But with Mary as long as you didn't say 'fuck' or anything near it she was happy. The punchline to it was that Ken said to me quite sheepishly: "Don't tell anyone we've had a letter from Mary Whitehouse congratulating us." He screwed it up and bunged it in the bin. We didn't want that label on us that we were Mary Whitehouse approved, good boys. It destroyed any street cred we may have had.

RC: You arrived at a time when the series was changing a little from its original family premise, did you have any favourite characters?

I really liked Colin Baker's character because he was so evil. Colin played him to the hilt. Detached, remorseless, almost sociopathic. He was I felt the only deeply interesting character within the piece, the rest just sort of fed a rather commonplace storyline about a trucking firm that had its ups and downs. Merroney had an element of danger about him. We made him quite witty with his put downs too. With *Lovejoy*, when it started Ian McShane used to come on and do a short monologue to camera. As soon we discovered Ian could do this so brilliantly, the monologues got longer and more complicated. We were feeding the actor rather than the character. And the same happened with Colin. He was so good at the ice cold witticisms, that we kept shoving in these lines that would stand out. We made it his show really. Colin was so good we just kept building and building him. It is so easy to get rid of characters or actors if they are not serving the series. I remember at the end of the first series of *Howards' Way,* Gerry Glaister was having trouble with a group of actors thinking they were worth more than they really were. He was troubled by it, because being the BBC he only had a limited budget to make the show. He said to me at the end of the first series, "I want the last episode of the series with them all in a plane, with the plane about to go down in the sea. Those who keep asking me for more money will not live." Lo and behold, the next series the plane didn't crash because they had magically all fallen into line. There was none of that really on *The Brothers* though. It was more fun than that, we had our private villains within the team, but by and large we just had a good time.

RC: Did you ever liaise with any of the actors on their character development?

No not on *The Brothers*, it wasn't necessary. It's generally a bit of a thankless task including actors in this process. They don't know anything about dialogue. They know about their own part, but not about balance and dialogue flow. They just think in terms of their own part. It sounds very sweeping but generally true in my experience.

RC: Have you any specific memories of Ken Riddington and Bill Sellars?

I think Ken had more bite to him as Producer, you couldn't really pull one over on Ken. He was quite an astute person. He was fair minded and easy going – until he lost his temper. He lost his temper with me once and it was all the more frightening because I didn't know it was there. I think I was moaning and complaining about something, I was quite young then, and he suddenly rounded on me. We never had a crossed word again though. Bill Sellars was a bit of a chameleon. He tried to be all things to all men, including the actors. He tried to get his daughter a part in it at one point too.

RC: Did you attend many of the rehearsals or the recordings on *The Brothers***?**

I certainly attended all the rehearsal read-throughs. The recordings generally took place all over one evening. I would generally be there because you never knew what might be needed. Someone might say, "We are fifteen seconds short on this episode, could we have a duologue with these two characters on this set?" So I would get scribbling away and find a way of making up the shortfall. And that is why I think I was liked as a script editor. I could come up with the goods. One of the directors Christopher Barry once said to me, "At least we know you can push a pen Doug if we need you to." A lot of script editors would require time to think about it, time that they hadn't got, but I could come up with stuff almost at will, which is where I scored with the directors.

RC: Did you feel that there was a lot of support for *The Brothers* **within the BBC?**

No not really. It was a strange phenomenon really. In hindsight, it now has a sort of kudos to it. It was a bit vilified within the press. It was considered to be a rather silly, indulgent soap opera. I thought it was one of a whole spectrum of programmes that the BBC were doing and it fitted very nicely into that Sunday night slot. Traditionally it was a rather mild, cheaply produced slot. A sort of Joanna Trollope-esque story. From what I remember of it I think it could hold its own against anything comparable at the time. I did think it was a pretty good effort. We were doing an episode a week for goodness sake. The script would be read, then rehearsed and we would go into the studio and do it all in one night. The tele-cine stuff which was needed would be done elsewhere before hand, and that was an art in itself for an editor to make sure everything looked continuous. There was quite a bit of tele-cine work by the end I think. And it was always tele-cine not actually film, much like the news reels. Somehow it all worked and fitted in very well. I remember when I was working on *Z Cars*, I got two writers who had submitted a play to cut it down and fit it into the *Z Cars* format. And it was the first script to be completely done on tele-cine, in a pub just around the corner from the rehearsal rooms. It was quite innovative then. It was a complex thing to get off the ground. We sometimes used to have trouble with the big lorry manufacturers. I once remember speaking to the CEO of DAF lorries. He started to complain he had seen a Volvo lorry in the show, a Mercedes lorry, a Scania. He complained quite strongly that it was advertising for his competitors by any other means, and not for them. So we had all that to cope with as well, and we had to be careful we didn't favour one make over the other. They were subsequently delighted when a lorry drew up in the show with the DAF logo clearly seen. They would have paid thousands for that on ITV.

RC: Have you any theories why *The Brothers* **became so popular overseas, in Europe and Scandinavia particularly?**

Absolutely none. I couldn't understand it. No more than I can understand why *Midsomer Murders*, which I worked on right at the beginning, had gathered such a global following. Evidently one BILLION people have seen it worldwide. I just can't account for it. All I can tell you is that when we sat in some basement cinema for a viewing of the pilot, John Nettles was very adrift. He was saying "I don't know it this is going to work, I'm a bit worried about it." A billion viewers later and they are still demanding more. I find it extraordinary that it was so popular in Sweden and the Netherlands. Colin was always going on tour in plays around Sweden. Colin did tell me about an incident which I think may be significant. He was appearing in somewhere like Malmo, doing a personal appearance. He got up on a podium and gave a little speech with jokes and anecdotes. Then the man running the event announced 'Signed photos of Colin Baker can be obtained over there..." and pointed to a table. The crowd apparently surged forward, knocking the actual person Colin out of the way in order to get their hands on one of these signed photos. He was irrelevant in the stampede for a souvenir. It's a strange old business television. It's the illusion people want to follow.

RC: Do you think the format could be resurrected for a modern audience?

I think it probably could, but I don't think it should. I feel quite irritated by the BBC sometimes. They pick up their old successes and re-work them. I am not saying I know what to put in their place. *The Forsyte Saga* for example was a brilliant piece of television. Then it was brought back by ITV I think. Only for four episodes or something, and it wasn't anything like as good as that original had been. I think we have to get and find something new and inspiring, because it is out there. *Black Mirror* for example is a great way of making reasonably priced television for a modern audience. I wish the BBC would put a greater emphasis on finding new writing, new ideas. There was been a suggestion that *Lovejoy* might come back. Thank goodness that is not happening. And it can't happen because Ian McShane purchased the rights to the book as soon as he left the series precisely in order to prevent a re-invention happening. He proved to be a very shrewd man.

RC: Do you think *The Brothers* and Lovejoy come from a golden age of television production?

I think so. A friend of mine, Betty Willingale who has written and produced so much, says that television should be rough around the edges. It shouldn't be so slick and smooth as to slip out of your minds. It must have some faction that an audience or a writer can grip onto. It should have its mistakes, it shouldn't be so perfect that nobody wants to know it. I agree with that. And then, when *The Brothers* was being done, because of the amount we did, and the amount of drama the BBC was churning out each week, you could really learn your craft. Script editors, writers, directors, actors – were all learning their craft from the mistakes being made daily in offices and on sets. Those opportunities are long gone. It has got to be right first time. That's a shame. A lot of *The Brothers* was made flying by the seat of your pants. These days *Midsomer Murders* will go through 10, 12 or 14 drafts of the script. To me, by then, the script is as dead as a door nail.

SERIES SIX (1976)

The gap between production of Series Five and Six saw some of *The Brothers* heading out on the road. This time appearing in theatre plays. Jennifer Wilson and Colin Baker joined forces in a production of Daphne Du Maurier's *September Tide,* whilst Kate O'Mara and Robin Chadwick appeared in a tour of Brian Clemens thriller *Shock!* Robin was reunited in this production with Annette Andre who had toyed with his affections as the wily Sally Woolf in the first series. Both plays did good business over the summer months as the show rode the crest of a popular wave. But it was back to the boardroom in October as the cast were recalled from their extra-curricular activities to go before the cameras for the sixth series. A new producer was in the chair by this time. Bill Sellars had started out at the BBC as a director, then gained experience as a producer on a number of series including *Compact* (1965), *The Doctors* (1970), *Owen M.D.* (1971) and *Circus* (1975). Douglas Watkinson stayed on as script editor whilst the writers pool was widened to include contributions from several newcomers to the show. These included Simon Raven who had scored a major success with the historical drama *The Pallisers* for the BBC. Ray Jenkins came to the show from hard hitting crime dramas Callan and The Sweeney. Also on board was Brian Finch who had cut his teeth on *Z Cars*, *The Tomorrow People* and episodes of *Coronation Street*. Added to a healthy dose of Crisp and Paice, this was perhaps the most varied set of writers ever to join forces on *The Brothers*.

The Hammonds returned to BBC1 on Sunday 25th January 1976, with ITV batting back with a movie premiere showing of Michael Caine in *The Italian Job*. 'Red Sky At Night' was on good form, and a central plot device was the use of David going to France to suss out business alliances only to fall foul of calculating femme fatale Therese d'Alambert, played by Francoise Pascal. Pascal went onto to score a major hit in the now un-PC ITV comedy *Mind Your Language,* but here she displays her devious side with some entrapment. David is sharing her bed, she gets him drunk and he owes £11,000 (around £75,000 today) in casino debts which D'Alambert promptly pays. But the payback is greater than expected. 27 year old Pascal had carved a career as a successful model and actress and was the latest in a series of love interests for David. She only appeared in two episodes and The People claimed to know why in February 1976. 'David Loses His New Love' spouted the feature. "First his wife in *The Brothers* was killed in a car crash and now it seems his new romance is to be nipped in the bud. For Therese D'Alambert, the rich scheming lady who snapped up David on a holiday-come-business trip is being phased out after only two episodes. The reason? Francoise Pascal who plays Therese is expecting a baby in July and her doctor has advised her not to work again until after the bird. 'Therese was originally going to appear in four episodes,' said producer Ken Riddington 'But now we've got to get rid of her fast. David certainly fell in love and they slept together but it won't turn into a lasting affair.'

It is generally felt among the cast that the story of Edward and Jennifer adopting a baby went too much into the realms of soap melodrama. The boy's real mother turns up wanting him back, cue much heartache and misery for Jennifer. As the story dragged on over two series, it came as something of a relief to the actress herself when Jennifer Hammond pulled herself together and re-joined the board on full thrusters showing that she could out perform Mary's mollycoddled brood whenever she chose. The series again made showbiz headlines when the Sun newspaper ran an article with the headline *Truth about the Brothers and booze*. "They call them the Boozing Brothers – the TV series that is top of the tipplers' league. Recently the Mothers' Union made that accusation in their report to the Annan Comittee on the future of broadcasting," wrote Gordon Blair. "They said the BBC's Sunday night series placed too much emphasis on drinking, and that the Hammond brothers and their friends 'always seem to have a glass in their hands.' But when I talked to Ted, the oldest brother played by Paddy O'Connell, he had some unprintable remarks to make about the Mothers Union. "What do they want us to do? Pretend that nobody drinks?" he asked." He went on to reveal that the

FRANCOISE PASCAL REMEMBERS

I was hooked on the series when I first watched it. I loved the characters, specially the matriarch of The Brothers. Jean Anderson was a force to reckon with. I loved her character, besides my friend Kate O'Mara was in it and that was enough for me. So you can imagine when I got the part of Thérese D'Alembert how excited I was to be in this popular and well-loved series. I did enjoy the character of Thérese, she was not a challenge, she was a character that I have met many times in my life, schemers and money grabbing women. So I actually played her like a woman that I knew in my travels. I enjoyed playing her. I know I was well known for one role Danielle in Mind Your Language, but I have played roles that are very demanding in the past before The Brothers. I was in a series with Denis Quilley and Ferdy Maine in 1970 shot in France and England for the BBC I think, I played Ferdy Maine's daughter and that was pretty taxing because I had to hate my father and in real life I loved my own father until his death. A hard one to act. It has been so long ago, I loved working with Robin, and Mike Pratt was a friend of Kate O'Mara and he use to tease me something rotten. Mike told Robin in the scene at Lydd Airfield, "This one, hands off, she's trouble". Mike used to tease me because I was a long time girlfriend of Richard Johnson so he used to call me "Hands off". Haha! I really liked Mike. Robin was aloof sometimes but a nice guy to act with and we worked on our scenes several times, he was a giving actor. I became pregnant whilst filming the series, I did not leave it because I was pregnant, my role was only for two episodes. It was for no more than that. I was told that I would be back in the series but nothing came of it in the long run. Lydd was very cold and windy. I had a velour suit on which kept me warm, but not that warm, if you know what I mean. I loved that burgundy suit, it was my own. The BBC can be tight with the budget. I do enjoy filming on location. I loved the way they decorated my apartment and Robin was a charmer. It was difficult to get to know the rest of the cast as they were so together in the series. Colin Baker was one that I became friends with to this day. As a matter of fact I have a role for Colin in my new film that I am producing. I love Colin's acting. He is so cutting and can be a bitch of a man. I like working in studios also. Mind Your Language was always in the studio. Yes I love working in the studios specially going to the bar after finishing filming. That was fun. My opinion is that no, The Brothers should not be repeated as it is so passé, so old that what happened in those days does not happen today. What made the series was the actors Jean Anderson and The Brothers, Richard Easton, Robin Chadwick and lovely Patrick O'Connell. The matriarch who kept her family together and also the shipping made the series, as many people related to that especially in Europe. The script was terrific, the intrigue, the messy relationships. The writing was really superb to speak and to act, all good viewing and good TV.

the white wine used in the programme was diluted ginger ale and the red wine was in fact Ribena. It is certainly true that reaching for a cup of tea or coffee was sometimes alien in the series. Simply everybody seems to drink spirits, and occasionally offer someone else a lift home when clearly they had been having a high old time at the bar! The series again made showbiz headlines when the Sun newspaper ran an article with the headline *Truth about the Brothers and booze*. "They call them the Boozing Brothers – the TV series that is top of the tipplers' league. Recently the Mothers' Union made that accusation in their report to the Annan Comittee on the future of broadcasting," wrote Gordon Blair. "They said the BBC's Sunday night series placed too much emphasis on drinking, and that the Hammond brothers and their friends 'always seem to have a glass in their hands.' But when I talked to Ted, the oldest brother played by Paddy O'Connell, he had some unprintable remarks to make about the Mothers Union. "What do they want us to do? Pretend that nobody drinks?" he asked." He went on to reveal that the white wine used in the programme was diluted ginger ale and the red wine was in fact Ribena. It is certainly true that reaching for a cup of tea or coffee was sometimes alien in the series. Simply everybody seems to drink spirits, and occasionally offer someone else a lift home when clearly they had been having a high old time at the bar!

Don Stacey failed his flight medical and exited the series. It was an exit that was forced on the production team. Sadly Mike Pratt was battling cancer, and ill health forced him to bow out of the show after six episodes. It was the final television acting assignment of a long and hugely successful career. He passed away on 10th July 1976, with the showbiz community in shock at his premature death aged just 45 years old. Most of the series regulars appeared at a benefit concert in Mike's honour on 8th August at the Aldwych Theatre in the West End, where they were joined by such luminaries as Lionel Bart, Harry H. Corbett, Glenda Jackson and John Le Mesurier in celebrating Mike's life and work.

Mike's final episode 'Tender' written by Eric Paice, found favour with the viewing audience. The BBC Audience Report stated "This episode was received enthusiastically by its admirers in the sample. They seemed to welcome the emphasis in tonight's drama on the business side of Hammond Transport rather than on personal relationships. This made it for them, particularly interesting." The subject of that cad Merroney was never far away from their thoughts though. "...several remarking with obvious delight that now Jenny had resumed an active business role, Paul Merroney had at last got a 'well deserved come-uppance'. Some felt this renewed concentration on financial problems made Eric Paice's 'Tender' the most satisfactory in the current run." The panel found it impossible to single out particular performances it seemed "The actors and actresses lived the parts they played" and "Each one complimented the others" were typical reactions to that weeks performances. 21% of the UK viewing public tuned in, a good solid regular core audience pitted against ITV's 25.8% with the impressionist show *Now Who Do You Do?* followed by Dick Van Dyke in the star movie *The Comic*.

Industrial espionage is once again the order of the day with the arrival of the future Mr. Hyacinth Bucket, Clive Swift as the sly Griffith Trevelyan, employee of the now liquidised RAI Transport. He arrives at Hammond's door offering information on the business affairs of RAI in order that the highest bidder could get their lucrative oil rig contract. It is a double bluff though, he has also sold his services Matthews Transport who use Trevelyan to proffer false information about the schedules and costs involved. You have to get up earlier in the morning to bluff Ted Hammond though when it comes to haulage. He smells a rat and disaster is averted at the eleventh hour. That old rival Kirkman's leaps into the fray at this point with a very tempting offer of 80p a share in a buy out deal for the controlling shares of Hammond Transport's board. The directors are all tempted, but for differing reasons. Actor Jack May, the bombastic head of Matthews Transport, would find himself heard by a different generation when later in his career he voiced the character Igor in the popular animated series *Count Duckula*.

Ray Jenkins' 'Try, Try Again' was the seventy-fourth episode of the series, and featured another attempt by Ted to try to stay ahead of Paul Merroney by arranging a secret meeting with Christian Van Der Merwe. Merroney's seemingly faultess network of spies give him the opportunity to once again thwart Ted's efforts at regaining some control. The episode gained a 14.9% share of the viewing population, against ITV's massive 44.1% share with the first network showing of *The Guns Of Navarone*, the 1960 war film starring David Niven and Gregory Peck. Both started at 7.25pm and it seemed the majority of the available audience went for the flashy Hollywood epic. The Audience Report from those who watched, was not too damning either. "This episode, the eleventh out of thirteen, was well up to the usual standard providing more than moderate enjoyment for well over half the sample. The plot revolved around members of the Hammond family to institute new commercial ventures, the out-come affecting them both financially and psychologically. A section of those reporting saw this emphasis on business rather than personal problems as a continuing trend, many not only welcoming it but becoming closely involved in its complexities and eventual outcome." The pro-active stance by Edward and his brothers over control of the company was noted too. "The Hammonds are really taking control again, just like their old selves – decisive and acting on their own initiative." The playing of the cast was universally praised. "A substantial majority of the reporting panel were fully satisfied with the acting; there was little or no specific criticism of individuals, any criticism was attributed to the script not the actors." One summed up, "It is very difficult to find fault with. Congratulations to all concerned." The report finished with a summary: "Some of the reporting viewers took the opportunity to comment on the series as a whole. A few thought *The Brothers* had lost its drive and purpose, that it was becoming predictable and boring; most, however, expressed their enjoyment, feeling that now the family had begun to take charge, that this present series was at last matching the achievements of the past, and they noted that recent episodes had contributed to this trend." The final words of the report were less verbose: "92% watched the episode all the way through, 4% came in in the middle and 4% either tried a bit or switched off before the end." On the whole though, it seems that those sat watching The Guns Of Navarone on ITV had missed some good, solid BBC home made drama.

'The Bonus' (the series 75th episode to air) brought with it some filming in Holland as Paul Merroney sets up his deal with Christian Van Der Merwe. Whilst Merroney is away, the depot recieves a visit from April Winter, the daughter of Lord Winter, and new flame of Paul. Upon his return Merroney casually informs faithful Clare that April is his fiancee. Naturally feathers are ruffled and it is clear there is only room for one lady to worship at the Chairman's feet. The writing is on the wall for Clare as Carole Mowlam had decided to leave the series, and this is one humiliation too many. Ken Riddington intended for Liza Goddard to be waiting in the wings and April's relationship with Paul Merroney would be explored to great effect in the next series.

'Birthday' written by Ray Jenkins ended the *The Brothers* current run. The Hammonds' are summoned to Mary's house to celebrate her birthday, Sir Neville Henniswode tags along but it's far from a jolly affair. Mary is steadfast against merging with Van der Merwe and insists on having her say on the latest direction for the company. At a meeting of the shareholders, Mary along with representatives of haulage rival Kirkman's, attempt to disrupt the vote on merging with the Dutch company. But Merroney has played his hand and the vote goes through. Hammonds is now part of a conglomerate. The series finale saw the final appearances of both Carole Mowlam, who as Clare has lost in the battle for Merroney's affections, and Carleton Hobbs, who was sadly to die two years later, aged 80. Mowlam particularly had become a popular member of the team, and everyone was sad to see her go. But an ongoing series like *The Brothers* thrives on change and Norman Crisp and Bill Sellars were already hard at work on preparing a mammoth sixteen week run for the autumn of 1976. As the ever loyal television audience were waiting patiently for the return of their favourite fifty minutes of Sunday night drama. However in the break between series The People newspaper bore a startling headline in its 16th May 1976 edition. BROTHERS AT THE END OF THE ROAD ran it's headline. "*The Brothers* will be off the road and off our screens by the end of the year," predicted an article by Peter Oakes. "A BBC producer has been instructed to look for a new show to replace the serial," it continued. "Norman Crisp one of the creators of *The Brothers* told me 'In theory the next series is the last.' As yet no definite decision has been made on the future of *The Brothers* which will have run for seven series. And Mr. Crisp said: 'There's a chance they might think again if the audience insists on watching it.' Personally I can't see the audience making much fuss about the end of the Hammonds. After a bright start the serial trickled away to the standard of less prestigious shows like *Crossroads*. But in case it gets a reprieve writer Crisp isn't taking any chances. 'I am writing what should be the last four episodes. But I am not writing them as if the show is definitely finishing. I am leaving everything open so they can come back if they want to. Whatever happens there will be a long gap before the eighth series. The last two are being done straight off with hardly a break. It would be autumn 1978 before work could start on an eighth series.' Backroom feeling is that *The Brothers* has had a good run for it's money."

Clearly the writing was now on the wall for Hammond Transport Services and this time not even the devious ploys of a quick thinking Paul Merroney could save it.

Patrick O'Connell promoting the show in the Netherlands

Contact sheet for the closing titles photo 1974.

IN CONVERSATION WITH
JENNIFER WILSON

RC: How did Jennifer Kingsley come about for you?

Jennifer Wilson: I think it all started because I was playing opposite George Cole in the series *A Man Of Our Times* playing a mistress. My husband [actor Brian Peck] was working for Gerry Glaister at the time on a series called *Codename*. Gerry said to Brian that he thought I was terrific in the role and that he himself was thinking of making a series about a mistress. So I think Jennifer Kingsley started with *A Man Of Our Times* to be honest. Sometime later Gerry called me into his office after I had recorded a *Dixon Of Dock Green* and asked me to read the script of the first episode. I read the script and thought it was just terrific, and I was told that Jean Anderson would be playing the wife. As Gerry described it all to me, it just sounded better and better. I had always been quite a goody girl , so playing a mistress first in *A Man Of Our Times*, then in *The Brothers* was a marvellous change.

RC: Can you remember what your impressions of the first script were?

Oh it was marvellous, just marvellous. Norman Crisp was a really good and very experienced writer. What was so good was the family of boys, these three brothers. And Jean's character. The nuisance was I'd agreed to do a series called *The Doctors* for the BBC and the dates clashed. I hadn't signed a contract but in those days any verbal agreement was considered binding. Nobody said to me "Well it's the BBC as well, so we'll get you out of it", I was just told "Well you better get out of it with your agent somehow!" I had a fortnight of worry before it got sorted. The other show said, "If we can find the right person to replace you, then we will let you go and do *The Brothers*" and eventually they did. The night before I was called into Gerry's office I had had a road accident. A car had driven into the side of my car and so I was very shaken. Then I had to go and do this large part in the *Dixon Of Dock Green* episode, so by the time I got up to Gerry's office I was just rambling away about my accident.

RC: Had you worked with any of *The Brothers* cast before?

I hadn't worked with anyone I don't think, although my husband had worked with Jean Anderson, so he knew her.

RC: What do you remember of that first day of filming around the grave?

Only that is was so cold, that we were all passing around a bottle of brandy underneath our coats in between the shots. We found a pub nearby and gathered around the fire to keep ourselves warm before we were forced out into the cold again for more filming. Thankfully things got better when we went into the studio. Those scenes around the table when I took my ring off were incredible. I got so many letters from around the world saying how powerful that moment was when it was revealed Jennifer had born Robert Hammond's baby. Glyn's anger particularly I remember.

RC: Did you have an inkling you might have a success on your hands?

None of us ever thought it was going to be as big as it was. We just thought they were very good scripts. All the characters had strong motivation. Such a diverse set of characters, all opposing each other. We did think we would get asked to do some more I think, but at the end of it all there was nothing. Then we waited nearly a year for them to put it out. The BBC had no intention of making any more but the reaction to that first series was so strong, and they got so many letters about it, that they were suddenly faced with having to get everyone back together, almost by popular demand. At the end of the first series when the BBC bods were supposed to come to see us, we all thought we were going to be asked to do a second lot. But when they said "I don't think we'll be doing any more" you should have seen our faces! We were absolutely stunned. We all trouped to the pub and shoved some booze down, and commiserated with each other. It was a job yes, but it was also something that we had all loved doing. Most of us were in young middle age at that time and there were financial implications. A lot of us had counted on a second series in order to pay off some of our mortgages. It was a terrible shock. But then a year later, when we were all doing other things, we heard that the BBC wanted us all back. Glyn wanted too much money to come back, and he tried to hold the BBC over a barrel. I think a lot of it was to do with Glyn's agent, because I think Glyn was very upset when they re-cast and he didn't come back. I loved him but he could be a bit fiery and bolshie. Then Paddy O'Connell came in and ended up being a big success but it took people a little while to adjust to a new Edward.

RC: You also found yourself in a prime-time Sunday evening slot from 1973 onwards.

Back on those days we had 'personality' newspaper critics. There was an Australian named Clive James, who was normally very scathing with his criticisms, and he just adored it. And a few other people who had prominent newspaper columns came out in praise of the show. Papers like The Times, we had excellent notices.

RC: What did you like or not like about Jennifer Kingsley.

Well, there were a few things I didn't like about her. I never thought really that I should have had that whole baby storyline. They put that in to give me another chance at being a mother, but Jennifer had already been a mother with Barbara. In those days you were middle aged at 40 so I always thought Jennifer Kingsley would never have wanted to have had another go at motherhood. One thing I remember from doing all that baby stuff was with our director Vere Lorrimer. Vere was so lovely, one of the nicest men. There was a shot where I had to get the baby into the car with me, this tiny little thing who was only a few weeks old

I think. I tried to get in gracefully but it was difficult. The mother was standing only a few feet away and Vere was shouting "Push it in, get it in the car" as if it were a doll. This poor tiny little baby. It was very funny. Another thing I didn't like was that I felt she wasn't as kind as she could have been to Edward. A little bit condescending at times. I felt she could have been a bit warmer. I liked the fact that she had a good business brain on her. I am not at all business like, my husband does all that side of things for me, and I felt the writing was very strong and at times she knew more than the Hammonds. I also liked the mother – daughter thing, the sequences I had with Barbara. I had a daughter of my own roughly the same age so I could associate with that. I think those scenes worked really well. I did like Jennifer. There was a few times though when she was a bit silly. I thought a lot of people would have been shocked that she wanted to marry the son of the man whom she'd had an affair with and born a child with, but funnily enough they weren't. Jean and I were travelling on the train to Birmingham one time and a woman rushed up to us, and hit Jean lightly with her umbrella and said "Let Jennifer marry Edward you old so and so..." It was very funny. We laughed and laughed. You would think that people would feel desperately sorry for Mary Hammond wouldn't you? But no, they were desperate for Jennifer and Edward to get together.

RC: The scenes filmed at Ralph Hilton Transport in Greenwich looked very chaotic, with lorries coming and going all the time. Was it chaotic to film?

It was very much a working depot. They give us some space to record, but did carry on working around us. Some of the girls in the canteen used to peer out of the window to look at all the filming going on. In some ways it helped, it made the situation very real to have all this madness with the lorries going on as we did our dialogue. If they had cleared the area of all that stuff, the scenes would not have looked nearly as authentic.

RC: Did you feel that some writers wrote for you better than others?

Yes I did. I was quite close to Norman Crisp in that I had done television plays of his before *The Brothers* so I think he knew my way of playing scenes, he knew how to write for me. Eric Paice was like Norman's other arm, they wrote those early series between them. I thought in the beginning Eric wasn't quite as good as Norman, but after a while he started to write some very nice scenes for me. We did have a lot of new writers coming in later. It's inevitable on a long running show that actors feel certain writers write better for their particular character than others. I have a feeling a lot of the baby scenes were written by the newer writers to the show, not Norman or Eric. I think when we had script editors on the show they felt the original cast had been around a long while, and favoured the newer characters so some of us felt a little side-lined. Fresh faces can help a long running series but you did lose some of the appeal of the family as things started to get fragmented. That worried me a bit. I worried there was too much of the business side of things, and some of the public did start to say that to me. Jean had a few scripts where she was given hardly anything to do. I know you cannot include everything in 50 minutes, but you can spread it a bit more evenly.

RC: Did you feel the show benefitted at all from moving to Pebble Mill?

I always liked Television Centre. There was a change, and it took a little while to get used to it. It was a bit of a fag going up to Birmingham every fortnight. One of the advantages of being there though was there was nothing to worry about as you would do if you were commuting from home. It was straight to the studio from the hotel and you could concentrate totally on the job in hand.

RC: How did the public approach you in the street? Was it as Jennifer Wilson or Jennifer Kingsley?

All actors will say that people never remember all the theatre or plays you have done, they just remember what you are doing now. It was mostly as Jennifer from *The Brothers* that they would greet me. With Jean it was the same. Mind you these days nobody has chance to read the credits, they whizz by so fast and are so tiny nobody knows who has been in a programme. It's awful. At least with *The Brothers*, and shows of that era, you had really strong credits sequences.

RC: When did you start you realise that *The Brothers* was being watched by a wider audience than just people in the UK?

It certainly didn't happen with the BBC because they couldn't be bothered to send it out to anybody. I think somebody from a television channel abroad would have seen it and requested tapes and sold it to their own network. Suddenly it really took off in Sweden, Norway, the Netherlands. Israel were mad about it. The BBC apparently took no notice of it and the channels had to go to the BBC and say "We'd like Series Two" or whatever. Nobody was pushing it at all. They couldn't be bothered. Whereas now they push like mad for their series to be bought by Europe or America. We were then asked to go over and do personal appearances abroad and I don't think the bigwigs at the BBC liked that. There were about five of us who were always going over to Europe. Instead of being pleased that we were promoting their show, they used to grumble about it in case we missed rehearsals or something. When we got the Christmas record out, which ended up with us all getting a Gold disc for our wall, Kate O'Mara and I went over there to do a signing. We got outside and there were hundreds of people surrounding the car, throwing themselves over the bonnet. These people just wouldn't get out of the way. We asked the driver what he was going to do. We thought he'd say he'd get out and go and get help. He just said "I shall drive through them!" Kate and I were appalled. We couldn't bear to look. On another occasion I went to do a signing and these British PR people said "Oh I think there will be about 30 or 40 people" coming along. They didn't seem to know much about the show at all. They got a long trestle table and we had our backs up against a big glass window which was behind us. Well, hundreds and hundreds of people turned up. They were all pushing forward and we were pushed against the glass. Brian was very worried. It was frightening. The English people didn't have a clue what to do. The police had to come and get us out of it. It was amazing really.

RC: Why do you think these countries were so keen on *The Brothers* and not other serials of the time?

I don't know really. It might have been the family thing might have struck a chord at the beginning. Maybe they could see themselves in the situations that some of the characters were in. Whether it be having an affair or juggling family and business. It was a warm show, not a cops and robbers series. It had its own niche because it was about real people.

RC: How did your husband Brian Peck come to play the bank manager who turned you down for the loan in Series 3?

That was the director [Philip Dudley]. He thought it was a great joke to have Brian do that. Brian was always telling me off for spending too much money. It was a lovely in-joke really. Brian was very busy with all sorts of work at that time so it was surprising he could fit it in.

RC: Do you think the show maintained its quality from beginning to end?

No, not really. It wasn't just me, there were four or five of us saying it wasn't the same as it used to be, although the public were still watching it avidly all the same. The newer directors and writers were pushing the newer arrivals to the show, and forgetting about the core of it sometimes. The family aspect was lost some of the time. I think, perhaps, the first four series were the best.

RC: Can I ask you about specific memories of the cast you worked with for so long. I know you were great friends with Jean Anderson.

I didn't know Jean before hand but we became great friends. We used to travel together up to Birmingham for the recordings. We had lunches together. We would visit each other. She came on holiday with us to Gozo. She came to visit us during the years we lived in France during the 1990s. She was always part of my life in some form. When she was very ill towards the end, she was 93, she suddenly had a tumour in her head. I don't know exactly what it was but it was very serious. She had a house in Penrith and we had a phone call from her daughter to say Jean is saying she would like to see you, I think to say goodbye. Brian and I raced through the night to get there and she was in a sort of coma by then. I sat and held her hand, talking to her. She knew that I was there, I could feel her squeezing my hand. She just slipped away. Jean was a lot older than me but we had this lovely closeness. We had such a lot of fun over the years, we both liked our Bloody Marys. The public could never believe it when they saw us out together having a good laugh and a tipple. They were so used to seeing us as enemies on the screen.

RC: Can I ask you about the rest of your fellow cast members. Starting with Glyn Owen...

Glyn and I were chums. He had a fiery disposition which used to annoy the boys sometimes, he was a bit full of himself actually. I loved him, he was a good artist and a very good actor. He was a bit mad, but we all are in this business. I got on very well with him.

RC: Patrick O'Connell

Paddy was a different kind of man. We had a very good working relationship, a fun relationship really. He would always stand up for me if there was any trouble. A good mate. After working together for so long you just get used to each other. I never had a crossed word with him. The other two used to get a bit annoyed with him because he liked a drink. He always thought of himself as an artist really, a painter. There always seemed a lot more things to Paddy apart from acting. He was very sweet when he came into the show. We were both very friendly with the actor Frank Finlay, and when he had been cast we met him for the first time at Frank's before he started working on the show.

RC: Richard Easton

Richard could be a bit of a prankster, but also a bit of a mixer. We would have a few words every now and again. He was very vocal about things he didn't like. Richard is an extremely good actor. Scenes with him were lovely. I think he'd had enough of *The Brothers* at one time. I have seen it happen over the years with various actors, and he decided to leave the series. I always thought he'd be back though, and he was.

RC: Robin Chadwick

I would get a bit cross with Robin. He was young and inexperienced. He used to think he was entitled to better things, and nobody is in this business. When I saw him again years later, when it was all over, he was the same old Robin. A bit bumptious still. Full of himself.

RC: Hilary Tindall

Hilary used to annoy me sometimes. We did see each other quite a bit, she used to come over to our house and then we'd go over to see her and Robin (Lowe, her husband). She could be quite critical on a persal level, perhaps telling me my hair was much too long or something. But maybe it was a bit of rivalry between two leading ladies.

RC: Julia Goodman

We got on fine, it was much the mother and daughter type relationship on screen and off. I was always telling her off for being late, she was always late. The cast used to get cross with her because of her time keeping. I treated her rather like my own daughter I suppose. She was much younger than me though.

RC: Gabrielle Drake

I didn't really know a lot about Gabby. You couldn't really mix with everybody. She was a kind, nice person.

RC: Derek Benfield

I used to call him Ruby. The reason for this, and it stuck for years, was because a script arrived and instead of saying 'Riley' it said 'Ruby'. That was the joke from then on and he became Ruby. I adored him. He loved his Bloody Mary's with Jean and I. We were very close, long after *The Brothers* finished.

RC: Margaret Ashcroft

I didn't know Maggie that well, enough to have a chat but we didn't visit each other or anything. I didn't know she had been so ill towards the end.

RC: Kate O'Mara

Kate was lovely. She came to see me several years back when I was in a theatre play in Birmingham. We didn't do that many scenes together. There was friction between our characters I think.

RC: Colin Baker

I got to know Colin quite well because we worked together in the theatre. He's a good actor and we got on fine.

RC: Mark McManus

Mark was a lovely lovely chap. I'll never forget, he thought he was going to stay on with the show. It was a terrible shock to him. Right at the end of the second series one of the directors said to him "Mark, I'm sorry we won't be seeing you next year" and he went completely white. I have never forgotten it. He was certain he was coming back, and it was a terrible shock. Obviously they had not told him he wouldn't be needed for the next series which was very naughty really, they should have made him aware much earlier. We had a lot of fun making that series though, he was very jokey and we got on really well. But he ended up alright because he got that wonderful series *Taggart*. He was superb in that.

RC: Mike Pratt

I didn't know him terribly well. A very nice man. I do remember enjoying scenes with him. He was a very gentle person. He had a charm, and was almost spiritual. He had a depth to him. He was spiritually perceptive. A bit of a hippy I think.

RC: And what about the the producers you worked with, Ken Riddington and Bill Sellars?

I got on well with Ken. He did at one point suggest I leave the series. Ken said I had done a lot of work in television before the series [as a character actress] and he didn't think I'd find it easy to go back to it afterwards. And he was right about that. He wasn't quite as intuitive as Gerry Glaister I don't think. He went on to do some marvellous things like *Tenko* though. Bill was OK.

RC: Did you know it was ending in 1976?

I knew it was going to end. I am sure. I felt it had run its course and the quality would go down. So it was the right time.

TIMOTHY COMBE REMEMBERS...

Timothy Combe directed several high profile dramas at the BBC during the 1960s and 70s. These included *Doctor Who*, *Z Cars* **and** *Angels*. **However, he directed seven episodes of** *The Brothers* **during the 1976 recording sessions and here recalls his time on the show.**

The first thing I would do when assigned to direct a series is meet up with the producer and story editor to discuss the script. I would have been sent the script in advance usually, if I had any comments to make on the script I would make that at the initial meeting. The length of the script would need to be sorted, although the script editor should have done their job it isn't always so. I would read it and time it, although difficult if there is filming. I would try and choose my production team if I had the chance, sometimes I would be told who I was getting but if I could I would request somebody who I knew and trusted. Its very important to have a good team working with you. Also build up a relationship with the producer if possible. In the case of *The Brothers* the producer was Bill Sellars whom I had first worked with on *The Newcomers* [1967] and then *The Doctors* [1970] which was filmed up in Birmingham. I knew Bill anyway, and we had a good relationship. He kept himself in the background pretty much and wasn't a frustrated director like a lot of producers are. It is tricky coming in as a new boy to an established team. You don't want to ruffle too many feathers but at the same time you want to make your mark. I always liked to think of myself as an actor's director. I had been at drama school myself and had done a bit of acting, not a lot but a bit, and I always felt it was important to work with the actors. Getting their performance and not worrying initially what the cameras were going to do. I would have a camera plan and work with the designer on how it is going to be shot. With a show like *The Brothers* it would have the same sets week in week out, so it was tempting to play around with it but other directors before you probably had similar ideas. So initially when I joined, and my first episode when I joined was 'Tender', I just spent time getting to know the cast and crew and them getting to know me without going out on a limb. I hadn't worked with any of the regulars before I don't think. I had worked on series and serials before and there is a disease which I call 'serial-itis'. That is to say an actor who has been in a serial a long time, and they want everything changed and done their way. They assume it's a permanent job which it never is and everyone is dispensable. With *The Brothers* I found everyone very professional, none of them had gotten serial-itis. I had a very nice time on the show, with the one exception perhaps being the time we went to Amsterdam to film scenes with Paul Merroney and Van Der Merwe. I think it was Bill Sellars who had been to Holland to do a recce of locations. He wanted to have a shot on the famous canals, in a boat. What he'd done was got on a tourist boat with his Dutch assistant director, and she'd fixed up this tourist boat. The scene was Merroney and Van Der Merwe having a deep conversation about business matters having a meal. It was a joke. *The Brothers* was big big viewing in Holland and we would have been laughed off the screen if we had used it. These tourist boats are not dining experiences, you are just meant to sit and admire the view. I asked the Dutch girl if she could get me a proper boat to shoot this scene, which we could go up and down the Canal on. It was all very last minute, we had only arrived the night before the shoot. It was traumatic. She tried her best but failed. I knew we had to find somewhere. I decided we would shoot on a boat and film shots of Amsterdam going by and somehow cut them together, mocking it up. We ended up in a marina. It could very well have been in England but was in fact in Holland. It was a bloody good scene actually, I remember getting nuances that weren't in the script. I was only disappointed we were on the long boat and not out on the canal in a nice yacht of some sort.

We filmed several times at Lydd Airfield which I had used as a child with my parents. It's not a busy airport. They would do anything for us, and were very very helpful. They had one or two Dakotas there as well as private planes. They used to say, "When we land to refuel at Le Touquet would you like any cheese or wine bringing back?" I asked them about fish as well. So I would go home armed with cheese and wine and lobsters. The depot at Burgh Heath is now a supermarket. Again they went out of their way to accommodate us, and couldn't have been nicer. We did our studios at Pebble Mill which was a bit akin to going from the West End out into Rep for the theatre. You are leaving your main base. Pebble Mill were very professional. I had first worked in Birmingham on *Swizzlewick* [1964] a series about a local Midlands council. Quite political. The cast knew they were coming to the end of their contracts and were a bit down. A bit un-punctual and carefree. Their hearts and souls were no longer in the work. Douglas Camfield was the the director on *Swizzlewick* and was a real task master to work for. We got the scripts and they were awful. Dougie said lets take them home and re-write them. So we both went away and re-wrote the thing. We later learned the scripts we were working on had been commissioned and rejected before as not being good enough. At that time the design office was a lovely Edwardian house in Carpenter Road. But when I went back with *The Brothers* there was this lovely new complex at Pebble Mill. Studios with terrific lighting, everything very slick. The crews were keen to show they were just as good as London if not better.

I remember working with Carleton Hobbs during my episodes. I had chosen him because when I was at Webber Douglas we had the Carleton Hobbs Award which was to do with voice work. I had always wanted to meet him and he was getting on by then so I was happy to cast him as Sir Neville. I cast Carmen Du Sautoy at the beginning of her career as Van Der Merwe's daughter. I found her through a casting breakdown for agents for the character, she came and read for me and was very good. Carmen went on to have a lovely career as an actress and is still going. I cast a young Caroline Langrishe too. It is satisfying when you find some nice young talent who then go on to prove your faith in them. Clive Swift was another casting, he has that lovely voice which can bring a bit of mystery to a part. Before he became a foil for Patricia Routledge in *Keeping Up Appearances*. Bill Sellars I think cast Joby Blanshard as Van Der Merwe. That was not mine. I was watching my episode 'Manoeuvres' last night and I think it comes over as quite slick. Some of the dialogue is quaint but on the whole it stands up pretty well. It's a different style of shooting to today, but very comforting to watch. I didn't find it jarred at all. I also watched the Merroney wedding episode which we filmed at a little church in Graffham in West Sussex. It was the church where my wife and I got married. Her parents had a little cottage just by the church, so I brought my children down and had them running around as wedding guests along with my wife Angela Ellison, who is an actress. We recently went back there for our 50th wedding anniversary. That was of course where Colin met Liza Goddard. I kind of had my suspicions that something was going on. I heard from people who were staying with them at the hotel that they were together as a couple. A couple of episodes later we were down at Lime Grove studios for some reason, and Colin came up to me and said "Tim, I wonder if I can have the afternoon off?" I was trying to say 'you can't just go off without a good reason' when Richard Easton piped up "He's getting married!" We must have been rehearsing so I let them go off and get married. I loved all the cast actually. Richard Easton was a very good actor and Colin Baker was excellent as Merroney. We had a little drama with Paddy O'Connell. He decided he wanted to become a painter and in the middle of rehearsals took off for Holland, and I phoned Pat - his wife - who managed to trace him. He was going to give the acting up. I don't think he really liked the part he was playing, he had decided what he really wanted to do was paint. We had to write him out of the episode and change all the lines. We were re-writing on a Saturday afternoon and giving revised scripts to the cast for the recording on the Monday. Fortunately Paddy didn't have a lot to do in that episode, but it was dramatic and traumatic. But fortunately I thrive on situations which keep me on my toes. I liked

Paddy a lot. You never knew if he was going to learn his lines. He had an edge to him. Robin Chadwick was a good actor, I think he was from New Zealand. I did the last episode that Mike Pratt appeared in, he was a good strong actor who played the scene very well. I had no idea he was so ill. Another bit of casting of mine was Terence Frisby as Simon Winter. It was completely against type. There were so many public school actors I could have cast but favoured Terry. I had seen him in a play somewhere. He was really good. Just the sort of person I wanted. I used him after that in a Richard Harris play for Innes Lloyd, *When The Boys Come Out To Play* about a firms day out on the golf course. He was also very well known as a writer for the comedy *There's A Girl In My Soup.*

SERIES SEVEN (1976)

The gap between series on screen had brought press coverage of the real life marriage between Colin Baker and his new co-star Liza Goddard. They tied the knot in Hampstead on 12th July 1976 during recording of the new series. The Sun leapt in with some tabloid reporting of course. "I can't understand it," they quoted Liza as saying, "Usually kissing an actor is all part of the job. But it suddenly gets a lot more complicated when the actor is your husband." Liza went on, "It was very sudden. I had never wanted to marry anyone before. But I wanted to marry Colin more than anything. He felt the same. At first we set the date for next year. Then we changed it to the end of this year. Finally we couldn't wait any longer." There was certainly no time for a honeymoon. Recording had started in May with barely a gap since series six had wrapped. Despite the pervading air of 'will they or won't they commission a further series?' all involved were giving it their best shot. A somewhat welcome development was the seventh series would be sixteen episodes in length, three more than had been the norm.

With Eric Paice having departed the series for good, three writers were contracted to provide episodes in addition to Norman Crisp – Ray Jenkins, Brian Finch and series newcomer Elaine Morgan. Morgan was an experienced television scriptwriter who had started her screen career in 1956. In the interim she had added her name to the credits of several BBC Sunday Night plays, *Dr. Finlay's Casebook*, *The Doctors* and *How Green Was My Valley* to pick out just four of her many scripting commissions. She was incidentally, the only female writer of episodes throughout the entire canon. Perhaps fitting she should pen the episode entitled 'The Distaff Side'. Another lady Cicely Cawthorne was appointed as script editor for this block of filming, meaning that the polish of the show was down to another lone female. N.J. Crisp addressed the recent influx of new writers to the Liverpool Echo: "In the original days, Gerry (Glaister) and I worked together a lot. Then he had to retreat and I carried on writing most of the scripts. It was very demanding. I did have other matters to attend to and the writing and the amount of work was a strain on my health. Now I take a lesser hand in the scripts. This time, of the sixteen episodes, I have written four." Further commenting on the devising of plots and the coming and going of lead actors, Crisp had this to say: "When actors want to be released, we find a way to make the characters depart and adjust the script accordingly. Gabrielle Drake wanted to leave the series so we made Jill die in a car crash. Richard Easton asked to season out so Brian had a nervous breakdown. With Hilary Tindall, a divorce seemed the most natural let-out for Ann. Thus the story is shaped by the characters themselves."

This seventh series was graced with a new set of opening and closing titles. Again set to Dudley Simpson's majestic theme music, the opening showed a montage of lorries and aircraft symbolising the expanding horizons of Hammond Transport. Whilst the closing credits were displayed over a shot of the view seen from a vehicle travelling on a motorway. (It was actually the same short bit of film repeated several times). If this was to be the last hurrah of Hammonds, the production was going out with some style. As the Hammonds gather for Paul's nuptials to April, the ailing Sir Neville Henniswode is on the verge of appointing his successor at the bank. Rather inconveniently April's brother Simon Winter is Merroney's rival for the position. All rather awkward. Meanwhile Jennifer manages to have a vehicle accident on the way to the wedding, she runs over a man on a bike. Naturally the BBC Research Department were on the case soon afterwards. "One feels it is a real family and gets so involved in events" reported one panel viewer. "Corny but irresistible" said another. The report further went on to note "If the characters of Colin Baker as Merroney, 'a man with half his thoughts on the bride and the other half on his business', and Jean Anderson as Mary Hammond stood out in some opinions, the acting on the whole was usually applauded. So too was the production; in particular reporting viewers quite often commented that the costumes, setting of the church and the marquee and 'general atmosphere of chaos' of the wedding had been well done, several remarking with admiration on the attractive country setting." More fierce critics in the report bemoaned that the wedding storyline was simply 'catering to the Mums' and had dominated the episode to a distracting degree. And among what the report described as 'stray criticisms' that "in parts – such as the 'switch' in filming when Brian was toasting the bridesmaids – it has seemed jumpy." With a 19.3% of the audience share, as opposed to the 17% for ITV against the imported American series Hawaii Five-O, the seventh series had indeed got off to a terrific start.

Several newspapers jumped into the fray with a verdict on 'To Honour And Obey', the opening episode. The Colchester Evening Gazette judged it thus: "It was one of those fairly ordinary Moss Bros receptions – striped marquee, a belted earl giving away his daughter and all that. Just the sort of junket you might expect The Brothers to be involved – as spectators only, of course. And everything went the way you'd expect from a series where the business and human interest has been laid on with a fairly heavy hand. There was the bridegroom Paul Merroney with half an ear to the telephone for news of the dying chairman. Edward and Jennifer are at the beginning of another "sorry darling" marathon in a road accident. The unexplained absence of the Merroney parents – who'd have thought his dad grew prize veg? – and an enterprising new brother-in-law to broaden the scope a little. Ray Jenkins certainly got the series off to a ripping start. The introduction of Liza Goddard – in reality Mrs. Colin Baker – strengthens the already formidable team of forceful ladies in this show. Too much I fancy even for Jean Anderson, the long time programme matriarch, to keep her crown for long." Over at the Evening News the headline was *Oh Brother! Almost As Bad As Real Life.* "When the time comes – and it may not be all that far distant – for television drama to be created by computer, *The Brothers* is the sort of thing we may expect," expounded Ronald Higham. "You feed in popular themes – sex, family rivalry, big business, high society, boardroom scheming – and out pops an efficient package deal of predictable situations, plastic characters and women's magazine type dialogue." Not a fan than Ronald? Apparently not, there was more. "A marquee on the lawn, champers galore, toastmaster, speeches, bad jokes, the lot. It was almost as excruciatingly tedious as a real wedding." He summed it up by writing "With such tortuous goings on and such monied skulduggery in high places how can we fail to be gripped? Well it's not difficult. Still I must learn to live with The Brothers for they're going to be with us for a long time." Well, actually Ronald only the next fifteen weeks as it turned out. The Observer's summary of the episode echoed what millions of viewers might have been saying at the time "Now that it's back I wonder all over again how life was ever supportable without it." The writer goes on to conclude "...watching The Brothers is like talking to your analyst only less expensive. The message of the show is that if the firm needs Edward and Jenny, then life needs you. Bill and Gwen Riley are there to reassure the plebs that to stay ordinary is a way of being above it all."

No sooner had viewers revelled in the picturesque setting of the wedding, then a surprise was heading their way for the second episode. The much missed Ann Hammond was back, albeit brief-ly. Hilary Tindall returned to the series for a trio of appearances, to let us know what had happened to Ann. As it turns out life has not been the rosy party she had expected away from dull Brian. Drifting from one hopeless relationship to another has led her to think that the security of being married to Brian was no bad thing after all. She has in tow her daughter Carol, this time played by Debbie Farrington, the third in the series of Carol clones. When we last saw her some two years previously, Carol had been a slightly daffy schoolgirl. Now she seems to have gained about five years in age and become a rather all too knowing hippy. She insists on calling her grandmother "Mary" and positively bristles whenever her mother is in the same room. What's worse she gets on famously with Jane Maxwell, now seriously interested in Brian. Incidentally, the episode 'Home And Away' which sees Ann's return has the distinction of being the longest ever episode of The Brothers, coming in at 52 minutes and 14 seconds. We get that bit extra Ann Hammond for our money, which is never a bad thing.

A very welcome addition to the cast as far as viewers were concerned was Christine Absalom. Paul Merroney had been without a permanent secretary since the departure of Clare Miller, so Judy Vickery is hired. She is everything Clare isn't. Shy and nervous, she is intimidated by Merroney and frequently annoys him by asking (perfectly reasonable) questions. He in turn is rude and be-littling. It was comedy gold to replace the cool all knowing Miller, with her antithesis and both Baker and Absalom played it to perfection. Miss Vickery made a trio of appearances, the creation of Elaine Morgan. Miss Vickery would have been a shoe-in for a return in the eighth series, how-ever as it is Christine Absalom's three episodes provided us with some rare comedy moments in the show, and Judy Vickery remains a very memorable visitor to the offices of Hammond Transport.

MARGOT HAYHOE REMEMBERS...

Margot Hayhoe worked for many years at the BBC as a production assistant and production unit manager, before progressing to a role as associate producer. She worked on the final series of *The Brothers* in the capacity of Production Assitant. Here Margot recalls her time at Hammond Transport:

RC: How did you come to work on *The Brothers*?

As a BBC staff Production Assistant in Drama Serials I was allocated to work on three episodes.

RC: What did your job entail?

I would find the locations for the film inserts and work out a film schedule, liaise with the Designer, Costume and Make-up, Technical departments. Book the extras for the filming and studio. Book the transport and film equipment. Go on the filming recce then attend the filming as Assistant to the Director. Then into rehearsals at Acton Rehearsal block, produce a recording order and camera plan for the technical run and travel to Birmingham Pebble Mill for the video recording, liaising with the cast, passing on instructions from the Director in the gallery, keeping the studio working to time. I also had to keep these episodes on budget and be responsible for the safety of crew and cast.

RC: What are your memories of the cast, crew, producer and directors? Were there any people specifically who stand out in your memory?

My director was Mary Ridge who was a very experienced director who worked meticulously on producing a detailed film shooting script and camera script. She was quite serious but very loyal and protective of her team. Bill Sellars was the Producer having taken over at some point I think from Gerard Glaister, in my position I didn't have much contact with them. The cast by the time I joined the show for the last series Eps. 12, 14 and 16 were very settled in their characters and ways. Obviously the stand out players were Kate O'Mara, Colin Baker and Patrick O'Connell. I have happy memories of all the cast. I can remember Kate being teased about her newly enhanced boobs which she took in very good humour inviting anyone to give them a squeeze. I had worked with Colin before on 'War and Peace' and was very happy to do so again. Jennifer Wilson was a bit reserved. Liza Goddard was good fun. Derek Benfield and Margaret Ashcroft were lovely. I was rather taken with Peter Blake in episode 14! A sad memory is that Anthony Nicolls got news during rehearsals of the cot death of a grandchild. Naturally he was given time off.

RC: Are there any specific memories of studio or location recording that spring to mind? Was it easy recording the location scenes at Kinloch's Provision Merchants at Epsom with all those lorries?

Filming location scenes at the lorry depot were difficult as we had to work round the continual comings and goings of the 'real' lorries which slowed down the amount we could shoot there. I can't remember if we used Kinloch's, I think there might have been a change somewhere during during the preceeding series. I do seem to remember that there was a lot of discontent at the original choice which was made by Gerry Glaister for being too far away from base and too noisy. One of the more memorable sequences I worked on was in episode 14. This was the sequences on the ferry from Newhaven to Dieppe and scenes in the streets of Dieppe. This filming was done in one day. It was fairly hair-raising in that we had to film the lorry driving onto the ship and film the loading doors shutting from the docks but manage to get back onto the ship before it sailed, to do shots on deck with Jennifer Wilson, without holding up the departure. We then all leaped off to go through customs and into the streets to get those scenes. Then back on board to film the dialogue scenes at the bar which didn't need daylight on the return to Newhaven. We did have a second camera so I was allowed to go off with the cameraman on the ship to get establishing, PoV shots. A very long but rewarding day. The other film sequences I remember were the Garden Centre sequences in episode 12 with Jean Anderson and Margaret Ashcroft at the Toad Hall Garden Centre near Henley which was good fun with two such good actresses. Another slightly hard shoot was in Belgravia with Colin Baker and Liza Goddard, walking and talking with extras passing by. This had to be shot on a Sunday but, as all shops in those days were closed on Sundays, a lot of negotiation had to be done to get the shop owners to put on their lights etc. The final episode was mostly studio and the party scene was quite a challenge. However we were then able to use that set for the wrap party!

RC: Was working at Pebble Mill in any way different to working at TV Centre in your job?

Apart from the travel from London and having the stay away from home, the only difference to my mind was that the crews at Pebble Mill were willing to help each other and make slight compromises in getting shots whereas the London crews were competitive and would push harder to get exactly the best shots. All the crews in all the Regions were very friendly and professional.

RC: Why do you think the series was so well received back in the 1970's and drew such huge ratings? Would such a series be made today?

Good scripts with strong characters. Family feuds are popular. The acting was strong with good looking artists. There were so many different genres of series made at that time. So many different themes. Obviously there were far fewer channels in those days and no internet, VHSs or DVDs which accounts for the ratings. I think this type of family based series could be popular again as a change from all the Detective / Police/ Medical series which flood the networks.

STEVE UBELS REMEMBERS

There was a guy called Ted Rhodes who was the second in command, who basically looked me up in Spotlight [the actors casting directory] and that was it, I was called in to audition. My father was Dutch and I was raised in Holland until I was 8 years old. I then came to England. I kept up the language a bit and was advertised in Spotlight as a British actor who could speak Dutch.

I had of course seen The Brothers but I wasn't really a fan, I didn't watch it regularly but I had seen a couple of them. My mother who is also an actress had worked for Gerry a few times too. Essentially when I was in The Brothers, as I remember it, one or two of the regular actors in the show were thinking of leaving and I was brought in as a possible replacement. The whole story of the Dutch and English companies merging meant that my character could easily be brought in. The cast were extremely helpful. It represented a break for me. It was the first time I had played a decent part on television. Both Liza Goddard and Colin Baker were very helpful, very generous. Offering me a lot of advice because they had been doing it for some time already. Working at Pebble Mill was very gentle. Very straight forward. Most of the other stuff I have done has been action based. Soldiers and spies. Paul Van Kepe wasn't sinister in any way, he was straight forward. He did have a suggested affair with Liza Goddard's character but as the series ultimately wasn't going to come back, I think they abandoned that story arc. I didn't really experience any fan reaction on the street. I did though have a full page in a Dutch magazine about me and my role which was exciting. It was really big news in Holland. I have relatives there and they were all talking about it. There were some ideas being floated about for future storylines. The idea was the Dutch side would come and take it over. I would then have taken the place of Paul Merroney and headed the company. That was the loose idea. We never got to develop it fully, as I said when it became clear it wasn't coming back, that side of it just petered out.

CHRISTINE ABSALOM REMEMBERS

I got the part of Miss Vickery, in The Brothers, in the autumn of that long hot heady year of 1976. I was so excited. I had watched The Brothers for years, it was a regular Sunday evening date, with the whole family. I went to meet the wonderful Mary Ridge, dressed as smartly as I could, and hopefully looking like a Secretary, as instructed by my agents. I had been struggling to cope with contact lenses for months, and much to my agents chagrin I didn't wear them for my interview because my eyes were just too sore. Actually I think it was the glasses that swung it my way, and the fact that I lied about being able to touch type. (Well, we did lie in those days!)

I just remember the enormous fun of rehearsing at The Acton Hilton, proper rehearsals, with a terrifying Producers' Run at the end of the week. Then decamping to Birmingham for the rehearse and record weekends. Everybody was delightful, and made me feel very welcome and part of the gang. I loved my scenes with Colin Baker, I seem to recall a lot of laughter, and forgive me for telling you that one week I did win the 'comedy' prize – a much coveted soft toy, which was handed on week by week to the next worthy winner.
I
t was my first really decent part on television, but I was never made to feel like a novice, I was nurtured. I was very ill with a perforated ear drum about half way through recording my episodes, and the care I was given was generous and loving. That probably sounds very mushy, but it is true.

When the episodes were screened I remember shopping in Marks and Spencer in Southend, and noticing quite a lot of whispering going on. When I got to the till the cashier said "Are you starring in The Brothers at the moment ?" I was quite overwhelmed. 'Starring' was an overstatement but the question made me very proud.

At this mid series point, *The Brothers* was still giving ITV a run for it's money. Although flashy American series The Bionic Woman had a 22.7% share of the audience, The Brothers were not far behind with a very healthy 19.7%. "If not perhaps great drama the series is fairly compulsive viewing," summarised the Audience Research for Elaine Morgan's debut script 'The Distaff Side'. "Occasionally the viewers felt that the story had moved too far away from the original conception of Hammond Transport ('Where are the lorries?'), that it was getting unrealistic and concentrating too much on petty domestic squabbles. The overall response was nevertheless, very cordial, viewers finding the plot interesting and realistic, with a good balance between business and personal matters. 'An absorbing episode; skilful build-up of tensions and shifts in relationships and a few intriguing new threads.'" The stalwart cast were also at the receiving end of the praise. "The acting was usually commended – indeed, those taking part had become so completely identified in viewers' minds with the characters they played that they often found it difficult to judge them objectively. However, this was a good all round performance, most would have agreed, small groups having particular praise for Colin Baker and Liza Goddard as Paul and April Merroney and for Christine Absalom as the new secretary."

However the popular press were by now adept at cutting The Brothers down to size. Paul Foster in his Eye On TV column for a national newspaper opened his attack on the episode 'Celebration' by Brian Finch with: "The Brothers is just about the most unimaginative, repetitive, padded-out piece of soap opera on the box." Ouch! He was not finished there though. "The main characters are all unsympathetic, unattractive people. Mary Hammond has become a peevish, interfering old trout, who looks as though there's a smell of bad eggs under her nose. Brian is weak, David spineless, Edward's a pain in the neck, and Jenny looks permanently miserable. Merroney is an icy male chauvinist, his wife a drippy snob and Jane Maxwell has all the appeal of a calculating machine. The Rileys are working-class bores. The whole wretched bunch are held together by almost non-existant plots, family squabbles, boardroom politics and inconsequential trivia. Sunday's saga typified the lack of acting with barely any development of the storyline. Apart from Jenny being upset over a summons for dangerous driving, the episode was waffled out with chunks of dialogue that went nowhere. It's definitely time Hammond Transport came to the end of the road. It's certainly long been barren of any compulsive elements." A little harsh perhaps Mr. Foster. Clearly he was out of step with *The Brothers* loyal following.

The Sunday Times leapt into the fray with an article praising the series as "sophisticated" from a business point of view. "Behind the expansion has been the shrewd advice of 64-year-old Dick Howe," it went on to say, " who has been picking up a modest £400 a series as financial adviser to the scriptwriters of *The Brothers*. They create all the domestic trials and tribulations, but Howe makes sure the lorry routes are right, loads arrives on time, what the cargoes should be. When the Hammond board meets, it is Howe's expertise that makes the cross talk ring true. "For example," says Howe, "Merroney was wanted out for a week so one of the scriptwriters phoned me to ask what to do with him. My son-in-law who is in the transport business had been telling me about these lorries being abandoned on the road between Istanbul and Tehran so I said "'why don't we send Merroney to Turkey?'" He admits he doesn't know if the scheme to salvage the trucks is viable. He'd have to look into it, but he points out that the lorries are worth £30,000 apiece." Howe had been a prisoner-of-war and imprisoned in hte infamous castle Colditz, becoming escape officer for three and a half years. He found himself as adviser on Glaister's BBC drama about the period Colditz, and by association landed a role advising on Hammond Transport. "Before the start of each series, the scriptwriters, directors and producers and Howe get together round a table either at the studios or at his office in Regent Street: "We discuss what might happen and all throw in ideas. When the scriptwriters are writing the series they ring me up to ask what Merroney or someone would do in a certain situation." Sure enough increased trade with the Middle East – based out of Tehran – was a major storyline of the final run . Paul pressures his fellow directors into voting for a scheme of operating service centres used for maintaining vehicles along the difficult trade route. The haulage industry were quick to spot the flaws of this storyline as trade publication The Journal Of Commerce were quick to point out. "We've been doing this route now for over 10 years" said a director of real life haulage firm Astran International, "We don't need service centres along the route – all that's needed are decent parking facilities." Clearly feathers had been ruffled, and he went on the offensive – seemingly oblivious to the fact the show was not a documentary – "If Hammond Brothers have got enough money to open these centres, perhaps they could afford to pay me a retainer and then I'd really show them how to run the Middle East!" he tells the reporter seemingly angry at plans the Hammond Board have voted to put through. A further example of how events in the show reflected real life, and how issues raised in the show proved provocative to the widespread viewership. But if there were criticisms from some quarters, the show was still wowing audiences across Europe. The Birmingham Post reported "It [The Brothers] is the top television series in Sweden and is also very popular in Finland, Belgium, Holland and Iceland. Members of the cast are treated like pop stars when they visit some of these countries. Women's magazines in Finland and Holland have organised competitions based on the series and brought prizewinners over to Birmingham to meet the cast. Mr. Bill Sellars, series producer, said yesterday: "We do not really understand why it has such massive success in these countries. There is hardly a car on the streets in Sweden on a Thursday night when The Brothers is on. Almost everyone stays at home to watch it." The Brothers which ends its seventh series here on Sunday week is seen in nine countries including New Zealand, Israel and Dubai." The Times too reported on the success of the show in Sweden, reporting from British week in Kalmar. "The winner of the darts competition received his prize and a kiss from none other than Jennifer Wilson." Robin Young further went on to say "Miss Wilson is a popular heroine in Sweden because she stars in the BBC television series The Brothers, which is easily the most popular show on Swedish television. Her presence in the town was the cause of great excitement. Several men stopped me in the street to ask: 'Do you know where she is staying?'" Clearly a case of what goes on tour, stays on tour!

One spin-off from the show took the cast on a surprising journey. They had been invited to make a Christmas record. The cast descended on Chappell Studios in London on 22nd and 23rd November 1976 to record a festive LP intended primarily for the Netherlands. The tracks were recorded in character as much as possible, with Derek Benfield and Margaret Ashcroft having a crack at a 'Winter Wonderland / Sleigh Ride' medley. Kate O'Mara gave a spirited (although not entirely in tune) 'The Holly and The Ivy' and Robin Chadwick showed off a reasonable light entertainment voice with his version of 'We Need A Little Christmas' from the Jerry Herman musical Mame. Perhaps wisely Jean Anderson chose not to sing and instead gave a reading of 'The Christmas Story' with music by Bach. There were further treats from Richard Easton ('Cantique de Noel'), Liza Goddard ('Rudolph The Red-nosed Reindeer'), Jennifer Wilson ('Have Yourself A Merry Little Christmas') whilst Patrick O'Connell and Colin Baker dueted on 'Good King Wenceslas'. All those involved also provided a unified 'Twelve Days Of Christmas'. Colin Baker's natural sense of fun was evident during his solo rendition of 'White Christmas' where he cheekily changed the lyric to "May your days be Merroney and bright". The tracks were all recorded to a lone piano accompaniment. The tapes were then flown back to Phonogram Studios in Hilversum where producers William Duys and Otto Vriezenberg added an orchestral backing. The whole affair was mixed, pressed and in stores in time for the Christmas of 1976. It sold like hot cakes too, with each of the cast members being awarded a Gold disc for their efforts. It is true, and indeed fair, to say that the record gets by on goodwill and will never win any awards for the quality of the vocalists, but it remains a unique foray into the recording industry for the Hammond family. Derek Benfield went one better and recorded a vocal version of the series theme tune entitled Ol' Bill, released as a single record which was part of an exclusive offer by Truck Magazine in the UK. As the series edged ever nearer its finale, another surprise return during the seventh series is Barbara Trent, played as ever by Julia Goodman. In the show Barbara is holidaying back in the UK after emigrating to Canada with her husband Johnny. However it turns out that there is more to the visit than meets the eye. Johnny has been having an affair and Barbara needs some breathing space to know where their relationship goes from here. Julia stayed for the last four episodes of the series thus giving her the distinction of being in both the first and the last episodes of the show, an honour she shared with five of the actors in the episode. Another storyline which is central to final episodes is the a motorcycle accident for Ronnie Riley, teenage son of Gwen and Bill. We have thus far only heard talk of the Riley siblings Ronnie and Sally, so it comes as a surprise to see him in his hospital bed, clearly at a low ebb physically and emotionally. Ronnie was played by Robin Langford who had been seen in the BBC's all star War & Peace with Anthony Hopkins, but would go on to a regular role as Corporal Veit Rennert in another Gerry Glaister drama Colditz and in the BBC's sci-fi drama Tripods. In the penultimate episode, 'The Ordeal' Gwen is very much left alone at the hospital agonising over the fate of her son whilst Bill is missing in Holland. He has been undercover investigating the smuggling of illegal immigrants in lorries through the continent, as it turns out the Hammond lorries are not involved but it keeps him out of contact with Gwen during those vital first hours when Ronnie is in hospital. It is a touching performance by Margaret Ashcroft in a situation that we all hope we never have to experience. 'The Ordeal' also sees the final appearance in the show for April. Liza Goddard is at her steely, cold best – giving Merroney a taste of his own medicine – as they have one last encounter before she flies, against his wishes, to spend Christmas with her old flame Rex Burton-Smithers in Barbados. April by now has seen Paul for what he is, and that he married her as an entrée into the best social circles. He in turn says that he married her because he loves her. It is all too little, too late for April and we see her chauffeur drive off for the airport.

The sixteenth and final episode 'The Christmas Party' sees the company at yet another crossroads. A Rights Issue (the issue of extra shares) has been put into place to raise capital. With the Hammond brothers' finances meaning they could not increase their share quota, it would see their control of the company reduced to 34% meaning for the first time they could band together to defeat any proposals. Merroney goes one step further and suggests abandoning the Hammond name altogether for something more adventurous. He is soon shot down in flames by Ted. Norman Crisp, naturally sensing the end of the show, brought it to a conclusion which left the futures of everyone open ended. Merroney no longer has the absolute support of the bank where he has also ruffled too many feathers. With Simon Winter now in charge and Merroney's marriage to his sister on the rocks, the future could be rather more bumpy than he would like. The Christmas Party looks like being a jolly affair. Brian seems to be cosying up to Jane, Ted and Jenny are enjoying a thawing of their ups and downs but Mary is keen to have the final word on the future of the company her husband founded. Despite some incredible dance moves shown by David (the choreographer is not listed, perhaps for fear of reprisals) Mary shoots down Merroney in front of the others. As he informs them he intends staying in the UK to supervise the Rights Issue, Mary has her say: "You will have achieved everything you set out to do. You will have destroyed Hammond Transport Services... You took a family business and used it for your own ambitions. Something it took my husband a lifetime to build, is now at the mercy of anyone with enough money. I wouldn't have thought any one man could do so much damage. But you have. You're what they call 'a winner' aren't you? You win every time." Viewers were at least glad Mary Hammondhad lost none of her fire as the series reached its climax, going head to head with another ITV bionic import The Six Million Dollar Man.

Above: Merroney Mania in Holland
Below: Recording the Christmas album in London, 1976

IN CONVERSATION WITH
LIZA GODDARD

RC: Were you a fan of _The Brothers_ before you became a member of the cast?

Liza Goddard: Well, because I was working so much I didn't really get the chance to follow it, but I did see a number of episodes and thought it was terrific. At that time it was one of the most popular television series on the BBC, so to be asked to be in it was a real thrill.

RC: How did you get the part of April Winter?

As far as I can remember, I was sent a script. At the end of the day, everything comes from the script and when I read that short scene at the end of Series 6, I thought the character sounded like terrific fun. It was very much setting the scene for what was to come in the next series. Carole Mowlam was leaving and I was the woman who would replace her in Paul Merroney's life and affections. When we recorded the episode [The Bonus] I was heavily pregnant with my son Thom so they had to put me in a big fur coat to hide the bump.

RC: What do you remember of filming _The Brothers_ in Birmingham?

Mostly I remember what a hot summer it was. For a lot of it, we were boiling. In those heady days we used to get ten days rehearsal for each episode, it was like doing theatre really. Those huge windows at the Acton rehearsal rooms made it like a green house. We sweltered. The team at Pebble Mill, both in front of and behind the camera, were like a family. Being away from home for the studio sessions was like being on tour. There was a lovely party atmosphere to it all. We knew the scripts were good, and we took our work seriously, but we used to have as many laughs as we could.

RC: Were the cast a tightly knit team?

Oh yes it was a lovely ensemble to be a part of. The show had been going for a long time before I came into it, but they made me feel so welcome. Jean Anderson was a lovely lady, very much the star of our show and the head of the company of actors. She used to sit and do the Telegraph crossword. Richard Easton was a very close friend of Jean's, and a very highly cultured man. He became a big star on Broadway. A very intelligent actor. We all adored Paddy O'Connell. He was often hilarious, a delight to work with. Robin Chadwick I remember used to do his VAT returns in the rehearsal room. He had a very glamorous American wife, who made the very first Pecan Pie I had ever tasted. Delicious it was too. Ruby – Derek Benfield – was a complete darling. Such a lovely man. He was always writing plays, which went on to be very successful. They are still performed today. His daughter Kate Plantin is a very well respected casting director. Kate O'Mara was always barking mad, She would come into rehearsals and say "I've been up all night painting scenery!" She used to cover herself in fake tan. Kate spent all her money putting on Shakespeare with her theatre company. A smart cookie and very talented actress.

RC: You did of course marry Colin Baker in real life shortly after you joined the series.

Well that turned out to be a mistake, but for the time we were together we had great fun. Colin is a terrific actor and the scenes between April and Paul were, I thought, superbly written. We went on to work again together in 2007 when we toured as husband and wife in the restoration comedy *She Stoops To Conquer*. He is a dear man, but we were just not right for each other in marriage.

RC: How did the public react to you on the streets?

I'd had some success before with *Skippy* and *Take Three Girls*, so in a way I was used to being recognised for certain work I'd done. There was no abuse like you get now with social media. Everybody loved The Brothers and so being stopped and recognised as April meant people just wanted to tell you how much they enjoyed the show, which is a lovely thing.

RC: What are your memories of the international visits with *The Brothers*?

That was utterly amazing. Going to Sweden, or the Netherlands and finding the crowds like you've never seen. It really was a phenomenon out there. In Israel it was bigger still. It was like being a rock star. I remember we were all sat on a coach at the Wailing Wall and masses of people were surrounding it, rocking the coach from side to side. I signed so many autographs, I forgot my name. I think I signed as Robin Chadwick at one point! As an actor you never expect to get that sort of reaction for the work you do, and it remains a very vivid memory from my career. At the end of the day we were just jobbing actors being treated like Hollywood stars. I think we all liked to play hard though, Maggie Ashcroft and Derek Benfield were definitely the leaders of the party animals.

RC: How did the production compare to other television series you have been in?

It was very similar to doing a Bergerac actually where I played the jewel thief Phillipa Vale. Everyone cared hugely about the show from the producer down. We were all committed to making it as good as it could possibly be. I remember the producer Bill Sellars coming into rehearsal one day with a terrible toupee. No one mentioned it at all. It was really weird because he looked as if he had a dead squirrel on his head. But Bill and his team looked after us all so well, it was a pleasure to go to work.

RC: Why did you think the BBC dropped *The Brothers*?

I've really no idea. It was massively popular when we finished. But back then the BBC had so much wonderful drama, I suppose you can't go on forever. Nobody ever got in touch to say we're ending it though, we just sat there waiting for the phone call which never came.

RC: Do you think *The Brothers* could be re-made for today's television audiences?

I don't see why not. It was a damn good story. It pre-dated the American shows like Dallas and Dynasty. It was perfect Sunday night viewing. When I was walking the dog the other day I met a man who had been the manager for Luckings, the theatrical removal firm. They used to move up to 120 theatre productions every weekend from one end of the country to the other. Perhaps packing up a show in Aberdeen and driving it down to Plymouth in time for a Monday night opening. All the haulage people must have masses of interesting stories. I met Eddie Stobart once and interviewed him at Truckfest [for Anglia TV's Liza's Country in 1998]. It was one of the very few times he was interviewed because he was a very shy man. He only did it because he was a fan of The Brothers. Eddie started out sleeping in his cab on the road. There is loads of potential to bring back a show like The Brothers in a modern style.

RC: Was *The Brothers* special or just another job to you?

I do have a special attachment to The Brothers. It's one of the things I am very proud of. There was a fantastic camaraderie within the company. It was just the most marvellous time for me.

The Merroney's reunited. Liza and Colin in She Stoops To Conquer (2007)

END OF THE ROAD

The final episode of *The Brothers* was transmitted on Sunday 19th December in its usual 7.25pm slot (just three days after the final studio session). Norman Crisp knew that it would at the very least be the last series for a while, possibly the last episode of all and brought the programme to a natural conclusion. Paul Merroney has put through a Rights Issue and the Hammond brothers effectively stand to lose control of the company their father founded. Private lives are at a crossroads, and Mary puts Merroney in his place. Of course the viewers wanted more. *The Brothers* was still rating healthily in the UK, but it was the end of the line. It has been suggested by Colin Baker that the BBC accounts department simply forgot to budget for the show, with the producer Bill Sellars being moved sideways to start pre-production on the first series of *All Creatures Great & Small*, which would hit the screens in January 1978, becoming one of the best loved Sunday night serials ever. But Norman Crisp had pre-warned of its demise at the beginning of 1976. Maybe the word around the BBC was that cuts were coming and the axe was about to fall on *The Brothers*. As far as the UK was concerned, it was the last time *The Brothers* was to be seen on terrestrial television. Official confirmation of the series cancellation came in The Sun on 28th July 1977, 'TV Favourites Chopped By The BBC' ran the headline. "Out go shows like *The Brothers* and *Softly Softly*," it continued. Shaun Sutton is quoted as saying "Some have been on a long time. In some cases the actors have had enough, in others we have had enough." The tapes wouldn't be used again until the satellite channel UK Gold dusted them down in the mid-1990s for a complete re-run.

Overseas it was a different matter. Television companies in Sweden and the Netherlands would happily have paid for more episodes had they been available. But, they were satisfied with a compromise of repeating the show from the beginning several times over during the following years. Rather later in the day it seemed *The Brothers* was suddenly becoming very popular in Israel. The show was the first contemporary soap opera to be broadcast there, and against all the odds the middle-class in fighting of the Hammonds had captured the imaginations of ordinary Israelis. It became an absolute must not miss series going out every Wednesday at 8pm in a mammoth near two year weekly run of episodes. The cast – having been used to Hammond-mania in Europe - suddenly found the situation even more frenzied in Israel. The Jerusalem Post reporter Catherine Rosenheimer attended a Variety Club gala dinner in Tel Aviv where *The Brothers* cast were guests of honour:

"The eight members of the cast of *The Brothers* (only Edward and Jane were missing) seemed overwhelmed by the reception they had got here. There were moments when their visit even got out of hand. Police had to be called in when they visited the children's ward at Hadassah Hospital; and despite compare Shaike Ophir's repeated requests not to pester the actors for autographs during the dinner, they were left little peace to swallow their soup." Breaking the news to the newspaper's readership that there were in fact no more episodes of the show to come, Rosenheimer also gave a glimpse of the entertainment the cast gave the revellers at the Variety Club event. "To wind up each of the four Variety Club dinners they attended last week, each of the actors presented a rather unlikely 'party piece' – with great charm, it must be added. Who would have thought to hear Mary Hammond reciting poetry; or Bill and Gwen singing old Sinatra songs and Hebrew nursery rhymes. David Hammond wound up his Fred Astaire singing number with a fierce Maori war dance; Jennifer sang extracts from the new London musical *Bar Mitzvah Boy*, Merroney and April sang a duet while Brian, a professional opera singer among other things, sang Ivor Novello and Cole Porter numbers. They finally wound up singing Hanukka songs in chorus. An elegant, emotional and slightly wet-eyed Jean Anderson concluded the variety dinner, adding that when she was told, in a Galilee modhav, that she was like a "real Yiddishe Mama" she felt very proud. "Mary Hammond's been called a great many things – I think that's one of the nicest."

Although it wasn't the show that was exactly making the headlines, one of its stars certainly did. Barely had the final episode gone to air when in January 1977 Patrick O'Connell had failed to turn up for rehearsals of a theatre tour of the John Osbourne play *The Entertainer*, and announced he had left Britain to be an artist in Amsterdam. It was all good copy for the national press. 42 year old O'Connell had previously gone missing during rehearsals of *The Brothers* in February 1976 but had been persuaded to return, reportedly by cast confidante Jean Anderson. With family and friends worried about his behaviour, Paddy was persuaded to return to the UK a few days later. He offered the Daily Mail an assessment of the situation:

"I know it's difficult for people to understand why I went to Holland. But I simply had to do it. To me, the problem was simple, I am an actor, but I want to be a painter. Only to others the situation is complicated. I did have a nervous breakdown. But that means one thing for one person, and another thing to someone else. To me, it was depression and the source of that was my frustration with my acting career. I have wanted to give up acting and become a painter for the past five years. Finally, I felt that if I didn't do it now I never would. I apologise to those involved in *The Entertainer*. But I felt that if I could give up such a good part, I must be serious about my painting. I was reluctantly burning my bridges so I would have to go ahead. And to quote Edith Piaf: No regrets."

The Queen's Silver Jubilee year also brought with it a satirical novel by former script editor on *The Brothers*, John 'J.V.' Stevenson entitled *The Dotty*. It told the behind the scenes story of a fictional series 'Three Men And A Woman'. There was little room for disguise in the novel if you are aware of the major backroom and front of the camera figures on *The Brothers*. As The Sunday Mirror pointed out: "There's the actress who's ready to do almost anything to get her role enlarged; the man-eating secretary; the script writer who quits because he's fed up with writing "trash"; the actor who costs a fortune in re-takes because he can't remember his lines; the leading man with a hair transplant..." The only known reaction from a cast member comes from Jennifer Wilson who offers, "Oh, he has been a bitch hasn't he?"

Although the actors all moved onto other things, some found it easier than others. In an article for the Daily Mail in 1979, Robin Chadwick told Charles Catchpole: "I thought *The Brothers* would make me, but it destroyed me," he says. Having been forced to find work on a building site, Robin shares his plans to go to America to re-launch this career. He further adds, "Being in a series like *The Brothers* is one of the most potentially harmful things an actor can do... Your expectations are built up so high it is a shattering blow when you hit the ground and find no one wants you. I think many of my former colleagues are in the same boat, although they may not admit it. They may say they're busy, but how many of them do you see on television now? Actors in a soap-opera type of series are disposable. The TV companies seem to take a snobbish attitude towards series like *The Brothers*. Actors in comedy series don't seem to have much trouble finding work. But after *The Brothers* no one wanted to know me. I didn't get any TV offers at all." There was a spate of stage work but seemingly that didn't appeal to Robin: "But they were not exactly what I had in mind. Perhaps I expect too much, but I thought I could do better than flogging around the provinces in some undistinguished pot boiler. I'm not greedy, but I need to live. I never got more than £4000 or £5000 a year out of *The Brothers* before tax. When you discover that make-up girls are getting more than you after 15 years in the business, you realise something is wrong with British television." For the record Robin did move to the US and made a nice living as a stage actor including stints on Broadway.

It was perhaps the last time in the UK that *The Brothers* would make headlines. The show simply faded into obscurity. Just another show with a glittering past but now gathering dust on the shelves of the BBC Video Tape Archive. Time moves on. Then somewhat out of the blue in August 2002, an ITV series which looked at well loved television successes of the past - and attempted to reunite some of their casts - poured favour on *The Brothers*. *After They Were Famous* was a 50 minute prime-time celebration of the show, raiding the archives for a light hearted look at the Hammond brothers phenomenon. They even arranged a reunion dinner for several of the cast. And so for the first time around a table sat the original Ted, Glyn Owen, along with Jennifer Wilson, Robin Chadwick, Julia Goodman, Derek Benfield, Margaret Ashcroft, Colin Baker and Kate O'Mara, The production team even flew to New York to get an interview with Richard Easton in addition to nabbing Liza Goddard for an chat too. Sadly time constraints meant that a sequence where three of the cast visited the site once occupied by Ralph Hilton Transport was dropped from the final show. The retrospective exercise was repeated by the BBC six years later in February 2008 as part of their *Cult Of Sunday Night* strand. A mere 30 minutes was allotted so the tale was told again in a truncated form, although this time Gabrielle Drake was enticed to join in the celebrations.

A UK DVD release of the first series was issued in October 2006 which showcased just what a gripping series *The Brothers* had been. Naturally, by the end of the ten episodes loyal purchasers wanted more. However the collapse of DD Entertainment meant that any contracts to issue more series were voided rather quickly. Nine years later Simply Media had inherited the assets of DD, and they noted that sales of the first series had added up to a rather healthy tally over the years. So they dipped their toe in the water by finally issuing the second series in November 2015. It was met with enthusiasm by all those who had been frustrated by the apparent loss of further slices of the Hammond pie. As a result all seven series appeared in pristine digital disc format, probably the clearest viewing of the show anybody had ever had. A mammoth 92 episode box set was even set loose on the market. Finally the series could be appraised by those who had remembered the original broadcasts so fondly and also those who only knew the show by reputation. *The Brothers* had seemingly gathered even more admirers along the way.

Today *The Brothers* is slowly being re-evaluated now that the episodes have become available on DVD. It was a training ground in fast paced, serial television for many of the actors. Likewise its writers, producers and directors. Many had learned their craft on *The Brothers*. The show, now a period piece and a slice of social history, came from a time when BBC television was the envy of the broadcasting world. A global symbol of excellence. *The Brothers* might just be a footnote in that reputation, but it stands as a superb example of serial drama production in the 1970s.

The story didn't quite end with episode 92 though. Six months after the broadcast, in May 1977, Norman Crisp penned a short story which was serialised over four weeks by Woman's Own magazine in the UK and Prive magazine in Holland. Did it come from notes made for a possible eighth series? Who knows. But it did give us one final tantalising glimpse of the lives and loves of the directors of Hammond Transport... Over the page is an exclusive extract from that story.

Exclusive new serial **THE BROTHERS** by N. J. Crisp

Longing to know what happened to The Brothers after the last TV series ended? In this gripping four-part serial, we take up the story of Mary Hammond, her three sons and the women in their lives

THE FINAL CHAPTER BY N.J. CRISP

PART ONE: THE NEW YEAR

PROLOGUE:

The Staff Christmas Party was pleasant, but for some the season had its darker side. Paul Merroney could not bring himself to telephone his wife in Barbados – April had gone to stay with her old friend, Rex Burton-Smithers. The Rights Issue was going to be another victory, but he could take no pleasure in it. Instead he was tormented by jealousy at the thought of April with another man. Mary Hammond saw the Rights Issue, with some justification, as the end of Hammond Transport as a family business. To make matters worse, she was confronted by a lonely Christmas. Edward and Jennifer were going to Austria, and Brian was staying with a friend in the country. Mary tried to convince herself that this 'friend' was not that Jane Maxwell woman, but she was afraid to ask. So she would be alone with David. Bill and Gwen Riley were thankful that their son Ronald had survived the accident on his motor cycle, but he was in hospital, a paraplegic. Nobody knew if he would walk again. Edward and Jennifer had recognised their marriage had not turned out as they had hoped. Both tried to avoid thinking that this was inevitable. After all, Edward's father had been Jennifer's lover, years ago. She had borne his daughter. David sometimes felt that he was lost in the world where everyone else had somewhere to go. His wife Jill was dead, killed in a car crash. He had hoped he would find someone else... Brian and Jane Maxwell were the only two who were happy without reservations. They had decided to get married, although Jane had insisted that it be kept a secret. She knew Mary Hammond was not going to like it, and Jane respected Mary's strength of purpose...

The card had the usual Christmas inscription, and was signed "April". Beside her signature something had been scratched out. Merroney peered at it, trying to decipher what she had erased – probably some affectionate message she had thought better of... He was irritated to find that it merely said "Rex Burton-Smithers". The bitch had borrowed one of the man's personalised Christmas cards. Merroney sat moodily in front of the television set, without taking in anything that was happening on the screen. There was only one consolation. This wretched holiday would be over soon, and he could get back to work.

The depot was stirring lazily, but seemed more than half inclined to go back to sleep again. David was the only other director to arrive. "Dear lord," Merroney said. "What an example to everyone my Board of Directors sets."

"There's only a skeleton staff in to deal with urgent traffic," David pointed out. "Nothing much is going to happen until the New Year."

"Well at least you're here," Merroney said ungraciously.

"A good mark is not deserved," David said. "Mother was geared up to give us all a lavish Christmas. Instead, I have been the sole recipient of her maternal affection, mince pies and Yuletide spirit. I couldn't take another day. I fled to the only refuge I knew. This office."

"Never mind," Merroney said briskly. "Let's get started. We can try and think through an idea I've had for the future. Presenting a complete transport package to under-developed nations." "Meaning what?" David asked.

"Basically providing the know-how for efficient internal communications," Merroney said. "Setting up, operating skills, training. Perhaps providing a leasing arrangement for the hardware; for the lorries, repair facilities, sturdy short-range aircraft which could be used for freight as well as passengers and so on."

"They'd need roads and airstrips first," David said.

"Some association with a construction firm goes without saying," Merroney said. "Or we might acquire our own." He had forgotten to include that aspect in his précis. Somehow, he must stop his mind switching to April.

"Well I suppose it will kill an hour," David said indifferently. But after a while he grew steadily more enthusiastic. Merroney was surprised, and unwillingly impressed. David carried a great deal of the necessary information in his head. Files grew into piles on the desk. Merroney realised that despite David's casually flippant air, he had a real grasp of the complexities of road and air transport. Also, his rough costings struck Merroney as cautious and realistic. Lunch-time came and went before they noticed the time.

"Mother'll be on the war path," David said. "I told her I'd only be a couple of hours at the most." But he was nowhere in Mary Hammond's thoughts. She was arranging flowers on her husband's grave.

When satisfied that the blooms looked natural, yet symmetrical, she stood up, gazed at the simple headstone. The quiet cemetery was chilly, and she shivered. She would never solve the puzzle posed by the revelation of her dead husband's secrets, she knew that. Perhaps she had not shown him all she felt, perhaps she might have seemed unresponsive, and a passing infatuation for a younger woman she could have understood. But it had gone on so long; he had given Jennifer a child...almost like another marriage. 'But I loved you,' she cried inwardly and uselessly to the cold, carved inscription, "Robert Hammond". She turned and walked away from the indifferent grave. Robert had left no explanations, only a will providing, as he thought, for the future, in which he left Hammond Transport in equal shares to his three sons and Jennifer, to be run as a family business. Now, it had become a great public company and, with the success of the recent Rights Issue, the family could be outvoted by powerful outside shareholders. Had he foreseen that?

Meanwhile Edward and Jennifer were toasting themselves in front of a huge log fire. Jennifer was determined that it was all going to be fun. Edward was looking much more relaxed, she assured herself. It was doing him good. Edward's impulsive, last minute decision to spend Christmas in Austria had meant they had little choice of resort, and they had settled for a cancellation in Zell am See. The hotel was fine, and the little town was interesting, but all they had seen was a blanket of cloud enveloping the mountains. "I'm glad we came," Jennifer said. "It's been wonderful." She smiled at him, expecting a reply, but he said nothing. He lit a cigar, and stared into the recesses of the crackling fire as if trying to perceive something. When he did speak, he was resuming another conversation they had had before Christmas.

"I don't feel any differently, Jenny" he said. "Nothing's changed." He blew smoke into the air, and watched it rise. "It might be easier if it had," he said quietly. "Then I'd know what to do. We both would."

It was Jennifer's turn to be silent. Edward was right. Nothing had changed. Least of all the one thing they never talked about. To Jennifer is was as if that girl who had cared for the older man until the day he died, were someone else. And so, in a way, she was. The young Jennifer Kingsley was a different woman from today's Jennifer Hammond. Jennifer knew what the missing element was in her marriage. Edward was a kind and affectionate man. He would have made a loving, firm and devoted father. She also knew how it was possible to love two men in one lifetime. Robert had been her lover, and she could not regret that, even though, when she could have married him, she would not. But the years when she could have given Edward children were gone, spent elsewhere. She did, uselessly, regret that. But if she could wind the clock of life backwards, would she act any differently? Jennifer Hammond might but Jennifer Kingsley would not. She looked at Edward as he leaned forward and threw the butt of his cigar into the fire.

"Do you want to be anywhere else?" she asked quietly.

Edward shook his head. "No."

"Nor do I." Jennifer said. "That's something."

"It's quite a lot," he replied.

Brian was quite happy where he was, which was bending over the stove in Jane's kitchen, deep in the countryside of Kent. As on previous days, she was at the airfield. "Holiday or not, I can't expect my pilots to fly if I don't at least put in an appearance," she said. Brian was quite content to potter around the kitchen and prepare the evening meal. He could not help missing his children now and then, but there was no doubt he thought, this was the best Christmas he could ever remember. Impossible, now, to imagine that he had been married for so long to the tempestuous, sulky, self-willed Ann. The door slammed, and Jane flung herself full-length on the settee, and kicked off her black, slim-fitting boots. For such a lovely and slightly-built woman, her movements were often curiously masculine.

"There are snags to organising the transport of racehorses by air," she sighed. "If I weren't on the wagon, I wouldn't mind a stiff drink."

"Well..." Brian began hopefully. The one thing he had missed during Christmas at Jane's was the occasional soothing Scotch.

"No," Jane said firmly. "The meals you cook, I can't afford the calories. I have to work at keeping whatever figure I've got."

"Your figure is perfect," Brian said. "Worth every revolting lettuce leaf you consume."

But he knew her concern was for him and not for her shape. He wished she would not make such heavy weather of it. Perhaps he had taken to drinking a little too much when the divorce was going through, but that was before his breakdown and, these days, he merely liked the occasional glass, that was all.

"Go into the kitchen and put that thing out there on automatic pilot," Jane said. "Then come and make love to me."

Brian did as he was told. Ann had always made it only too plain that he was less than adequate. Jane made it crystal clear that he was more than adequate. Strange that, he thought, before all thought deserted him in favour of sensation.

The following day Bill Riley turned up at the depot. "You needn't have come in Bill," Merroney said. He exempted Riley from the strictures of his fellow directors. Riley could hardly have been enjoying himself much this Christmas.

"Oh well there's things to be done," Riley said.

106

"How's Ronnie?"

"Not so bad," Riley said. "They wouldn't let him come home for Christmas, so Gwen and me, we went to the hospital every day, like. They put on a good show. I must say; carols, crackers, Christmas dinner, presents off the tree and all that." He smiled, a strange tenderness on the face of the earthy, burly man. "Ronnie was given a firm date to go to the rehabilitation centre. That's all he's living for now. I reckon that was the finest Christmas present he had," he sighed. "It was a funny old Christmas though, right enough." He shook his head, sloughing off his personal problems and stabbed a powerful finger at the notes David had made on Merroney's latest scheme. "This construction angle; Kirkman's are good on the construction side. The best in Europe maybe."

Merroney shifted the conversation. He wanted to get Riley off the subject of Kirkman's, which would come up soon enough anyway. He wondered in what form. That he did not know yet. What he did know was that Kirkman's had added to their already substantial holding in Hammond Transport Services Ltd. by buying every possible share not taken up under the Rights Issue. Kirkman's were a patient and far-sighted company. One take-over bid for Hammond Transport had been thwarted, but that was at the beginning. Merroney had little doubt that Kirkman's would soon, in alliance perhaps with one of the more institutional shareholders, begin to make life difficult and unpleasant for the board of Hammond Transport. The Rights Issue had been necessary in order to get the Middle East Repair and Recovery scheme off the ground, in collaboration with their Dutch associates, but in business, as in life, there was always a heavy price to pay. Sooner or later, the bill would come in. Who was left to pay it was another matter. Neil Kirkman was an old acquaintance, and several guarded conversations had taken place recently. There might very well come a time, Merroney thought, when it would be wise for him to change sides. If he did, he would try to take Bill Riley with him. But none of the others. In their old-fashioned way, he was sure they would rather go down with the sinking ship, if it began to sink.

Ronald Riley greeted Mrs. Hammond politely. "Nice of you to come," he said. It was New Year's Eve, and Bill and Gwen Riley had driven Mary to the hospital. She had not liked to intrude on them over Christmas she said, but now, if they wouldn't mind...

"Of course not," Gwen Riley had said. "Ronnie'll be pleased." But this serious, intense, inward-looking young man did not seem to be especially pleased to see anyone, Mary thought. "...if you need transport..." Riley was saying.

"It's all right, Dad," Ronnie said. "An ambulance'll take me to the centre."

Mary did not know the boy well, but she was shocked by the apparent change in his manner. Lively, outgoing and humorous as she remembered him, he now only talked about his condition, possible treatment and people like him who had walked again. Well, that was natural enough...
"The doctor was saying you might be able to have a few days home first," Gwen said.

"I'd rather not, Mum," Ronnie said. "Not yet. Not like this."

"Don't be silly," Gwen said. "Nobody cares about that."

"I do," Ronnie said. "No, Mum, if you don't mind, I'd rather stay here. They are trained to look after people like me."

"Just as you like," Gwen said, giving him her warm smile.

Mary thought that beneath that smile, Gwen was hurt. Did her son not realise that? No, probably not. His world had contracted to the ward, the corridor, the bathroom and his wheel-chair. Gwen talked brightly, but Ronnie said little.

"Well," he said at last, looking at his watch. "I shan't be staying up till twelve. I'll be having my sleeping-pills soon; be off like a light."

"Ay, we best be making tracks," Riley said.

"I hope it all goes well at the rehabilitation centre," Mary said, "and..." She hurriedly bit back the conventional wish, but the glint of ironic amusement in Ronnie's eyes told her that he had completed it in his mind.

"Thank you Mrs. Hammond," he said. "If this is the year I walk again, it will be."
Ronnie watched them move along the corridor towards the exit, before he manoeuvered his wheel-chair round, and headed for the ward and the major drama which getting into bed represented these days.

"Bill and me, we're going to see the New Year in on our own," Gwen said, as they got into the car. "You'd be only too welcome to join us, if you like..."

"Thank you," Mary said, "I would, very much. David's going to a party, and the others aren't back yet, so I shall be alone."

"Oh ay," Riley said. "That'll be the Daltons' do. One of our major customers. We thought one of us ought to go."

"Yes, he said it was business more than anything," Mary said. She felt guilty. She had not entirely believed David, suspecting him of concocting an excuse when she suggested they book a table for the function at the Dorchester. She should be more trusting.

The Daltons' party was a slightly lesser evil than the Dorchester, David thought, as he edged his way through the crowd, but not much. There must be hundreds of people milling around the luxurious house near The Boltons in South Kensington. Eric Dalton ran a profitable supermarket chain and lived accordingly. David drifted from one chattering group to another.

"Oh, do you know Irene?" someone said.

"No..."

"David Hammond."

"How do you do," she said.

He had glimpsed her once before earlier, from the back, short fair hair topping a silver dress. Now he saw that she was striking looking, slender and tall. High cheekbones, a broad forehead and wide mouth gave her an unusual face which was certainly not pretty on first sight but was unconventionally beautiful at a second glance. David thought she was about thirty.

"Look I hate to talk shop," Eric Dalton said, as he took David's arm. "Excuse me," he said to Irene, and led David away. David cursed inwardly, and listened impatiently for the next twenty minutes. It was getting on for midnight before he was able to edge his way alongside Irene again. There was something about her which drew him irresistibly.

"Do you come here often?" he inquired.

She laughed. "Only when I'm invited, so the answer's no."

"Look," David said, making a desperate bid for the opportunity of some kind of intimacy, "When we've seen the New Year in, why don't we go to Tramp's?"

It was a long time before he had thought of going to that expensive discotheque for the trendy well-heeled, but suddenly, with this slim lady beside him, it seemed like a good idea.
"Thank you, David," he said, "but I'm afraid that really isn't my scene any more."

Midnight arrived, people cheered and surged around and David found himself being kissed by a stout matron. "Happy New Year" David mumbled, and set off to find Irene again. She was in the hall. A man in his forties was helping her on with her coat. They left together. She did not see David. For some reason, it had never crossed his mind that she was with someone like that. He took another drink and sipped it. Well, that was that. But it was not, and he knew it. He had no idea where she lived, or worked, or what her surname was. Eric Dalton would know.

"The girl I was talking to," David said, "Irene."

"Who?"

"Tall, slim, fair hair, wearing a silver dress..."

"Oh, Mrs. Nelson," Dalton said. "Works for that Marlow Economic Study Unit. We use their forecasts. What about her?"

"I wondered what she did, that's all," David said.

He walked for a long way before he even tried to find a taxi. He could not get that compelling, fascinating face of hers out of his mind. Quite unexpectedly, without looking, he had found someone. And she was married. Presumably, the man she had left with was her husband. And yet... had she been wearing a wedding ring? Forget it, he told himself. He saw a lone taxi, hailed it, and climbed in. No, face the truth, Married or not, he was not going to forget Irene Nelson. He gave the taxi driver a generous tip. He had thought of a splendid, cast iron, legitimate reason to invite her to lunch.

TO BE CONTINUED...

Launching the Christmas album in Holland, December 1976

After They Were Famous 2002
(ITV/Shutterstock)

EPISODE GUIDE

1972 - SERIES ONE

Regular cast:
JEAN ANDERSON (Mary Hammond) GLYN OWEN (Edward Hammond) RICHARD EASTON (Brian Hammond) ROBIN CHADWICK (David Hammond) JENNIFER WILSON (Jennifer Kingsley) HILARY TINDALL (Ann Hammond) JULIA GOODMAN (Barbara Kingsley) DEREK BENFIELD (Bill Riley)
Producer GERARD GLAISTER Associate Producer IAN STRACHAN

1. END OF THE BEGINNING by N.J. Crisp
Studio recording: 26th February 1971
Broadcast: Friday 10th March 1972 at 8.15pm, BBC 1
Running length: 44'54"
The death of Robert Hammond brings the inevitable grief to the Hammond family. However, there are shocks in store at the reading of the will. Robert has left his flourishing haulage business to the equal care of his three sons – and his secret mistress, company secretary Jennifer Kingsley. In addition he has made provision for Barbara Kingsley, his illegitimate daughter. Eldest brother Edward is gutted that he will not be getting the business as expected. He sets about trying to get the other beneficiaries to sell their shares. Brian's wife Ann is more concerned about how much ready cash will be available for a house move. Mary tries to come to terms with the fact that her husband had a life that she never knew about. Jennifer reveals to Barbara the secret of her parentage. David's grief takes the form of a confessional to girlfriend Jill. The new directors gather for their first meeting as a board.
Guest cast: JOHN WELSH (Mr. Cassell) GABRIELLE DRAKE (Jill Williams) GABRIEL WOOLF (Priest) IAIN REID (Young driver) DOMINIC CHRISTIAN (Nigel Hammond) NICOLA MOLONEY (Carol Hammond)
Directed by RONALD WILSON

2. DOWN TO BUSINESS by N.J. Crisp
Studio recording: 9th March 1971
Broadcast: Friday 17th March 1972 at 8.10pm, BBC 1
Running length: 47'54"
A tense first meeting of the new Hammond board results in Edward being elected as Chairman and Managing Director. Ann pays a visit to Mary, they discuss Robert. Barbara has much on her mind as she visits the grave of the father she never knew. Ted arranges finance and announces he is buying shares from whoever is willing to sell. Ann asks for Mary's help in getting Brian to sell his shares to free up cash for a new house. She then goes to the depot fearing Brian might make a big mistake. Both Barbara and Mary visit solicitor Mr. Cassell, both eager for information. David and Brian have refused to sell their shares to Edward. Brian then has to break the news to Ann, who takes the news badly.
Guest cast: JOHN WELSH (Mr. Casell) PHILIP TREWINNARD (Peter Lowman) SARAH GRAZEBROOK (Marion) KEN HOWARD (Mechanic)
Directed by RONALD WILSON

3. CONFRONTATION by N.J. Crisp
Studio recording: 9th March 1971
Broadcast: Friday 24th March 1972 at 8.10pm, BBC 1
Running length: 45'07"

Mary sends a note with Edward inviting Jennifer and Barbara to meet with her. Jennifer however is determined not to go. David continues to learn about aspects of the business. Ann conspires to get Brian and his former boss Mr. Stevens together in the hope that Brian can be persuaded to return to his former job. Ann meets a fellow parent at the school gates and finds she has an admirer. Mary arrives at the depot determined to that a meeting will take place. Jill's evening with David is not the cosy romantic night she would have liked and accuses him of becoming boring. Ann uses all of her wily cunning to charm Mr. Stevens. An awkward evening at Mary's house turns sour as Mary lets her true feelings about Jennifer out into the open.

Guest cast: PETER COPLEY (Mr. Stevens) GABRIELLE DRAKE (Jill Williams) MICHAEL FORREST (Terry Foster) KEN HOWARD (Mechanic) ROD BEACHAM (Albert) SARAH GRAZEBROOK (Marion) NICOLA MOLONEY (Carol Hammond)
Directed by PHILIP DUDLEY

4. DECISIONS by N.J. Crisp
Studio recording: 30th March 1971
Broadcast: Friday 30th March 1972 at 8pm, BBC 1
Running length: 48'19"

Ann has a heart to heart with David and Brian about the future. Brian accepts their father was more canny than he realised by dividing up the business. David tries out a new power boat. Barbara visits Ann in an attempt to find out more about Robert Hammond. A new sales rep, Frank Walker, makes an impression on Jennifer. David gives his decision to Edward. Edward then makes a counter offer to Brian. He doesn't get the answer he wanted. In fury Ann sets off to see David and plays the femme fetale.

Guest cast: MICHAEL HAWKINS (Frank Walker) GABRIELLE DRAKE (Jill Williams) PHILIP TREWINNARD (Peter Lowman) SARAH GRAZEBROOK (Marion) TERENCE BROOK (Storekeeper) DOMINIC CHRISTIAN (Nigel Hammond) NICOLA MOLONEY (Carol Hammond)
Directed by ERIC PRICE

5. THE PARTY by N.J. Crisp
Studio recording: 9th April 1971
roadcast: Friday 7th April 1972 at 8.10pm, BBC 1
Running length: 48'04"

David takes an opportunity to learn the business from the ground up. He takes an idea to Jennifer and in the process encounters his half sister Barbara. The Birketts, an important client, throw a party and the Board of Directors of Hammonds are all invited. Mary is worried that the party will become a gossip ground for family issues. David uses the party as an opportunity to finish with Jill, and Ann is determined to make the most of her night without husband Brian in tow.

Guest cast: GABRIELLE DRAKE (Jill Williams) PHILIP TREWINNARD (Peter Lowman) MICHAEL HAWKINS (Frank Walker) GEORGE A. COOPER (Birkett) CHRISTOPHER ROBBIE (The Man) MARJORIE SOMMERVILLE (Mrs. Birkett) SARAH GRAZEBROOK (Marion) ROBERT TAYMAN (Photographer) DERRICK SLATER (Charlie)
Directed by RONALD WILSON

6. TURNING POINT by Eric Paice
Studio recording: 20th April 1971
Broadcast: Friday 14th April 1972 at 8.10pm, BBC 1
Running length: 48'34"

Brian is concerned about Ann's movements after the Birkett party as cracks in their marriage continue to widen. David touts for business with paint mogul Sir John Borret and appears to secure a deal. Jennifer proposes a new accounting system for the business. Edward meanwhile smells a rat over the Borrets deal, but his opposition to major financial outlay to accommodate the new Borret deal is overridden in a Board vote. He fears the first moves against him have been made.

Guest cast: MICHAEL HAWKINS (Frank Walker) HAMILTON DYCE (Sir John Borret) ANNETTE ANDRE (Sally Woolf) PHILIP TREWINNARD (Peter Lowman) JAMES COPELAND (MacDonald) GRAHAM WESTON (Carter) SARAH GRAZEBROOK (Marion) DOMINIC CHRISTIAN (Nigel Hammond) NICOLA MOLONEY (Carol Hammond)

7. THE PERFECT DAY by Eric Paice
Studio recording: 30th April 1971
Broadcast: Friday 21st April 1972 at 8.10pm, BBC 1
Running length: 47'46"

Work begins on building a storage facility for the Borret paint. The firm has borrowed substantially so it's future depends on the success of the contract. David and Sally get to know each other better. A looming dock strike suddenly brings dark storm clouds over Hammonds. Financially they are stretched to the limit so if the strike continues for a short period the firm could be placed in a perilous situation. Has Sir John played a cunning hand? An emergency board meeting brings the full extent of the situation home.

Guest cast: MICHAEL HAWKINS (Frank Walker) HAMILTON DYCE (Sir John Borret) ANNETTE ANDRE (Sally Woolf) TERENCE BROOK (Forbes) PETER LONGBOW (Fred) STEVE EMERSON (Mechanic) BRENDA STEPHENS (Woman in café)

Directed by ERIC PRICE

8. CRISIS by Eric Paice
Studio recording: 11th May 1971
Broadcast: Friday 28th April 1972 at 8.10pm, BBC 1
Running length:

The strike by Docks workers spells potential disaster for Hammonds Transport, thanks to the extra financial outlay for the Borret's contract. Mary begins to feel unwell. She summons Barbara for a chat. Ann continues to put pressure on Brian to move to a larger house but then finds out his salary has been frozen. David wonders if Ted will step in and try to buy their shares. Bill and David attempt to cross the picket line.

Guest cast: ANNETTE ANDRE (Sally Woolf) HUGH MORTON (Dr. Marsh) DAVID MORRELL (Thomas) BRIAN COBURN (Fitzgerald) IAIN REID (Peters) LAURENCE BEATTIE (Customs officer)

Directed by RONALD WILSON

9. WORM IN THE BUD by Eric Paice
Studio recording: 21st May 1971
Broadcast: Friday 5th May 1972 at 8.10pm, BBC 1
Running length: 50'10"

Sir John invites the Hammond Board to lunch - but he has an agenda to trap them as the strike reaches it's conclusion. Mary offers her house to Ann and Brian in order to help the cracks in their marriage. Sir John makes his move at the lunch. Edward turns him down. News come through that a deal may be in the offing for the strikers. It could be that Sir John has underestimated the situation. Following an extravagant shopping expedition Ann finally leaves Brian.

Guest cast: HAMILTON DYCE (Sir John Borret) ANNETTE ANDRE (Sally Woolf) LEONARD FENTON (Walpole) JOHNNY BRIGGS (Minicab driver) CORBETT WOODALL (Newscaster) SARAH GRAZEBROOK (Marion) JOHN PAYNE (Head waiter)   Directed by PHILIP DUDLEY

10. FULL CIRCLE by Eric Paice
Studio recording: 1st June 1971
Broadcast: Friday 12th May 1972 at 8.10pm, BBC 1
Running length: 49'02"
With the strike over, Hammond's can finally look to the future with possible expansion plans. Ann is finding it harder than she thought away from her husband and Ted is growing closer to Jennifer. Mary however is more determined than ever to have her say on the matter. Bill is none too impressed by Ted's proposal of working towards a directorship.
Guest cast: ANNETTE ANDRE (Sally Woolf) RALPH MICHAEL (Mr. Stewart) JOAN HEATH (Mrs. Stewart) EVE PEARCE (Nurse Carpenter) SARAH GRAZEBROOK (Marion) DAVID HARGEAVES (Reynolds) DEREK MARTIN (Van driver)   Directed by RONALD WILSON

1973 - SERIES TWO
Regular cast:
JEAN ANDERSON (Mary Hammond) PATRICK O'CONNELL (Edward Hammond) RICHARD EASTON (Brian Hammond) ROBIN CHADWICK (David Hammond) JENNIFER WILSON (Jennifer Kingsley) HILARY TINDALL (Ann Hammond) JULIA GOODMAN (Barbara Kingsley) DEREK BENFIELD (Bill Riley) GABRIELLE DRAKE (Jill Williams) MARK McMANUS (Harry Carter)
Producer GERARD GLAISTER
Gabrielle Drake does not appear in episodes 11 and 22
Hilary Tindall does not appear in episodes 11, 12, 21
Derek Benfield does not appear in episode 22

11. A FAMILY GATHERING by N.J. Crisp
Studio recording: 16th & 17th October 1972
Broadcast: Sunday 14th January 1973 at 7.25pm, BBC 1
Running length: 49'29"
Mary Hammond returns from recuperation abroad, determined to drive a wedge between Edward and Jennifer. Harry Carter, of Carter's Express Deliveries, puts in an impressive offer for land adjoining the Hammond depot - land Edward thought was already promised to his firm. It seems Brian's separation from Ann has distracted him from his responsibilities to the firm. Mary's insistence that her sons attend her homecoming supper conflicts directly with Barbara's 18th birthday party.
Guest cast: JOHN WELSH (Cassell) SARAH GRAZEBROOK (Marion) CHRISTOPHER COLL (Bailey)
Directed by QUENTIN LAWRENCE

12. WHEELS AND DEALS by N.J. Crisp
Studio recording: 27th October 1972
Broadcast: Sunday 21st January 1973 at 7.25pm, BBC 1
Running length: 49'59"
When Mary finds a phone number in Edward's pocket she learns an ex-girlfriend is back on the scene. It is another weapon in her war against Jennifer. Brian is instructed to find out any information on Carter – no matter what the method. Mary visits Barbara and gives her a very personal 18th birthday gift. David has a chance encounter with Jill Williams. Brian gets on well with his children's former teacher, Pamela Graham. Jennifer has to accept that Mary has driven a wedge between her and Ted.
Guest cast: ANNA FOX (Pamela Graham) CLAIRE NIELSON (Nancy Lincoln)
Directed by PRUDENCE FITZGERALD

13. THE TROJAN HORSE by Eric Paice
Studio recording: 6th & 7th November 1972
Broadcast: Sunday 28th January 1973 at 7.25pm, BBC 1
Running length: 49'52"
The stand-off with Carter continues but David reckons that Carter isn't in as strong a position as he makes out. Mary continues to manipulate the lives of her children but with Edward she may have gone too far.
Guest cast: ANNA FOX (Pamela Graham) JAMES COPELAND (Eddie MacDonald) BROWN DERBY (Michael Harris) SARAH GRAZEBROOK (Marion)
Directed by QUENTIN LAWRENCE

14. SNAKES AND LADDERS by Eric Paice
Studio recording: 16th & 17th November 1972
Broadcast: Sunday 4th February 1973 at 7.25pm, BBC 1
Running length: 48'53"
Carter finally lays out his conditions for the take-over. With a seat on the Board at the top of the list, the Hammond Board takes a vote. Jennifer and Barbara clash over her future plans. Ann confronts Brian about his new lady friend after finding lipstick on a glass at their home. Barbara convinces her mother to attend Carter's party unaware that Mary has been invited too.
Guest cast: MEREDITH EDWARDS (Parker) CLAIRE NIELSON (Nancy Lincoln) SARAH GRAZEBROOK (Marion) JANE COLLINS (Penny) CHRIS TRANCHELL (Felix) RAY MARIONI (Waiter)
Directed by TERENCE WILLIAMS

15. LABOUR PAINS by N.J. Crisp
Studio recording: 30th November 1972
Broadcast: Sunday 11th February 1973 at 7.25pm, BBC 1
Running length:
Harry Carter has cunningly invited all the Hammonds around to his apartment for drinks. One by one *The Brothers* drop out, which leaves Mary and Jennifer the only guests that turn up! Barbara is in awe of her new art tutor Nicholas Fox and at the depot trouble is brewing between the Carter and Hammond drivers...
Guest cast: SARAH GRAZEBROOK (Marion) CLAIRE NIELSON (Nancy Lincoln) ANNA FOX (Pamela Graham) MEREDITH EDWARDS (Parker) JONATHAN NEWTH (Nicholas Fox)
Directed by PRUDENCE FITZGERALD

16. NEGOTIATIONS by N.J. Crisp
Studio recording: 14th December 1972
Broadcast: Sunday 18th February 1973 at 7.25pm, BBC 1
Running length: 49'37"
With strike action threatened, the Union is called in to settle the conflict with the two sets of drivers. Carter is determined that the Union won't have a say in the way he handles the unrest, but Ted is a much more experienced negotiator. David falls for the charms of Jill's flatmate Julie.
Guest cast: MEREDITH EDWARDS (Parker) KENNETH WATSON (Reg Turner) CLAIRE NIELSON (Nancy Lincoln) ANNA FOX (Pamela Graham) GILLIAN McCUTCHEON (Julie) JONATHAN NEWTH (Nicholas Fox) MALCOLM KEITH (Car salesman) ELIZABETH CHAMBERS (Mother) SARAH GRAZEBROOK (Marion) PATSY KENSIT (Toddler)
Directed by TERENCE WILLIAMS

17. DECLARATION OF INDEPENDENCE by N.J. Crisp

Studio recording: 28th Decemeber 1972
Broadcast: Sunday 25th February 1973 at 7.25pm, BBC 1
Running length: 50'21"

Ann's continued bating of Brian reaches a climax when she interrupts his evening with Pamela. The firm sinks deeper into debt, Ted pressures Brian into keeping them afloat. Barbara and her mother clash over her friendship with Nicholas. Guest cast: ANNA FOX (Pamela Graham) CLAIRE NIELSON (Nancy Lincoln) GILLIAN McCUTCHEON (Julie) SARAH GRAZEBROOK (Marion) JONATHAN NEWTH (Nicholas Fox) PETER DIAMOND (Stanley Miller) CHRIS WEBB (Dennis Yates)
Directed by PHILIP DUDLEY

18. ERRORS OF JUDGEMENT by N.J. Crisp

Studio recording: 11th January 1973
Broadcast: Sunday 4th March 1973 at 7.25pm, BBC 1
Running length: 49'08"

Hammond Transport is struggling to complete its delivery commitments. Barbara intends to go to Paris with Nicholas and Ann is using all her wily skills to gain Mary's support as she makes a move to keep Brian onside. A Board meeting reveals the extent of Hammond's troubles. The cash flow is perilous. They need to recoup their debts urgently.
Guest cast: GILLIAN McCUTCHEON (Julie) ANNA FOX (Pamela Graham) JONATHAN NEWTH (Nicholas Fox) CLAIRE NIELSON (Nancy Lincoln) SARA CLEE (Sue) JOHN FORGEHAM (Mortimer) PATRICK DURKIN (Fry) DAVID JANSON (Benson)
Directed by MARY RIDGE

19. STORM BIRDS by Eric Paice

Studio recording: 25th January 1973
Broadcast: Sunday 11th March 1973 at 7.25pm, BBC 1
Running length: 49'24"

The drivers strike continues over the use of Harry Carter's non-Union drivers. A full meeting of the Board members and Union representatives is made more difficult by Carter antagonising the Union. Jill and Julie call on Mary but Julie does not endear herself to the Hammond matriach. Negotiations falter and Hammond Transport is starting to flounder under the weight of the problem. Brian discovers Ann has been making secret visits to the family home.
Guest cast: ANNA FOX (Pamela Graham) KENNETH WATSON (Reg Turner) GILLIAN McCUTCHEON (Julie) SARA CLEE (Sue) DAVID McKAIL (Jim Waters) EDWARD BROOKS (Bob Nash) JAMES APPLEBY (Morphett)
Directed by PHILIP DUDLEY

20. TIGHT ROPE by Eric Paice

Studio recording: 8th February 1973
Broadcast: Sunday 18th March 1973 at 7.25pm, BBC 1
Running length: 50'05"

Whilst Harry wines and dines Jennifer, Ted arranges a late night meeting with Reg Turner and Bill. Ann arrives home unexpectedly to find Pamela waiting for Brian. Tom Parker has left the country, he owes Hammond Transport a lot of money. Without it they are sunk. Jill receives some devastating news. Carter plays a masterstroke to end the stalemate.
Guest guest: ANNA FOX (Pamela Graham) KENNETH WATSON (Reg Turner) GILLIAN McCUTCHEON (Julie)

DAVID McKAIL (Waters) EDWARD BROOKS (Nash)
Directed by RONALD WILSON

21. A MARRIAGE IS ARRANGED by Eric Paice
Studio recording: 22nd February 1973
Broadcast: Sunday 25th March 1973 at 7.25pm, BBC 1
Running length: 48'25"
With the lorries back on the road, concern grows about the whereabouts of Tom Parker. Barbara is finding her trip to Paris with Nicholas Fox is not all she wanted it to be. Mary invites Jill to lunch and together they conspire to get David to the alter. Brian's discreet enquiries about Parker shows that he is in trouble, making finding him more urgent. Ted flies out to Parker's last known whereabouts in Corfu in a desperate bid to sort out the debt. Whilst he is away Carter makes a move for the Chair in the Board meeting.
Guest cast: ANNA FOX (Pamela Graham) CLAIRE NIELSON (Nancy Lincoln) ALISON GRIFFIN (Debbie) JONATHAN NEWTH (Nicholas Fox) FRANCIS GHENT (Peter Whitehead) JOHN SERRET (Garcon)
Directed by RONALD WILSON

22. WOMEN ARE TRUMPS by Eric Paice
Studio recording: 8th March 1973
Broadcast: Sunday 1st April 1973 at 7.25pm
Running length: 50'03"
Edward has returned with grave news - Parker is going bankrupt. He also decides Carter has to go and gives him three options on which he can leave the company. But Carter wants buying out and cash is the one thing Hammonds do not have. Jill reveals the extent of her inheritance - £250,000. It occurs to Jill she might have the means to save Hammond Transport. With Pamela out of the picture, Ann and Brian start rebuilding their marriage.
Guest cast: GILLIAN McCUTCHEON (Julie) CLAIRE NIELSON (Nancy Lincoln) ALISON GRIFFIN (Debbie)
Directed by MARY RIDGE

23. NO HARD FEELINGS by N.J. Crisp
Studio recording: 21st March 1973
Broadcast: Sunday 8th April 1973 at 7.25pm, BBC 1
Running length: 49'24"
The Hammond Board vote to buy out Harry Carter. He parts company on good terms with everyone - except Mary Hammond. David is not happy that Jill's money alone is keeping the business afloat. Ann plays her final hand in her game to get husband Brian to take her back. Despite constant bating from Julie, David marries Jill.
Guest cast: GILLIAN McCUTCHEON (Julie)

1974 - SERIES THREE

Regular cast:

JEAN ANDERSON (Mary Hammond) PATRICK O'CONNELL (Edward Hammond) RICHARD EASTON (Brian Hammond) ROBIN CHADWICK (David Hammond) JENNIFER WILSON (Jennifer Kingsley) HILARY TINDALL (Ann Hammond) JULIA GOODMAN (Barbara Kingsley) DEREK BENFIELD (Bill Riley) GABRIELLE DRAKE (Jill Hammond) GILLIAN McCUTCHEON (Julie Lane) JONATHAN NEWTH (Nicholas Fox)

Producer KEN RIDDINGTON Script Editor SIMON MASTERS

Derek Benfield does not appear in episodes 26, 27
Jonathan Newth does not appear in episodes 27, 34, 35
Gillian McCutcheon does not appear in episodes 28, 29, 34, 36

24. THE HAMMOND ACCOUNT by N.J. Crisp

Studio recording: 7th June 1973
Broadcast: Sunday 3rd February 1974 at 7.25pm, BBC 1
Running length: 44'48"

Hammond Transport Services is once again in the position for expansion, thanks to Jill's guarantee. It appears everyone is optimistic for the future, however David is strangely reluctant. He proposes advertising for new accounts. However the search for an Advertising Agency to handle the campaign brings with it two unexpected faces from the past. Bill is cautious about a new scheme being introduced involving the drivers. Barbara returns from months abroad with some shocking news for Jennifer.

Guest cast: TERENCE BAYLER (Anthony Bromley) MALCOLM STODDARD (Johnny Trent) ROBERT MacLEOD (Rogers) IAN LISTON (Wilkins)
Directed by RODERICK GRAHAM

25. THE NEWLY WEDS by N.J. Crisp

Studio recording: 21st June 1973
Broadcast: Sunday 10th February 1974 at 7.25pm, BBC 1
Running length: 44'33"

Barbara attempts to placate her mother over the news that she has secretly married. But her new husband knows she is a heiress which makes Jennifer even more suspicious. Ted wants a meeting with Johnny Trent so he can find out more about his motives. Bill confesses to Jennifer that all is not well at home, his wife Gwen is not happy living in their house any longer. Mary welcomes the newly weds into her home. Jill returns to find that Julie is once more back in their lives. Ann has an encounter with Nicholas Fox which leaves her shaken.

Guest cast: MALCOLM STODDARD (Johnny Trent)
Directed by RODERICK GRAHAM

26. SUSPICIONS by N.J. Crisp

Studio recording: 5th July 1973
Broadcast: Sunday 17th February 1974 at 7.25pm, BBC 1
Running length: 44'28"

With plans underway to improve Hammond Transports links with Europe, David travels to Dover to look at sites for a potential new depot. Barbara and Mary chat frankly about Jennifer. Brian's new competitive drive in business excites Ann, but she is consumed by thoughts of Nicholas. David's resistance to the plans for expansion leads to a clash with his elder brothers. He seeks comfort from Julie, but he arrives home to find Jill in suspicious mood.

Guest cast: MALCOLM STODDARD (Johnny Trent)
Directed by PHILIP DUDLEY

27. TUG OF WAR by N.J. Crisp
Studio recording: 19th July 1973
Broadcast: Sunday 24th February 1974 at 7.25pm,. BBC 1
Running length: 44'55"
David openly opposes the plan for a new depot at Dover, causing Brian to go behind David's back and appeal directly to Jill. Ted convinces Mary into inviting Jennifer around for dinner, it is an invitation neither are looking forward to. Jill is convinced that David and Julie are having an affair, meanwhile David is furious that Brian has approached Jill without his knowledge and appeals directly to Ted. A new lorry driver, Jim Barker, turns up wanting a job but his motives are less than honourable.
Guest cast: GILLIAN McCUTCHEON (Julie) MALCOLM STODDARD (Johnny Trent) ANNA FOX (Pamela Graham) FRANK JARVIS (Jim Barker) JOHN BARCROFT (Lowe)
Directed by RODERICK GRAHAM

28. HIJACK by Eric Paice

Studio recording: 2nd August 1973
Broadcast: Sunday 3rd March 1974 at 7.25pm, BBC 1
Running length: 47'02"

Ted and Bill travel to the Continent as the first shipment for Hammond Transport heralds a new era for the company. However they are unaware they are being followed. Nicholas Fox continues to exert his charisma over everyone, and issues a charm offensive against Ann on a trip to an Art Gallery. On the way back to the London depot, the lorry driven by Bill and Jim is hijacked. The lorry is soon found but the load is missing. Suspicion immediately falls on the two drivers, but when Jim's background check comes back clean it is Bill who remains the strongest suspect.

Guest cast: HUGH SULLIVAN (D.I. Parsons) BRIAN GRELLIS (D.S. Pritchard) FRANK JARVIS (Jim Barker) PAUL HALEY (Harvey) YVONNE BONNAMY (Isobel) JOHN BARCROFT (Lowe)

Directed by PHILIP DUDLEY

29. RILEY by Eric Paice

Studio recording: 16th August 1973
Broadcast: Sunday 10th March 1974 at 7.25pm, BBC 1
Running length: 44'43"

Bill and Jim are both taken into custody. An incident in Bill's past on his police record puts him firmly in the hot seat for the hijacking. The dinner party is an uneasy gathering thanks to Jennifer's presence, and Gill is angered by an off-hand comment from Ted. Nicholas and Ann continues to circle each other whilst Jennifer demands to know the extent of Johnny's debts with the boutique. She also reveals her suspicions that Bill has known about her affair with Robert Hammond for years. Jill, finally exhausted with David's constant excuses, suggests a divorce. Mary learns that Julie is destroying their marriage and vows to intercede.

Guest cast: MALCOLM STODDARD (Johnny Trent) FRANK JARVIS (Jim Barker) HUGH SULLIVAN (D.I. Parsons) BRIAN GRELLIS (D.S. Pritchard)

Directed by RODERICK GRAHAM

30. TRADE WIND by Eric Paice

Studio recording: 30th August 1973
Broadcast: Sunday 17th March 1974 at 7.25pm, BBC 1
Running length: 44'43"

Barbara sees a way of settling Johnny's debts by borrowing against her future inheritance. Ann holds a dinner party inviting both Nicholas and Pamela Fox. David places the Board under pressure to release Gill's financial guarantee to the company. Barbara finds help with her loan from an ally close to home. Mary confronts Julie about her interference in David's marriage and the two clash. With Nicholas leaving for Brussels on business, Ann makes a confession as the situation starts to spiral out of control.

Guest cast: GILLIAN McCUTCHEON (Julie) JONATHAN NEWTH (Nicholas) ANNA FOX (Pamela Graham) JOHN WELSH (Mr. Cassell) JAN HARVEY (Briony) EBONY WHITE (Tina) JEREMY ANTHONY (Tom) ROGER FOSS (Ian)

Directed by PHILIP DUDLEY

31. ECHOES by Eric Paice
Studio recording: 13th September 1973
Broadcast: Sunday 24th March 1974 at 7.25pm
Running length: 44'35"
Julie continues to be an ever present temptation to David as she is appointed to work on the Hammond account by the advertising agency. Nicholas and Ann take another step in their continuing liaison whilst David clashes with Brian whilst standing in for Ted in the Chairman's seat. Ann uses Pamela as a confidante in her ongoing obsession with Nicholas. Ted and Jenny go sailing, and David tells his mother to stop interfering with his life.
Guest cast: ANNA FOX (Pamela Graham) STEPHEN YARDLEY (Alex Dyter)
Directed by RODERICK GRAHAM

32. AN IMPOSSIBLE DEBT by N.J. Crisp
Studio recording: 26th & 27th September 1973
Broadcast: Sunday 31st March 1974 at 7.25pm, BBC 1
Running length: 45'41"
Jennifer guesses the source of Barbara's loan and suddenly Johnny's debts assume unimagined importance. Ann seeks medical help for insomnia as she is wrestles with her feelings for Nicholas. The Hammond Board release Gill's guarantee and she tells David he is free now the company do not need her financial backing. Jennifer is furious with both Barbara and Mary and makes a drastic decision which will have repercussions for everyone at Hammond Transport.
Guest cast: ANNA FOX (Pamela) PAULINE WILLIAMS (Doctor Graham) FRANK MOOREY (Miller)
Directed by PHILIP DUDLEY

33. POWER FOR SALE by N.J. Crisp
Studio recording: 11th October 1973
Broadcast: Sunday 7th April 1974 at 7.25pm, BBC 1
Running length: 45'03"
Ted is floored by Jennifer's announcement and is mystified as to her reasons. A Dutch businessman Van Der Moewe is introduced to the Board by Nicholas Fox, he could be a great ally in their plans to expand their operations into Europe. With Ted refusing to accept that Jennifer is serious, she opens up her offer to the other brothers. The triangle between David, Jill and Julie continues to threaten their marriage much to the concern of Mary.
Guest cast: ANNA FOX (Pamela) MICHAEL TURNER (Van Der Moewe)
Directed by RODERICK GRAHAM

34. CONSPIRATORS by Eric Paice
Studio recording: 24th & 25th October 1973
Broadcast: Sunday 21st April 1974 at 7.25pm, BBC 1
Running length: 44'53"
The current situation sees Brian and David scrambling to raise cash in an effort to put themselves in the driving seat on the Hammond Board. Bill Riley confides in Mary and Edward the reason he wants to leave the firm. In an effort to keep open her options, Jennifer visits her Bank Manager but the news he has for her isn't what she was hoping. Jill is appalled to see David and Brian plotting against Ted and makes a decision regarding her role in the proceedings. When Ted finally finds out the reason for Jennifer's decision he sets about putting things back in their natural order, and this means putting his brothers in their place.

Guest cast: BRIAN PECK (Bank Manager) DENNIS CLEARY (Jim Saddler) PAT GORMAN (Tom Webb) JAGDISH KUMAR (Bus Conductor)
Directed by PHILIP DUDLEY

35. PERCHANCE TO DREAM by Eric Paice
Studio recording: 8th November 1973
Broadcast: Sunday28th April 1974 at 7.25pm, BBC 1
Running length: 44'41"
A desperate Ann tries, and fails, to fly to Brussels to be with Nicholas Fox. Barbara gives Mary news of a debt repaid. The family gather to celebrate David's birthday as they try to restore harmony. Ann's trip to see the children at boarding school leaves her ever more desolate, and Brian gets a shock at the end of the evening.
Guest Cast: ANNA FOX (Pamela) CHARLOTTA MARTINUS (Carol) NATALIA LINDLEY (British Airways Girl) SUE BISHOP (Hilary) WILLIAM EEDLE (Stan)
Directed by RODERICK GRAHAM

36. RETURN TO NOWHERE
Studio recording: 22nd November 1973
Broadcast: Sunday 5th March 1974 at 7.25pm, BBC 1
Running length:
Ann is taken to hospital as Brian endures an anxious wait. Julie continues to play games with David but this time it is she who gets the biggest surprise. Bill tells Ted that he and Gwen have found the house they want. Ted and Jenny set off on holiday as Ann and Brian try to come to terms with what has happened. On their return to see Mary with important news, they have a shock in store.
Guest Cast: ANNA FOX (Pamela) HILARY MINSTER (Doctor Johnstone) BONNIE HURREN (Sister) EDNA DORE (Woman In Waiting Room) DAVID PUGH (Motor Cyclist) DOUGLAS RAE (Ambulance Man)
Directed by PHILIP DUDLEY
N.B. There is no writer credited to this episode on any production paperwork. It is likely that it is an Eric Paice script which has he asked for his name to be removed from, following re-writes by the script editor.

1974 - SERIES FOUR
Regular cast:
JEAN ANDERSON (Mary Hammond) PATRICK O'CONNELL (Edward Hammond) RICHARD EASTON (Brian Hammond) ROBIN CHADWICK (David Hammond) JENNIFER WILSON (Jennifer Kingsley) HILARY TINDALL (Ann Hammond) DEREK BENFIELD (Bill Riley) GABRIELLE DRAKE (Jill Hammond) MARGARET ASHCROFT (Gwen Riley) MURRAY HAYNE (Martin Farrell)
Producer KEN RIDDINGTON Script Editor SIMON MASTERS
Gabrielle Drake does not appear in episodes 37, 38, 39, 47
Murray Hayne does not appear in episode 37
Margaret Ashcroft does not appear in episodes 43, 44, 45, 46
Hilary Tindall does not appear in episodes 46, 47

37. EMERGENCY by N.J. Crisp
Studio recording: 7th February 1974
Broadcast: Sunday 1st September 1974 at 7.25pm, BBC 1
Running length: 49'49"
Edward and Jennifer return from holiday, anxious to acquaint Mary with their marriage plans but find her collapsed with another heart-attack. Whilst Ted follows her to the hospital, Jennifer alerts the rest of the family to the situation. Ann and Brian return home early from Ann's recuperation to be closer to Mary. Mary questions Ted on his relationship with Jennifer and he is less than truthful. Ann receives a phone call from Nicholas Fox. Gwen Riley visits Mary in the hospital and they find they have more in common than they thought. Jennifer accepts that her relationship with Ted is doomed.
Guest Cast: ALEXANDER JOHN (Hospital Registrar)
Directed by RODERICK GRAHAM

38. SECRET MEETINGS by N.J. Crisp
Studio recording: 7th March 1974
Broadcast: Sunday 8th September 1974 at 7.25pm, BBC 1
Running Length: 48'53"
Brian arranges a covert meeting with Martin Farrell, the merchant banker who he hopes will oversee the public flotation of Hammond Transport. Ann continues her deception when visiting Nicholas Fox. Brian ropes in David at a further meeting with Farrell and they plot to get the proposal through the next Board meeting. Gwen is upset when she visits Mary, she opens up about her situation. At the Board meeting Brian deftly manipulates the meeting, resulting in Farrell being invited onto the Board. In retaliation Ted sounds out Bill Riley about being a director.
Guest Cast: JONATHAN NEWTH (Nicholas Fox) FRANK CODA (Cashier)
Directed by VERE LORRIMER

39. INVESTIGATIONS by N.J. Crisp
Studio recording: 21st March 1974
Broadcast: Sunday 15th December 1974 at 7.25pm, BBC 1
Running length: 49'53"
Mary asks Gwen to be her home help, in the process finding out that Hammond's might become a public company. Ted arrives with his new car and a reserved Company Chairman parking spot. Ted engineers that Bill will show Martin around the depot. Brian investigates the phone bill and queries a telegram sent from his account. He discovers the liaison between Ann and Nick. He confronts Nick in the office and obliquely warns him. Jennifer shows Martin around the Dover depot. David expresses an interest in taking motor racing lessons. Ted announces that he would like Bill on the Board. *The Brothers* decide that they must take it in turns to sit with Mary.
Guest Cast: JONATHAN NEWTH (Nicholas Fox)
Directed by RODERICK GRAHAM

40. HAPPY ANNIVERSARY by N.J. Crisp
Studio recording: 4th April 1974
Broadcast: Sunday 22nd September 1974 at 7.25pm, BBC 1
Running length: 49'26"
Brian is antagonistic towards Bill during a meeting of the Joint Consultative Committee. Ted presses Bill for a decision on his invitation to join the Board. Ann asks Mary about her husband and Jennifer Kingsley.

Brian admits to Ann he knows what has been going on. Jill presents David with a new penthouse flat but he is less than grateful. Bill wonders if he has done the right thing after his first Board meeting. Brian storms out calling Ann a "selfish whore".
Guest Cast: ROBIN FORD (Hall Porter) ADRIAN BRACKEN (Dawson)
Directed by VERE LORRIMER

41. PARTINGS by John Pennington
Studio recording: 18th April 1974
Broadcast: Sunday 29th September 1974 at 7.25pm, BBC 1
Running length: 49'40"
David gives in and accepts Jill's penthouse gift, he takes the day off work to be with her. Martin Farrell asks Jenny out to dinner. Bill confides to Martin his doubts. Ann visits Mary and confesses her affair and that that she does not love Brian. A lunch meeting with Paul Merroney seems to go well despite Brian being distracted. Ted storms around to David's flat and demands to know why he was not in work. Ann goads Brian during an argument and he retaliates by hitting her.
Guest Cast: COLIN BAKER (Paul Merroney) KEITH CAMPBELL (Head Waiter)
Directed by RODERICK GRAHAM

42. LONELINESS by John Pennington
Studio recording: 2nd May 1974
Broadcast: Sunday 6th October 1974 at 7.25pm, BBC 1
Running length:
Brian drives recklessly on his way from visiting Ann. He calls on Jennifer but she is about to go out for dinner with Martin. Ann arrives at Nicholas' apartment and finds Virginia, his second wife, in residence. Brian arrives at David's flat and he stays the night. Jill and David decide to move into the new penthouse straight away so that Brian can use the flat. David uses a vehicle from the depot to move house, Ted however is not happy when he finds out. Brian tells Ann he is starting divorce proceedings.
Guest Cast: MARJORIE YATES (Virginia Fox) RIO FANNING (Durkin) DAVID PURCELL (Logan) JOHN CANNON (Lorry Driver)
Directed by LENNIE MAYNE

43. HIT AND MISS by John Pennington
Studio recording: 16th May 1974
Broadcast: Sunday 13th October at 7.25pm, BBC 1
Running length: 49'16"
Ann and Brian are both finding it difficult adjusting to their new situation. Ann asks Brian if Nicholas can speak to him about the situation but he refuses. Jill is planning a flat warming party for the penthouse. Both Jennifer and Mary are invited. Jill reveals to David that she is pregnant. The Board of Directors are invited on a clay pigeon shoot in the country by Sir Neville Henniswode, chairman of the merchant bank who are handling the Hammond share issue. Edward grows concerned at the developing friendship between Jenny and Martin.
Guest Cast: MARJORIE YATES (Virginia Fox) CARLETON HOBBS (Sir Neville Henniswode) COLIN BAKER (Paul Merroney)
Directed by RODERICK GRAHAM

44. PUBLIC CONCERN by John Pennington
Studio recording: 31st May 1974 & 1st June 1974
Broadcast: Sunday 20th October 1974 at 7.25pm, BBC 1
Running length: 49'28"
Merroney attends a Board meeting and advises them that the bank has decided to proceed with the share issue. Arthur Naylor is intent on forming a local residents committee to object to the noise of the lorries. He presents a petition to Bill Riley. Arthur angles for a job at Hammonds in return for dropping the petition. Brian confides in Jill. He then goes to the boarding school and tells his daughter Carol that he and Ann are separating. Ted entertains local resident Mrs. Abbot and finds that Arthur has wavering support among the residents. Arthur tells the press that he has been harassed by workers at Hammonds. David takes to the race track for the first time. Bill offers Naylor a job, but he has a plan in mind. David wants the Board to sponsor him as a racing driver.
Guest Cast: COLIN BAKER (Paul Merroney) CHARLOTTA MARTINUS (Carol Hammond) CAROL HOLLAND (Sally) JOHN BADDELEY (Arthur Naylor) DAVID PURCELL (Logan) CHRISTOPHER GILBERT (George Lewis) NICHOLAS FIELD (Harry Blane) ALLAN DEUTROM (Charlie Royle) PATRICIA MASON (Mrs. Abbot) NATALIE KENT (Mrs. Naylor)
Directed by LENNIE MAYNE

45. THE RACE by John Pennington
Studio recording: 13th June 1974
Broadcast: Sunday 27th October 1974 at 7.25pm, BBC 1
Running length: 48'32"
Merroney attends a Board meeting and advises them that the bank has decided to proceed with the share issue. David announces that he is driving a car in a forthcoming Formula Ford race. The Board are concerned. Nicholas tells Ann that he no longer wants her. He later asks Brian to take her back. At the race meeting David starts off well but has to settle for ninth place. The Hammonds celebrate with champagne anyway. Meanwhile Jenny entertains Martin. Nicholas books a flight to New York in a bid to escape Ann's attentions, he asks her to leave his flat. Jennifer visits Brian and discusses her feelings for Martin... and Ted. Ann arrives a broken woman at Jill and David's apartment.
Guest Cast: JONATHAN NEWTH (Nicholas Fox) JOHN ROLFE (Haughton) ANTHONY MARSH (Race Commentator)
Directed by RODERICK GRAHAM

46. SATURDAY by Eric Paice
Studio recording: 22nd August 1974
Broadcast: Sunday 3rd November 1974 at 7.25pm, BBC 1
Running length: 49'36"
David is fussing around a pregnant Jill. Edward gets wind of a special Union Meeting being held at the depot. Edward demands to see the ring leader straight after the meeting. Gwen asks Mary about Bill's position in the company. She is worried change might affect their circumstances. Doug Walker puts the workers position to Edward and Jennifer – they want an improved deal including pensions if Hammond Transport is floated on the stock exchange. After lunch Jill is upset at David's attitude to Brian's separation and defends Ann. Walker makes a veiled threat of a strike on the day the shares are issued. Mary offers to look after Brian's children but Brian is very much against it. David is suspicious at Bill's motives. Brian picks up two girl hitch-hikers in his car. Distracted he knocks down a little girl on a bike.

Guest Cast: SEAN CAFFREY (Doug Walker) DENIS CLEARY (Jim Saddler) JACKIE ROHAN (Sheila) BRIGID ERIN BATES (Dawn)
Directed by GEORGE SPENTON-FOSTER

47. THE GUILT BENEATH THE GINGERBREAD by Eric Paice
Studio recording: 24th August 1974
Broadcast: Sunday 10th November 1974
Running length: 45'31"
Brian is in shock in the aftermath of the accident. The hitch-hikers have disappeared. The police question him closely. Gwen upsets Bill by wanting to borrow money from the company again for a new house. A meeting of the Joint Consultative Committee brings the workers grieVances to the fore. David confronts Bill about his actions regarding the workers demands. Brian's solicitor informs him he is to be charged for 'dangerous driving'. Brian makes things difficult for his defence. The Consultative Committee gets heated, with the pension scheme proposal at the heart of the negotiations. Mary heads back to London after a tip off from Gwen. Mary discovers Jennifer's ring has been left at her house. Brian heads to the hospital to ask about Karen Williams, whilst there he confronts her Mum and Dad. Ted manages to come to an agreement over the workers demands. Mary turns up at the depot and returns Jennifer's ring.
Guest Cast: TIMOTHY CARLTON (Solicitor) BRIAN SPINK (1st Patrolman) MICHAEL ELPHICK (2nd Patrolman) SEAN CAFFREY (Doug Walker) DENIS CLEARY (Jim Saddler) JAMES APPLEBY (Sid Thompson) BILL TREACHER (Williams) PAM CRAIG (Sister) JOANNA ROSS (Nurse)
Directed BY GERRY HILL

48. A BAD MISTAKE by N.J. Crisp
Studio recording: N/A
Broadcast: Sunday 17th November 1974 at 7.25pm, BBC 1
Running length: 49'42"
Amid a tricky shares issue, the Hammonds attend a meeting of prospective buyers. Ann weighs up her options now that Nicholas nor Brian are expected to be part of her life. Bill, Brian and Jennifer seem to be finding favour with the buyers but then Ted makes a speech which affects the meeting drastically with Ted too stubborn to make amends. Martin advises Jenny that Ted has done long term harm and it needs to beput right. Ann calls on Brian just as he is making an inventory of the house. The newspapers have got hold of the story. Paul Merroney is taking charge of the situation and instructs Ted to make a statement to the financial press. Jill has a heart to heart with David about her pregnancy. Ann continues to try and engage Brian but he seemingly isn't interested. A private investigator calls at the house with a dossier on Ann's affair with Nicholas.
Guest Cast: RICHARD HURNDALL (Clifton) COLIN BAKER (Paul Merroney) RICHARD HAMPTON (Prescott) PETER HUGHES (Barrington)
Directed by RODERICK GRAHAM

There was no episode of The Brothers broadcast on Sunday 24th November 1974 due to the televising of the Royal Variety Performance.

49. THE FALL GUY by N.J. Crisp

Studio recording: 7th August 1974

Broadcast: Sunday 1st December 1974 at 7.25pm, BBC 1

Running length: 49'38"

Prescott – the private investigator – persuades Ann that the evidence against her is overwhelming and that it is in her best interests to admit infidelity for the divorce hearing. Ted tells Mary her shortcomings regarding Jennifer. Martin tells the Board the share issue is looking good. Ted takes Jennifer out and asks if she intends to marry Martin. Gwen announces she is spending her savings on Hammond Transport shares. Market forces seem to be against Hammonds, as the financial market takes a dip just before the shares are issued. Jill however is determined to buy some with the last of her windfall. Nigel is at home with a sprained ankle giving Ann some leverage over Brian. The shares are down to 35p. Merroney instructs Farrell to salvage the situation and restore market confidence in Hammonds. Farrell puts it to Ted that he stands down as Hammonds' Managing Director. He takes the suggestion badly. He challenges Martin to try and get him out of the chair. Farrell systematically set about getting the support of the other directors. At the Board meeting Farrell presents a motion to remove Ted as Chairman and Managing Director.

Guest Cast: COLIN BAKER (Paul Merroney) RICHARD HAMPTON (Prescott)

Directed by OLIVER HORSBRUGH

50. THE CRUCIAL VOTE by N.J. Crisp

Studio recording: 5th September 1974

Broadcast: Sunday 8th December 1974 at 7.25pm, BBC 1

Running length: 49'10"

Ann brings the children to the depot. Edward and Jennifer call on Mary with the news of the Boardroom revolt. On a family outing, Ann flirts with Brian. All parties try to figure out how the voting might go. On the surface it looks good for Ted but the game is not over yet. Ann announces she is going to have the children at home. It is a ploy which Brian sees through. At the crucial vote, Farrell insists that Ted vacate the chair. David is forced into chairing the meeting. An impassioned speech by Farrell pleads for the future of the company, and asks that his fellow directors support him in removing Ted as Managing Director. Amid the threat of a takeover bid by Borrets, the vote is taken. Ted is removed and Martin Farrell installed as Chairman with Brian as Managing Director.

Guest Cast: ANNABELLE LANYON (Carol Hammond) JOSHUA LE TOUZEL (Nigel Hammond)

Directed by WILLIAM SLATER

1975 - SERIES FIVE

Regular cast:

JEAN ANDERSON (Mary Hammond) PATRICK O'CONNELL (Edward Hammond) RICHARD EASTON (Brian Hammond) ROBIN CHADWICK (David Hammond) JENNIFER WILSON (Jennifer Kingsley) DEREK BENFIELD (Bill Riley) MARGARET ASHCROFT (Gwen Riley) COLIN BAKER (Paul Merroney) CAROLE MOWLAM (Clare Miller) KATE O'MARA (Jane Maxwell) MIKE PRATT (Don Stacey)

Producer KEN RIDDINGTON Script Editor DOUGLAS WATKINSON

Richard Easton does not appear in episodes 56 – 62

Mike Pratt and Kate O'Mara do not appear in episodes 51 – 55

Margaret Ashcroft does not appear in episodes 55 – 58

Colin Baker does not appear in episode 61

51. LIFE GOES ON by N.J. Crisp

Studio Recording: 16th January 1975
Broadcast: Sunday 6th April 1975 at 7.25pm, BBC 1
Running length: 49'36"

Brian's divorce from Ann is finalised. He has been under severe strain over the intervening months and it is showing at work. Mary is certainly concerned about him. At the Bank it is revealed that Martin Farrell has handed in his resignation. With Sir Neville's blessing Paul Merroney subtly puts himself forward as a replacement. The directors debate on why a man of Merroney's stature at the bank should want a position with Hammond Transport. Bill takes Gwen for a day out – and much to her annoyance shows her the newest addition to the haulage industry. Ted has to spring to Brian's assistance when an important logistics problem faces the firm. At informal drinks, David and Jennifer question Merroney about his motives. At the penthouse block, David delivers some devastating news to a neighbour...

Guest Cast: LLEWELLYN REES (Sir Neville Henniswode) JOHN KELLAND (Solicitor) LINCOLN WRIGHT (Judge) FRANCES PIDGEON (Susan Collier)
Directed by LENNIE MAYNE

52. THE SELF MADE CROSS by N.J. Crisp

Studio recording: 30th January 1975
Broadcast: Sunday 13th April 1975 at 7.25pm, BBC 1
Running length: 49'19"

David finally feels able to talk about Jill's death. Brian is beginning to drink heavily in an attempt to placate the increasing pressures he feels under. David attempts to pick up his repaired Ford Cortina GT – but finds he cannot go through with it. On a visit from Mary, David finally releases the pent up grief. At a meeting of the directors, it is voted that an offer is made for Merroney as Chairman. As Merroney takes the chair, the directors get a sense that life under the new recruit will be very different. On a visit to his Doctor, Brian breaks down.

Guest Cast: STANLEY MEADOWS (Garage Foreman) MICHAEL ELWYN (Doctor IVan)
Directed by VERE LORRIMER

53. TIGER BY THE TAIL by Eric Paice

Studio recording: 13th February 1975
Broadcast: Sunday 20th April 1975 at 7.25pm, BBC 1
Running length: 49'45"

Paul sets out his stall as Chairman. As discussion centres on acquiring a sub-depot in Switzerland, he arranges for Ted and Jenny to go and investigate the possibilities. Brian's treatment continues but he is struggling to cope. Mary wants to invite Merroney to dinner. The depot is to get a facelift thanks to Merroney's plans for streamlining the business. Clare is seconded to Brian as his secretary, but her skills prove more insightful than Brian is prepared for. The psychiatrist recommends Brian goes into hospital for tests. At the dinner, Merroney warns David that Brian is not fit to continue as Managing Director, Mary cannot help but overhear.

Guest Cast: RONALD LEIGH-HUNT (Doctor Gloster)
Directed by LENNIE MAYNE

54. BREAKDOWN by Eric Paice
Studio recording: 27th February 1975
Broadcast: Sunday 27th April 1975 at 7.25pm, BBC 1
Running length: 48'48"
Jennifer and Edward are in Switzerland interviewing staff. Paul is putting the board under pressure to pass his plans for redevelopment of the depot. Mary visits Brian and finds him prickly and clearly unwell.
During a business lunch Brian reveals just how unwell he is to Merroney. Paul is surprisingly sympathetic and confides in Brian his own past problems. The Doctor advises Brian that he should be admitted to anursing home straight away, reluctantly Brian is forced to concede. Jenny and Ted decide to drive to a hotel for a break. With Brian now unable to continue as Managing Director, David and Bill intend on lobbying for Ted to be reinstated. David tries to contact Ted to urge him to get in touch urgently. On the
ski slopes, Ted and Jenny finally commit to getting married.
Guest Cast: LARRY NOBLE (Sam Johnson) RONALD LEIGH-HUNT (Doctor Gloster) RICHARD BASIC (Hercule) FREDERICK SCHILLER (Patron)
Directed by VERE LORRIMER

55. SPECIAL LICENCE by Eric Paice
Studio recording: 15th March 1975
Broadcast: Sunday 4th May 1975 at 7.25pm,BBC 1
Running length: 49'16"
Mary goes to visit Brian at the nursing home. Ted and Jennifer arrive back from Switzerland and immediately Paul insists on emergency measures to cover for Brian's absence. At a board meeting Ted is voted acting Managing Director. Ted is worried that Brian might sell his shares loosening control of the Hammond's in the company. Merroney meanwhile is visiting Brian. Jennifer agrees to let Mary host the wedding reception at her house. During a cosy evening, Clare sees through David's ruse of finding out what Merroney is up to. Jennifer visits Mary wanting a truce to hostilities. Ted and Jenny are married. At the reception Merroney reveals Brian has put his shares in Hammond Transport Services in trust to the bank.
Guest Cast: JACKI WEBB (Nurse) LAURIE WEBB (Superintendent) MIKE KINSEY, DAVID PURCELL (Lorry Drivers)
Directed by LENNIE MAYNE

56. FLIGHT OF FANCY by Eric Paice
Studio recording: 27th March 1975
Broadcast: Sunday 11th May 1975 at 7.25pm, BBC 1
Running length: 49'59"
The directors receive a summons for an early board meeting from Paul. Merroney has had word that an air cargo firm is on the brink of going into liquidation. He enlists David and Bill on a recce to check out the facilities. Mary calls Doctor IVan, who insists she goes for tests at the local hospital. During their fact finding mission the Hammond's directors encounter pilot Don Stacey who is less than helpful. Scouring the office paperwork they are intercepted by Jane Maxwell, an outspoken and forthright director of Flair Freight. Merroney sets about convincing her that a take over by Hammond's is the only way to save her company. Mary has discharged herself from hospital against medical advice. Merroney makes a return visit to Flair Freight where Jane informs him that she wants a seat on the board if Hammond's want to operate Flair Freight on her aviation certificate.

Guest Cast: MICHAEL ELWYN (Doctor IVan) RAYMOND MASON (Mr. Barrett) JOSEPH WISE (Customs Officer)
Directed by VERE LORRIMER

57. A VERY SHORT HONEYMOON by N.J. Crisp
Studio recording: 10th April 1975
Broadcast: Sunday 18th May 1975 at 7.25pm, BBC 1
Running length: 49'42"
Jennifer and Ted go to view a house with the intent of starting a family. There is trouble at the Dover depot, the men have walked out wanting parity with the London workers. Merroney tries to persuade Clare to get close to David and report back. Mary is concerned that Ann Hammond's latest relationship has made the gossip column of a national newspaper. Ted and Jenny go golfing, but Mary confides later that she is concerned about Jennifer being too old to carry a baby. Paul formally reports to the board that the merchant bank is now holding Brian's shares in trust. Ted and David voice concern that the Hammond's could be out-voted now that Brian's shares are no longer part of the Hammond family. Mary invites Jennifer to tea but old hostilities emerge. Ted surprises Jenny by buying the house.
Guest Cast: PETER BETON (Surveyor)
Directed by LENNIE MAYNE

58. BIG DEAL by N.J. Crisp
Studio recording: 24th April 1975
Broadcast: Sunday 25th May 1975 at 7.25pm, BBC 1
Running length: 49'48"
Jennifer and Ted are busy working on making their house habitable. Mary in some remorse wants to apologise to Jennifer. She writes to Jennifer, but gets no response. Paul wants a job evaluation scheme for the entire company and puts Bill and Jenny in charge. Don Stacey treats David to a flight. Ted discovers the airfield has tenants on a piece of land they own. Jenny attempts to contact Brian. David and Clare have dinner together but the atmosphere is awkward. Merroney attempts to gain Jane's support at the board meeting. Ted however brings up the farmland at the airfield, and Jane supports his criticisms. Paul agrees to dispose of the land at the request of the board. Paul is furious and intends that a holding company formed by himself and Clare will purchase the land which they will then sell on for a quarter of a million pounds.
Guest Cast: JOHN HARTLEY (Dennis Reed) TOMMY WRIGHT (Workman) MICHAEL GAUNT (Co-Pilot)
Directed by VERE LORRIMER

59. PACKAGE DEAL by N.J. Crisp
Studio recording: 1st May 1975
Broadcast: Sunday 1st June 1975 at 7.25pm, BBC 1
Running length: 49'52"
Merroney is still planning the sale of the land adjoining the airfield for his own profit. Union representative Reg Turner is called in regarding the job evaluation scheme. Bill and Gwen take Mary to the nursing home to visit Brian. David arranges for Don to take Clare and him for a flying trip. Brian tells Bill that he is not up to seeing Mary. David is given a chance to impress Clare by being Don's co-pilot on the flight to Beauvais. Mary is disappointed that Brian has refused to see her. Merroney plots with influential figures to ensure the sale of the the land. Clare cleverly gets David behind the wheel of a car again. Merroney visits farmer Bert Reed but doesn't find him the pushover he thought. Jenny visits the gynaecologist. Paul surprises everyone by appointing Bill as deputy Managing Directorof Hammonds.

Guest Cast: KENNETH WATSON (Reg Turner) MARCIA ASHTON (Mrs. Palmer) RAYMOND ADAMSON (Bert Reed) FREDERICK TREVES (Charles Daventry) NORMAN PITT (Barnes) MICHAEL GAUNT (Co-Pilot) PATRICIA PRIOR (Doctor's Receptionist)
Directed by LENNIE MAYNE

60. END OF A DREAM by N.J. Crisp
Studio recording: 8th May 1975
Broadcast: Sunday 8th June 1975 at 7.25pm, BBC 1
Running length: 50'05"
Paul is concerned that Clare's friendship with David might compromise his business affairs. Edward and Jennifer are preparing their new home. David test drives a new car. Paul advises that the land will be sold to Double M Developments Ltd. Negotiations begin under the new job evaluation scheme. Jack Cornish shows concern over the figures that will be available under the scheme. David takes Mary and Clare for a day out at Henley. Edward and Jenny hosts house warming drinks. Merroney turns up with an attractive companion much to Clare's surprise. Jenny is given the news that for health reasons she should not attempt to get pregnant. Naturally upset, Jenny is encouraged by Ted's assertion that they should adopt.
Guest Cast: JACK WATSON (Jack Cornish) KEN WATSON (Reg Turner) GEOFFREY ADAMS (Mr. Hollis) JOHN DAWSON (Porter) LAURENCE HARDY (Mr. Vaisey) RULA LENSKA (Fiona Lester)
Directed by VERE LORRIMER

61. THE JUDAS SHEEP by Eric Paice
Studio recording: 21st & 22nd May 1975
Broadcast: Sunday 15th June 1975 at 7.25pm, BBC 1
Running length: 49'24"
Jenny and Ted have an appointment with an adoption society. Helen Milmoss shows concern over their age regarding adopting a child. They are floated the idea of fostering two West Indian babies. Jack and Bill go to the airfield to talk about job evaluation, where they encounter Don. A problem develops over areo-engine fitter Bob Carr who is earning more money than his colleagues. Mary learns that Ted intends adopting a child. She cannot help but make it her business. During a visit from Dr. Ivan she learns that he might be able to help Ted with his adoption plans. Later, Mary lets slip the families unusual relationships during Helen Milmoss' visit. It is then revealed that they are not suitable candidates for the adoption after all on the grounds they have only been married a few months. Whilst in the depths of despair, Dr. Ivan brings the Hammonds an unexpected offer...
Guest Cast: JACK WATSON (Jack Cornish) PINKIE JOHNSTONE (Helen Milmoss) MICHAEL ELWYN (Dr. Ivan) FREDDIE EARLLE (Bob Carr)
Directed by LENNIE MAYNE

62. JENNIFER'S BABY by Eric Paice
Studio recording: 4th & 5th June 1975
Broadcast: Sunday 22nd June 1975 at 7.25pm, BBC 1
Running length: 50'00"
Jenny and Ted are busy preparing for the arrival of their baby. Merroney arrives back from Beirut with Clare is given the task of entertaining Sheik Abu during his visit. The problem of Bob Carr continues to stall the job evaluation negotiations. Clare finds that Abu is taking a shine to her. Don and Jane head up to London for business and pleasure. David finds he is consumed with jealousy at the thought of Clare entertaining another man. Mary manages to put a foot in it during a visit from Jennifer. Jane's opposition to Bob Carr's retirement sees Merroney try to get her onside. He threatens her with Don's contract renewal. David helps Clare out by inviting Sheik Abu to dinner with Mary and tips off Ted to Merroney's plans. At dinner, Sheik

Abu drops the bombshell that the company involved in the land deal is Double M Developments – Merroney & Miller. Paul instructs Clare to put a stop to her friendship with David.
Guest Cast: JACK WATSON (Jack Cornish) KENNETH WATSON (Reg Turner) CYRIL SHAPS (Sheik Abu) ELIZABETH CHAMBERS (Sister) PETER BALE (Barman)
Directed by VERE LORRIMER

63. WARPATH by Eric Paice
Studio recording: 18th & 19th June 1975
Broadcast: Sunday 29th June 1975 at 7.25pm, BBC 1
Running length: 49'53"
The Hammond family are enjoying the summer. Brian surprises everyone by his return. Merroney arranges for Clare to take a holiday to Bermuda, in order to get her out of the way in case awkward questions are asked about the airfield land deal. A newspaper gets hold of the story, and Jane seems rather pleased. Mary decides to buy more shares in Hammond Transport. Merroney tries to gain Bill's support in getting rid of Ted. At the board meeting in Paul's absence, Ted tries to get his fellow directors to support his motion for getting rid of Paul. However, Paul has been secretly taping the meeting. Paul sends a transcript of the meeting to Sir Neville at the bank. Jane and Paul fail to reach an agreement, Jane sets off to see Sir Neville. Clare says goodbye to David, but warns him that Merroney is at his most dangerous, especially as he might be falling out of favour with the bank. Ted takes a phone call telling him that William's natural mother wants him back.
Directed by LENNIE MAYNE

1976 - SERIES SIX
Regular cast:
JEAN ANDERSON (Mary Hammond) PATRICK O'CONNELL (Edward Hammond) RICHARD EASTON (Brian Hammond) ROBIN CHADWICK (David Hammond) JENNIFER WILSON (Jennifer Kingsley) DEREK BENFIELD (Bill Riley) MARGARET ASHCROFT (Gwen Riley) COLIN BAKER (Paul Merroney) KATE O'MARA (Jane Maxwell) CAROLE MOWLAM (Clare Miller) MIKE PRATT (Don Stacey)
Producer BILL SELLARS Executive Producer KEN RIDDINGTON Script Editor DOUGLAS WATKINSON
Patrick O'Connell does not appear in episode 73.
Margaret Ashcroft does not appear in episodes 69 , 70.
Kate O'Mara does not appear in episode 74.
Mike Pratt does not appear in episodes 70 - 76

64. RED SKY AT NIGHT by Simon Raven
Studio recording: 23rd October 1975
Broadcast: Sunday 25th January 1976 at 7.25pm, BBC 1
Running length: 49'38"
Mary is anticipating Brian's return from Italy. Jennifer is worrying about William's future with her and Ted. Ted harangues Paul about Brian's future with the company but Paul has his own reasons for wanting Brian back. Jane confides to David that she struck a deal with Paul about not causing waves about the sale of the land in return for renewing Don's contract of employment. Ted warns Jenny about giving up William with dignity if it comes to it. During the board meeting Brian sneaks into the offices at the depot. David confronts Bill about his worries that Brian may not be up to scratch after his breakdown. Brian waits for Paul in his office who then helps Brian acclimatise to being back. Mary goes to see Sir Neville, and he tells her that

her sons will have to prove their worth in the coming months. David is sent to France to investigate new areas of expansion. There he meets Therese D'Alambert, the daughter of an influential business figure. Don however has some words of warning. Jenny is getting desperate and asks Ted to offer William's natural mother money so they can keep him.

Guest Cast: CARLETON HOBBS (Sir Neville Henniswode) FRANCOISE PASCAL (Therese D'Alambert)
Directed by JOHN DAVIES

65. A CLEAN BREAK by Douglas Watkinson
Studio recording: 6th November 1975
Broadcast: Sunday 1st February 1976 at 7.25pm, BBC 1
Running length: 48'40"

Jennifer's desperation is doing her no favours with Dr. Ivan. Mary goes out to dinner with Sir Neville. Pat Hawkins visits Dr. Ivan and says she has definitely decided to keep William. He then finds out her husband Alan works for Hammond Transport. Jenny takes William to Suffolk planning for his future education. Paul is less than sympathetic to the Hammond's worries. Ted meets with Alan Hawkins and offers to help move his family to the Dover depot, plus gives him a cheque for William when he reaches the age of 18. Ted asks Gwen and Bill to give William back to his parents. David asks for more time in France to investigate possibilities then clashes with Paul over his criticisms of Ted and Jenny.

Guest Cast: CARLETON HOBBS (Sir Neville Henniswode) MICHAEL ELWYN (Doctor Ivan) IAN MARTER (Alan Hawkins) ELAINE DONNELLY (Pat Hawkins) PETER HOWELL (Headmaster)
Directed by CHRISTOPHER BAKER

66. RED SKY IN THE MORNING by Simon Raven
Studio recording: 4th December 1975
Broadcast: Sunday 8th February 1976 at 7.25pm, BBC 1
Running length: 48'10"

Mary has relayed Sir Neville's comments to her sons, they weigh up what it could mean for them. Clare shows concern at David's trips to France and in particular associating with Therese. Jenny shows little interest in events at the depot. Therese presses David for information on Paul Merroney.

Brian tackles Paul about the finance for the expansion. And the future of the Hammond family under the bank's powerful influence. Ted consults Dr. Ivan about Jenny's depression. Therese tempts David with a business proposition. The following morning a hungover David is told he lost gambling to the tune of £11,000. What's more, Therese has paid his debt and now David owes her the money. She suggests a way to repay the debt would be to award the fuel contract to her father's company. Dr. Ivan tries to talk to Jenny but she proves unresponsive. Merroney confides that Sir Neville wants to get rid of David as a way of 'bringing the others into line.' Merroney is determined that will not be the case. Don Stacey and David get an unwelcome reception from customs on their arrival back in England. Ted is forced into some plain talking with Jenny.

Guest Cast: MICHAEL ELWYN (Doctor Ivan) FRANCOISE PASCAL (Therese D'Alambert) MICHAEL SHEARD (Customs Officer)
Directed by CHRISTOPHER BAKER

67. ORANGES AND LEMONS by Simon Raven

Studio recording: 20th November 1975
Broadcast: Sunday 15th February 1976 at 7.25pm, BBC 1
Running length: 49'34"

Merroney heads to the airfield to find out exactly why Don and David were targeted by customs. Don tells Merroney about his theory that Therese tipped off customs to get at David. The Hammonds wonder where David has gone. He hasn't been in touch since the airfield incident. Gwen is frustrated that Bill's workload is affecting their life for the worse. Merroney tests Jennifer as he welcomes her back to the company. Unbeknown to everyone, David is laying low at Clare's flat. Gwen has had enough of playing second fiddle to Hammonds, and is determined to improve her lot. Merroney denies Bill's request for a holiday with Gwen. Brian intercepts David as he pays a low key visit to home. Ted receives a phone call telling him all the directors are being summoned to a meeting so that David can explain his actions. On arrival back at her flat, David and Clare find they have a visitor...
Guest Cast: CARLETON HOBBS (Sir Neville Henniswode)
Directed by JOHN DAVIES

68. WHEN WILL YOU PAY ME? by Simon Raven

Studio recording: 18th December 1975
Broadcast: Sunday 22nd February 1976 at 7.25pm, BBC 1
Running length: 49'52"

Paul makes an unexpected call on the Rileys. He informs them he is calling a special board meeting to hold David to account for his actions. Furthermore he enlists Bill's help in getting Ted to face up to his responsibilities as Managing Director. David reports events back to the full board. Bill motions that they get rid of David as a solution to the French problem. Merroney makes a special trip to Sir Neville's country house and reports that David's trip to France was clear of incident. Sir Neville later tells Mary that Merroney has lied to them in order to protect David. Jane works out Merroney's tactics for reuniting the board. Don offers Bill some words of advice on his marriage. Ted tries to reason with Bill and Jenny attempts to gain Jane's support. Bill suggests Jenny as a new executive sales liaison. Gwen shares her frustrations with Mary. Jane finds Don drunk on the afternoon of his medical. She attempts to sober him up. Merroney receives a message from David in France. He reports to the board he has received David's resignation.
Guest Cast: CARLETON HOBBS (Sir Neville Henniswode)
Directed by PHILIP DUDLEY

69. TENDER by Eric Paice

Studio recording: 3rd January 1976
Broadcast: Sunday 29th February 1976 at 7.25pm, BBC 1
Running length: 49'52"

The morning news carries reports of RAI shares suddenly dropping. Mary doesn't want Edward to go to France to find David. Don reports that he has failed his medical. Merroney spies an opportunity involving RAI. Merroney proposes that Brian returns to the board as a fully fledged director. Jenny surprises Merroney by being well ahead of him on the RAI front. She has information on a tender for oil rig installations that will be going begging with RAI's collapse. Griffith Trevelyan offers information in RAI contracts – for a price. Don asks Jane to marry him again but she refuses. He turns to Brian for someone to confide in. David arrives back from France having dealt with his debt. He offers words of warning about Trevelyan. Don confesses he is still in love with Jane. She knows they are at an impasse and one of them needs to make a clean break.

Mary relays Sir Neville's warning that the company has a Judas in the camp.
Guest Cast: CLIVE SWIFT (Griffith Trevelyan)
Directed by TIMOTHY COMBE

70. THE MOLE by Eric Paice
Studio recording: 15th January 1976
Broadcast: Sunday 7th March 1976 at 7.25pm, BBC 1
Running length: 49'07"
Griffith Trevelyan offers his services to Dennis Matthews of Matthews Transport. Merroney has already traced Trevelyan to Birmingham, where Matthews are based. He guesses that he is making a similar offer to their competitors in the tender for the oil rig contract. Dennis Matthews agrees terms with Trevelyan and his first task is to send him back to Hammonds to spy on their bid. Sir Neville takes Mary to look at his stables. The board debate engaging Trevelyan. It is decided to offer him a contract. David is suspicious of Jane's motives in supporting Paul. The company are working furiously to work out costings and schedules for their contract tender, based on information supplied by Trevelyan. Ted is suspicious of the figures Trevelyan has supplied. He asks Brian to get him some information via the accountant grapevine. It seems Trevelyan is supplying false figures from the old RAI contract. Jane tells Brian over dinner that Don is in Africa trying to get a job with a charter company. Merroney decides that will play Trevelyan at his own game by supplying false figures for their tender. Merroney flies to Birmingham to talk to Matthews directly. They turn the tables on Trevelyan. The contract is awarded to Winwigs of Edinburgh. Trevelyan has the last laugh.
Guest Cast: CARLETON HOBBS (Sir Neville Henniswode) CLIVE SWIFT (Griffith Trevelyan) JACK MAY (Dennis Mathews) HILARY MINSTER (Michael Parker) ELIZABETH MOOREFIELD (Muriel) ESMOND WEBB (Charles Rhodes)
Directed by PHILIP DUDLEY

71. THE CHOSEN VICTIM by N.J. Crisp
Studio recording: 29th January 1976
Broadcast: Sunday 14th March 1976 at 7.25pm, BBC 1
Running length: 49'41"
Merroney is at the airfield early, a refuelling stop by Luxury Air could be more than it seems. Brian is surprised by the upsurge of Hammond shares on the stock market. Ted receives a letter from Barbara in Canada, she has had a miscarriage. Gwen has found another dream house. Jane suspects Merroney is up to something again. Sir Neville informs Merroney that money will not buy him social standing. Merroney is more concerned with the activities of rival Kirkman's, who are buying up the shares. Gwen takes Bill to see the house she has her eye on. David reveals his true feelings to Clare, but he doesn't get the response he was hoping for. Jenny speaks to Barbara on the phone, and Ted announces that they are going to visit her. Bill finally gives in to Gwen's pestering about the house. At a special board meeting, Merroney reports that Kirkman's have bid for the remaining shares in Hammond Transport pitching their offer at 80p per share. They have pitched their bid perfectly.
Guest Cast: CARLETON HOBBS (Sir Neville Henniswode)
Directed by TIMOTHY COMBE

72. BLOOD AND WATER by Brian Finch

Studio recording: 12th February 1976

Broadcast: Sunday 21st March 1976 at 7.25pm, BBC 1

Running length: 49'43"

Gwen is thrilled about the prospect of gaining a windfall if Kirkman's buys the Hammond shares. Merroney sounds Brian out about his vote on the Kirkman's bid. Mary makes a social call on Jennifer, but Jenny knows exactly why she has called. She is lobbying against the share bid. Brian and Ted surmise the Kirkman's bid has been helped by some insider help. Sir Neville is once more impressed by Mary's forthright manner regarding the bid. Merroney has his own suspicions on who is advising on Kirkman's bid. Clare is offended by Merroney's assumptions about her personal life. Paul visits Bill at home as he wants to know how he stands on the forthcoming vote. Mary tackles David about his position on the vote. Jenny shocks Ted by declaring that she is for the takeover bid.

Guest Cast: CARLETON HOBBS (Sir Neville Henniswode)

Directed by PHILIP DUDLEY

73. THE DEVIL YOU KNOW by Brian Finch

Studio recording: 26th February 1976

Broadcast: Sunday 28th March 1976 at 7.25pm, BBC 1

Running length: 49'45"

Ted has been sent to Stockholm to buy some lorries, but Jennifer is worried that he won't be back in time for the Kirkman vote. Clare hands in her resignation to Paul and he is unable to talk her out of it. Merroney pays a visit to Mary in order to gain her support and drops a heavy hint as to who might be informing Kirkman's. Brian and Jane mull over the reason for Clare's resignation. Mary pays Gwen a visit. Merroney meanwhile delivers an alternative viewpoint of life under Kirkman's in order to influence Jane's vote. Bill has the Managing Directors job dangled before him. The board take the vote for accepting Kirkman's bid. Paul persuades Clare not to leave. Mary receives a flowers as thanks for her 'unholy alliance'.

Guest Cast: CARLETON HOBBS (Sir Neville Henniswode)

Directed by TIMOTHY COMBE

74. TRY, TRY AGAIN by Ray Jenkins

Studio recording: 11th March 1976

Broadcast: Sunday 4th April 1976 at 7.25pm, BBC 1

Running length: 46'40"

Mary has a mysterious appointment. Ted and Brian discuss merging with Dutch firm Van der Merwe. Van der Merwe himself is in London, so the brothers decide to try and sound him out in secret. Mary is shown around Gwen's dream house. Mary offers the money she needs but first they have to persuade Bill. Ted and Brian meet with Christian and put forward their ideas for talks between the two firms. The offer for talks is rejected, but Paul Merroney is annoyed that the Hammonds have gone about things in an unprepared fashion. He makes his own approach to Van der Merwe in the hope of rectifying the situation. Bill can see how much the house means to Gwen but he cannot commit to Mary's offer. Merroney persuades Sir Neville the financial risk is worth taking with Van der Merwe.

Guest Cast: CARLETON HOBBS (Sir Neville Henniswode) JOBY BLANSHARD (Van Der Merwe) CARMEN SAUTOY (Ika) VERNON NESBETH (Ogun)

Directed by CHRISTOPHER BAKER

75. THE BONUS by Ray Jenkins
Studio recording: 25th March 1976
Broadcast: Sunday 11th April 1976 at 7.25pm, BBC 1
Running length: 50'02"
Merroney takes a private flight to Amsterdam for secret talks with Van der Merwe. Clare is instructed not to reveal his whereabouts. Merroney gets a hair-raising trip from the airport by Christian's daughter Ika. Sir Neville fends off questions from David and Mary about Merroney's plans. Jane discovers Paul's whereabouts. The arrival of April Winter at the Hammond offices causes Clare some distress. Christian tells Paul about an hidden asset which Hammond's will inherit as part of the merger. When Paul discovers his deception has been discovered back in the UK, he seeks to return immediately. Edward is awaiting his arrival back at the airfield. Paul also drops the bombshell to Clare that April Winter is his fiancé. At a board meeting Paul outlines his plans for merging with Van der Merwe. He intends to put it before a Special General Meeting of the shareholders. Clare stuns the meeting by announcing her resignation.
Guest Cast: LIZA GODDARD (April Winter) CARLETON HOBBS (Sir Neville Henniswode) JOBY BLANSHARD (Van Der Merwe) CARMEN SAUTOY (Ika)
Directed by TIMOTHY COMBE

76. BIRTHDAY by Ray Jenkins
Studio recording: 8th April 1976
Broadcast: Sunday 18th April 1976 at 7.25pm, BBC 1
Running length: 49'44"
Paul tries to get Clare to stay. Later at the pub Clare is clearly upset. Mary is also upset about the boards merger decision. Clare tries to explain her actions to David. Mary arrives at the Rileys, and Bill agrees to accept her loan. But Mary has other reasons for calling. Christian instructs Paul to put a stop to his daughters romantic pursuits. At Mary's birthday party the host is determined to have her say about the merger. Paul is brutal delivering the news to Ika. At the SGM, Kirkman's representative tries to derail the proceedings as does Mary. The brothers are requested to keep her in line. Clare types out her resignation in the deserted offices. Sir Neville hints at his successor at the bank. Following news that the Dutch company have voted in favour, the SGM vote is taken, and is carried. Hammond's will merge with Van der Merwe.
Guest Cast: CARLETON HOBBS (Sir Neville Henniswode) JOBY BLANSHARD (Van Der Merwe) CARMEN SAUTOY (Ika) WILLIAM MERROW (Uncle Willi) STEVE UBELS (Paul Van Kepe) MICHAEL SPICE (David Gosper)
Directed by CHRISTOPHER BAKER

1976 - SERIES SEVEN
Regular cast:
JEAN ANDERSON (Mary Hammond) PATRICK O'CONNELL (Edward Hammond) RICHARD EASTON (Brian Hammond) ROBIN CHADWICK (David Hammond) JENNIFER WILSON (Jennifer Hammond) DEREK BENFIELD (Bill Riley) MARGARET ASHCROFT (Gwen Riley) COLIN BAKER (Paul Merroney) KATE O'MARA (Jane Maxwell) LIZA GODDARD (April Merroney)
Producer BILL SELLARS Executive Producer KEN RIDDINGTON Script Editor CICELY CAWTHORNE

Liza Goddard does not appear in episode 92

77. TO HONOUR AND OBEY by Ray Jenkins
Studio recording 20th May 1976
Broadcast: Sunday 5th September 1976 at 7.25pm, BBC 1
Running length: 50'41"
It's Paul's wedding day, Brian as best man is charged with getting him to the church. Lord Winter admits to finding his new son-in-law dull. News on the ailing Sir Neville is not good. Paul confides in Brian that Sir Neville has been a second father to him. He also fears he will lose the race to be Sir Neville's successor. Although Sir Neville has been refused visitors, Paul reasons he will see Mary and tries his best to get Mary as his messenger. Late for the wedding, Jenny knocks a cyclist off his bike with the car. The boy's father intends to press charges for dangerous driving. Simon Winter tells Van der Merwe that Paul will never again be the favourite son at the bank. April delivers the news that Sir Neville has only hours to live.
Guest Cast: JOBY BLANSHARD (Van Der Merwe) ANTHONY NICHOLLS (Lord Winter) TERENCE FRISBY (Simon Winter) STANLEY LEBOR (Faulkner) GARY FAIRHALL (Boy with bicycle) MARJORIE WILDE (Sir Neville's housekeeper)
Directed by TIMOTHY COMBE

78. HOME AND AWAY by Ray Jenkins
Studio recording: 4th June 1976
Broadcast: Sunday 12th September 1976 at 7.25pm, BBC 1
Running length: 52'14"
Jenny helps Ted pack for his three week business course, despite her worry about the driving charges. Mary makes a phone call but hangs up when a voice answers at the other end. Jane lobbies for more aircraft. Over lunch Mary tells Jenny that she has had a letter from her grand-daughter Carol. She wants to visit and to see her father. Mary is concerned about Brian's affair with Jane and how it may look to Carol. At the business course, Edward displays his fears for the way his company is going and his ability to understand it. Carol arrives at Mary's and is far more mature than she is prepared for. David takes April to lunch in Paul's absence. Bill reveals that they have lost the house they had put in an offer for. Jane pitches her request for new aircraft and expansion of the airfield to Paul and Christian. Ann Hammond turns up at Ted's business course. Jane is furious that her proposal has been turned down. Gwen is understandably upset, she is at a crossroads in her life. Jane is defensive at the board meeting, especially when Brian has to put a realistic viewpoint. David however is backing Jane's plans. Carol arrives at the depot to see Brian and meets Jane. Back at Mary's Brian is shocked by another visitor.
Guest Cast: HILARY TINDALL (Ann Hammond) JOBY BLANSHARD (Van Der Merwe) DEBBIE FARRINGTON (Carol Hammond) JEFFREY WICKHAM (Lorrimer) DENNIS EDWARDS (George Bannerman) ANDREW LODGE, WILLIE PAYNE (Course members)
Directed by MARY RIDGE

79. INVITATIONS by Ray Jenkins
Studio recordings: 16th & 17th June 1976
Broadcast: Sunday 19th September 1976 at 7.25pm, BBC 1
Running Length: 49'55"
Brian is uneasy at Ann's arrival. She is eager to know Brian's plans for the future. Gwen gets up in the middle of the night and starts stripping the wallpaper. Brian and Ann row about Carol, Mary tells them to row elsewhere. David sees an opportunity and involves Jane in his scheme. They go to Henley to visit Ted to discuss his ideas. Gwen has got the bit between her teeth with big plans to give her house a make-over. April is busy planning a flat warming party. Her brother Simon arrives with news of a disappointment for

Paul over the finance he is after. Ann and Carol continue to be at loggerheads. Ann confides in Mary her own inadequacies. Jane wonders where her and Brian stand. During another argument with Brian, Ann finds herself talking to Jane on the phone. April would rather David kept Simon away from Paul during the party. Ann turns up at the airfield to confront Jane. David admits he cannot sell Van der Merwe's left hand drive trucks in the UK. He offers an alternative solution which averts a clash between Paul and Simon. Jane cannot agree to what Ann is asking.
Guest Cast: HILARY TINDALL (Ann Hammond) DEBBIE FARRINGTON (Carol Hammond)
TERENCE FRISBY (Simon Winter) CAROLINE LANGRISHE (Lynn) RAYMOND LLEWELLYN (Man at party)
Directed by TIMOTHY COMBE

80. THE FEMALE OF THE SPECIES by Brian Finch
Studio recordings: 30th June 1976 & 1st July 1976
Broadcast: Sunday 26th September 1976 at 7.25pm, BBC 1
Running Length: 50'27"
Jenny is on her way to the airport, she is flying to Canada to see Barbara. Carol is coming to stay for a few days again with Mary. Paul is off on another business trip to Amsterdam. David tells Jane that he feels there is an imbalance between the two merged companies. A bored April turns up at the depot, Ted takes her for lunch. Ann calls Mary, she has no idea that Carol has come to visit. April has invited Ted to dinner as they are both alone for the evening. Ted reveals what he has learned about himself and also the difficulties in his marriage. After helping at a playgroup, Gwen has ideas for a future. Jane spends the day with Carol whilst Ann and Brian try to figure out what to do about her. Brian thinks he is being used as a lever by Carol to get rid of her mother's boyfriend. Carol and Ann leave having reached an understanding. Jane refuses Brian's offer of dinner. She has other plans.
Guest Cast: HILARY TINDALL (Ann Hammond) DEBBIE FARRINGTON (Carol Hammond)
Directed by MARY RIDGE

81. MANOEUVRES by Brian Finch
Studio recording: 14th & 15th July 1976
Broadcast: Sunday 3rd October 1976 7.25pm, BBC 1
Running length: 49'26"
David and Jane talk at the airfield. They have a scheme together which must be kept secret for the time being. David meets with Simon Winter asking for the banks blessing for his independent project. Jenny returns from Canada with news of Barbara and Johnny. Gwen tells Bill of her new plans for her own play group. During supper, Simon drops hints to Paul about the C41 scheme making him suspicious. Jane then gets wind that Paul has suddenly shown interest in the C41 project again. Paul visits Simon and puts a spoke in the works for David and Jane. Jennifer finds out that Ted and April had supper together whilst she was away. Brian tackles Merroney about his part in David and Jane's failure. During a family meeting where David appeals for family unity, Brian is very much opposed to the C41 project. Brian appeals to Paul to reconsider the project as a Hammond concern for the sake of the company.
Guest Cast: TERENCE FRISBY (Simon Winter) JUDITH FIELDING (Beryl)
Directed by TIMOTHY COMBE

82. ARRIVALS AND DEPARTURES by Elaine Morgan
Studio recording: 28th & 29th July 1976
Broadcast: Sunday 10th October 1976 at 7.25pm, BBC 1
Running length: 50'02"

Paul Merroney's new secretary Miss Vickery finds that working for her new employer is a bigger challenge than she was expecting. Mary is feeling quite unwell, she turns to Gwen for help. Jane finds that the locals are objecting to the airfield expansion plans. Brian and David argue about who should stay at home and look after their mother. Paul is about to fly away on business when April receives some terrible news. Paul's reaction shocks her. Mary is not pleased that Brian and David are looking after her under sufferance. Jane and Brian have a meal together as they attempt mend bridges. Miss Vickery tells Ted that a Mrs. Merroney needs pick up from the train station. Ted finds a rather different Mrs. Merroney to the one he is expecting...

Guest Cast: NORAH FULTON (Mrs. Merroney) CHRISTINE ABSALOM (Judy Vickery) ROBERT BLYTHE (Marsh) BRENDA LAWRENCE (Fiona) LEWIS WILSON (Dr. Johnstone)

Directed by MARY RIDGE

83. THE DISTAFF SIDE by Elaine Morgan

Studio recording: 11th & 12 August 1976

Broadcast: Sunday 17th October 1976 at 7.25pm, BBC 1

Running length: 48'59"

David drives Mary to stay with a friend in Buckinghamshire to convalesce, Brian tells him not to hurry back as he wants the house to entertain Jane. Ted and Brian wonder what they are going to do with Paul's Mum. Both Paul and April are out of town. Gwen arrives to take Mrs. Merroney to stay with them. Paul arrives back from Beirut early, much to Miss Vickery's surprise. April rushes around to Gwen's to take charge of Mrs. Merroney. April is still annoyed with Paul but Mrs. Merroney puts her right about family loyalties. Jenny disapproves of Jane's burgeoning relationship with Brian. Merroney calls a board meeting. David is delayed by a spare tyre. Merroney announces a letter of resignation from David. Jane has to confess that the planning office have not yet passed plans for the airfield expansion. Jenny spies on Jane and sees her leaving with another brother.

Guest Cast: NORAH FULTON (Mrs. Merroney) CHRISTINE ABSALOM (Judy Vickery) ROBERT BLYTHE (Marsh) PHILIP JACKSON (Garageman)

Directed by CHRISTOPHER BAKER

84. CROSS CURRENTS by Elaine Morgan

Studio recording: 25th & 26th August 1976

Broadcast: Sunday 24th October 1976 at 7.25pm, BBC 1

Running length: 49'48"

Mary is back from her trip. Ted and Jenny are at loggerheads, the subjects of April and Jane are raised again. April accuses Paul of "cheque book diplomacy" when finding a place for his mother to live. The next morning April tells Paul he should be taking his mother to the station rather than going to work.

Brian decides to balance the pros and cons for the Tehran project. Jane receives a visit from one of the protest committee. Paul comes up with a solution to Jane's problem, but as ever it comes with strings attached. Paul dispenses with Miss Vickery's services. Jenny is growing increasingly paranoid about Ted's whereabouts. On a visit to Mary she blurts out that Jane is involved in a ménage à trios with David and Brian.

Guest Cast: NORAH FULTON (Mrs. Merroney) ROBERT BLYTHE (Marsh) CHRISTINE ABSALOM (Judy Vickery) MITZI ROGERS (Mrs. Preston)

Directed by MARY RIDGE

85. RIPPLES by Brian Finch
Studio recording: 9th September 1976
Broadcast: Sunday 31st October 1976 at 7.25pm, bbc 1
Running length: 48'52"
Gwen detects something is wrong with Mary. Ted is back from his trip but has time away helped his marriage? Mary spills the beans to Gwen about what is bothering her. Merroney interviews Miss Dawes, a potential new secretary, whose cold and efficient manner is the equal of Merroney. Mary wants Ted to intercede in the 'Maxwell affair' but he refuses. Jane interviews Chris Felton, she needs a pilot to fly the C41's expected shortly. Ted is furious at Jenny's indiscretion. Mary turns up at the depot and has stern words for Jane Maxwell. Then she tells Brian of Jane's deception. It causes friction between *The Brothers*. Jane agrees to Merroney's terms. At the board meeting, to everyone's surprise, Paul suggests a deputation be sent to Tehran to find out more information before a vote can be taken.
Guest Cast: AMANDA BOXER (Julia Dawes) VINCENT MARZELLO (Chris Felton)
Directed by CHRISTOPHER BAKER

86. CELEBRATION by Brian Finch
Studio recording: 23rd September 1976
Broadcast: Sunday 7th November 1976 at 7.25pm, BBC 1
Running length: 49'05"
Bill and Brian are off to Tehran to prepare a report for the merged companies. The Dutch representative is Paul Van Kepe. Jane is excited at the prospect of the arrival of the C41 planes, she decides to throw a party to celebrate. Mary worries about David. Paul arrives at the flat with Van Kepe, he will be staying the night which annoys April. Jenny has word of her court date over the accident. Merroney instructs Van Kepe on how to deal with Brian's objections in Tehran. Paul is called to Amsterdam on business. Jenny reveals to Ted just what has been eating at her all day. April attends Jane's party with Van Kepe. Merroney arrives during the evening with dire news.
Guest Cast: STEVE UBELS (Paul Van Kepe) BRIAN HAUGHTON, CY TOWN (Guest at party)
Directed by MARY RIDGE

87. WINDMILLS by Brian Finch
Studio recording: 7th October 1976
Broadcast: Sunday 14th November 1976 at 7.25pm, BBC 1
Running length: 49'31"
Two weeks on and Jane is still tortured by the missing plane and its pilot. Jenny is understandably nervous as she prepares to go to court. David buys Jane some perfume, he is increasingly drawn to her. The insurance investigator Harvey McKay arrives with some reservations. Mary invites Jane to her house, her reason remains unclear. Paul calls Jane to account for her actions hiring the pilots for the C41's. It seems one of them is not who he claimed to be. The two Paul's have an uneasy dinner at the flat. Mary asks Jane if she is in love with David. And she also asks her to turn down any marriage proposal. Van Kepe wonders if he is being used by April in her battle of wits with Merroney. Paul informs Jane that thanks to him everything should be alright with the insurance claim, but in return he needs her vote. Brian however tells Jane that the insurers would pay anyway. She has been conned.
Guest Cast: STEVE UBELS (Paul Van Kepe) MICHAEL SHEARD (Harvey McKay)
Directed by CHRISTOPHER BAKER

88. THE GOLDEN ROAD by Brian Finch

Studio recording: 21st October 1976
Broadcast: Sunday 21st November 1976 at 7.25pm, BBC 1
Running length: 50'05"

Jane has a puncture as she sets out to work, Brian gallantly steps in to help her. Brian uses the opportunity to sway her vote. Paul goes to work on Bill and then dangles a rather large carrot before David. Jane confronts Paul about his claims regarding the insurance claim, she declares any alliances are off. Gwen confesses to Bill she has sent their son Ronnie £25 to help him out as a student. Paul calls on Bill to accompany him to see Ted and Jenny. Meanwhile April has been stood up for dinner. Jane refuses David's offer of marriage, telling him they can only be friends. Ted remains steadfast against the Middle East scheme. Jane breaks both good news and bad news to Brian. Ted advises David to move back in with Mary. Brian however informs David that he doesn't stand a chance up against Van Kepe for the top job in the Middle East. The vote is taken. Despite Brian's protest the scheme goes through.
Guest Cast: GRAHAM KENNEDY (Delivery boy)
Directed by MARY RIDGE

89. OUT OF THE BLUE by N.J. Crisp

Studio recording: 4th November 1976
Broadcast: Sunday 28th November 1976 at 7.25pm, BBC 1
Running length: 49'25"

Barbara lands back in the UK unbeknown to the family. David makes efforts to move back in with Mary, but she refuses. Jenny is equally surprised and delighted to see her daughter. Brian is concerned about Hammond finances with new projects being discussed by the merged companies. He feels Paul is rushing through the Tehran project to the tune of £500,000. He insists Paul refers the commitment back to the Hammond board. Barbara is evasive over her reasons for Johnny not accompanying her. Edward gets word that an illegal immigration racket is being operated from the continent and all haulage firms are being investigated. April is getting fed up of being ignored by Paul. They have had an invitation to Barbados for Christmas by Rex Burton-Smithers, an old flame of April's. Paul is dismissive, he hasn't got the time. But April is determined to go. Gwen isn't thrilled that Bill will be going undercover to Holland. Brian reveals the major skeleton in the Hammond's closet to Jane. Paul finds the finance he is after from the bank won't be forthcoming. He suggests to the board a Rights Issue to raise the finance. But this puts the Hammond family dominance of the company into question.
Guest Cast: JULIA GOODMAN (Barbara Trent) ANTHONY NICHOLLS (Lord Charles Winter) STEVE UBELS (Paul Van Kepe) JOHN PULLEN (Det. Chief Inspector) JOHNNY WADE (Taxi driver)
Directed by CHRISTOPHER BAKER

90. THE KNOCK ON THE DOOR by N.J. Crisp

Studio recording: 20th November 1976
Broadcast: Sunday 5th December 1976 at 7.25pm, BBC 1
Running length: 50'21"

The Rights Issue is causing much consternation and debate among the directors. Jane doubts that Mary has accepted Jennifer, she feels it is a mask. Paul appeals to Lord Winter for help in getting April to change her mind about going to Barbados without him. Barbara questions Brian about his marriage troubles. Paul tries to talk to April at the riding stables, but she is cold and resolute. On the ferry Jenny spots Bill but he is undercover and wants it to stay that way. He pals up with a fellow driver in an attempt to get information.

April tells Paul not to use her father in their disagreements. Mary summons her sons for a meeting about the Rights Issue. She is angry that the Hammond holding will be reduced to 34%. Gwen receives a late visit from the police with some terrible news.

Guest Cast: JULIA GOODMAN (Barbara Trent) ANTHONY NICHOLLS (Lord Winter) RICHARD BORTHWICK (Policeman) PETER BLAKE (Scotsman)

Directed by MARY RIDGE

91. THE ORDEAL by N.J. Crisp

Studio recording: 2nd December 1976
Broadcast: Sunday 12th December 1976 at 7.25pm, BBC 1
Running length: 49'04"

Gwen has rushed to the hospital where her son Ronnie is in a bad way. She phones Ted in order to contact Bill in Holland. Nobody seems to know where he is. Mary arrives at the hospital to support Gwen. April tells her father that she has changed her plans for Barbados, she is flying out as soon as possible. David admits his affair with Julie Lane to Barbara. Bill finally arrives home and Gwen admits how bad the accident is and what it may mean for the future. Plans are in place for the forthcoming Christmas party and Jennifer is tasked with supervising it. Jane advises Brian to watch his drinking if they are to make a go of it together. The doctor tells Bill that there is every chance that Ronnie will be paralysed from the waist down. As April departs for Barbados, she and Paul have one last frosty conversation during which she delivers some home truths.

Guest cast: JULIA GOODMAN (Barbara Trent) ANTHONY NICHOLLS (Lord Charles Winter) ROBIN LANGFORD (Ronald Riley) PENELOPE HORNER (Dr. Wincott)

Directed by CHRISTOPHER BAKER

92. THE CHRISTMAS PARTY by N.J. Crisp

Studio recording: 16th December 1976
Broadcast: Sunday 19th December 1976 at 7.25pm, BBC 1
Running length: 51'33"

Barbara admits to her mother that Johnny had an affair and that is why she has come home. Ronnie is determined to go to the medical rehabilitation centre to help his condition. Jenny reveals the cracks in her marriage to Barbara. Ted warns Paul over trying to change the name of the company. Barbara makes the decision to return to Canada to give her marriage another chance. Brian advises Paul to follow April to Barbados. He decides to call April but at the last minute he ducks out of speaking to her. Brian and Jane kiss under the mistletoe. They agree to get married. Mary is determined to speak her mind to Paul before they depart. Ted and Jenny are going to spend Christmas in Austria, to see if their marriage can survive.

Guest Cast: JULIA GOODMAN (Barbara Trent) ROBIN LANGFORD (Ronald Riley) PENELOPE HORNER (Doctor Wincott) SALLY LEWIS, EVGENY GRIDNEFF, MAX MASON, BERNIE SEARL (People at party)

Directed by MARY RIDGE

Paul Merroney signeert de nieuwe kerstelpee van de Hammonds

Kom dat beleven bij Caminada morgen 4-5 uur

De Hammonds nu ook op een klankrijke kerstelpee met onvergetelijke melodieën. Vers van de pers bij Caminada. Een unieke Philipsplaat. Die moet u beslist kopen. En laten voorzien van een handtekening van Paul Merroney himself. Hij is er maar even. Alleen morgen van 4-5 uur Haastige spoed is daarom zeker geboden.

20.25

caminada
een plaat
van een zaak.

WHATEVER HAPPENED TO THE BROTHERS?

JEAN ANDERSON continued to work well into her 90s. It would be some years before she found another television role which captured the public imagination. Again for producer Ken Riddington she created the role of Joss Holbrook in the second and third series of *Tenko* (1982-84). Jean continued as a working actress appearing in roles in such prominent series as *Keeping Up Appearances*, *The House Of Elliot*, *Trainer* and *Inspector Morse*. Jean's final screen appearance was in Samuel Beckett's *Endgame*. She died in her adopted Cumbria, aged 93 in 2001.
Number of Brothers episodes: 92

RICHARD EASTON continued acting establishing himself as one of the great names of British and American theatre. Whilst in the UK he worked sporadically in television and film including *Doctor Who: Time Flight*, *The Brief* and Kenneth Branagh's *Henry V*. A move to America proved advantageous when he won a Tony Award for his Broadway performance in *The Invention Of Love*. Easton worked solidly on Broadway. Most notably his productions have included *The Rivals*, *The Coast Of Utopia* and Duncan in *Macbeth*. He has also managed a spate of appearances on American TV: the title role in *Benjamin Franklin*, *Law & Order: Special Victims Unit*, *Mildred Pierce* and *Boardwalk Empire*.   Richard passed away on 2nd December 2019,
Number of Brothers episodes: 85

ROBIN CHADWICK (b. 1939) continued with theatre roles, but eventually moved to America and carved out a niche in American theatre. His Broadway productions have included *The Circle* and *Shadowlands*. In addition Robin has played many Shakespearean roles and Ebaneezar Scrooge in several productions of *A Christmas Carol*. He is now retired and living in New Jersey with his wife Susan.
Number of Brothers episodes: 92

JENNIFER WILSON (b. 1932) returned to the theatre following the end of *The Brothers*. She toured in a huge amount of plays before leaving to live in France during the 1990s. Ten years later she returned to the UK to resume her acting career and found guest roles in television series such as *Last Of The Summer Wine*, *Casualty*, *Doctors* and *Coronation Street*. On stage she found herself appearing in Agatha Christie's *The Mousetrap* in the West End and Agatha Christie's *Witness For The Prosecution*. With her husband Brian, she is now back in the south of France once more, enjoying a sunny retirement.
Number of Brothers episodes: 92

GLYN OWEN went on to become a stalwart guest actor in numerous television series. He found his last great television role once again for Gerry Glaister in Howards' Way playing Jack Rolfe, the owner of the Mermaid boat yard. The show ran for 78 episodes between 1985 – 1990. Glyn even released a record "I Wish I Could Love You Again" in character written by Simon May. His last screen role was in the movie Pandemonium (2000). Glyn passed away on 10th September 2004, aged 76.
Number of Brothers episodes: 10

PATRICK O'CONNELL continued acting and painting. He was in the production of *Loot* with Leonard Rossiter during which the comedian died in his dressing room. He found a regular role in the wartime series *We'll Meet Again* playing pub landlord Jack Blair for ITV.   In the late 1990s Patrick retired from acting and public life. He passed away aged 83 on 10th August 2017.
Number of Brothers episodes: 81

DEREK BENFIELD toured in his own play *Caught On The Hop* immediately following the end of *The Brothers*, co-starring with Margaret Ashcroft and Richard Easton. Television guest roles followed including *Hi-de-Hi!*, *First Of The Summer Wine* and *Poirot*. He also scored a regular role as Patricia Routledge's husband in *Hetty Wainthropp Investigates*. As a playwright his plays continue to be performed at theatres around the world. Derek passed away on 10th March 2009 aged 82.
Number of Brothers episodes: 89

HILARY TINDALL left the show to perform in theatre. Her productions are many and varied and include *A Little Night Music*, *The Owl And The Pussycat*, *The Heiress* and a season in the West End in N.J. Crisp's thriller *Dangerous Obsession*. Hilary also made some notable television appearances in the Swedish serial *The Ship Builder*. Her UK screen work includes *Tropic*, *Nice Work*, *Tales Of The Unexpected*, the mini-series *A Kind Of Loving* and *Poirot*. She passed away aged just 52 on 5th December 1992.
Number of Brothers episodes: 48

JULIA GOODMAN (b. 1951) appeared in a wide range of television series after she left *The Brothers*. Among them were the spy drama *The Lotus Eaters*, *Chalk And Cheese*, *Fanny By Gaslight*, *Kelly Monteith*, *Gems*, *Grange Hill*, *Inspector Morse*, *Coronation Street* and *The Bill*. Julia was a founder member of the British Actors Theatre Company along with Kate O'Mara and Peter Woodward. In 1989 she started Personal Presentation, a hugely successful company dedicated to training professionals with skills of presentation and confidence in the corporate and business sector.
Number of Brothers episodes: 35

GABRIELLE DRAKE (b. 1944) remains a much in demand actress in theatre and on television. She appeared with comedian Kelly Monteith in his highly rated BBC series, and then as Nicola Freeman in *Crossroads*. A wide array of guest roles in many high rating series have followed including *Peak Practice*, *The Inspector Lynley Mysteries*, *The Royal*, *Coronation Street* and *Doctors*. In addition Gabrielle's theatre work has included *Lady Windermere's Fan*, *Loot*, *The Rivals* and Lady Bracknell in *The Importance Of Being Earnest*. She has also published a book in tribute to her brother Nick Drake.
Number of Brothers episodes: 39

MARGARET ASHCROFT continued as a jobbing actress following her role as Gwen Riley. She performed with the Royal Shakespeare Company in *The Bundle* soon after *The Brothers* finished. Other theatre productions included Agatha Christie's *Cards On The Table*, *The Killing Of Sister George* and Alan Ayckbourn's *Seasons Greetings* in Stockholm. Maggie reunited with Colin Baker on stage in a summer season of the comedy *Not Now Darling*. Although Maggie was never again to find a high profile television role like Gwen, she gave memorable performances in *The Bill*, *McCallum* and *Heartbeat*. Margaret was incapacitated by a stroke which ended her career, she passed away on 25th October 2016 aged 85.
Number of Brothers episodes: 45

COLIN BAKER (b.1943) went on to become the Sixth Doctor in *Doctor Who*, a role which made him famous worldwide. He continues to play the role in audio plays. In addition he has been seen in many television series including *Blake's 7*, *Jonathan Creek*, *Doctors* and as a contestant in *I'm A Celebrity Get Me Out Of Here*. Colin has also appeared in numerous theatre productions encompassing plays, pantomimes, musicals and light opera. He continues to tour the world appearing at Doctor Who conventions.
Number of Brothers episodes: 46

CAROLE MOWLAM continued finding work in *Coronation Street* shortly after the series finished and in the West End opposite Richard Todd in *The Business Of Murder* and on tour in Francis Durbridge's *The Small Hours*. With her husband Antony Rouse she adopted two children and only worked sporadically during their upbringing. Carole sadly passed away on 14th April 2015, aged 75.
Number of Brothers episodes: 26

KATE O'MARA went from strength to strength following the demise of *The Brothers*. She played similar strong ladies inlcuding Katherine Laker in *Triangle*, Caress Morell in *Dynasty* and Laura Wilde in *Howards' Way*. Guest roles have included a reunion with Colin Baker in *Doctor Who: Mark Of The Rani*, *Absolutely Fabulous*, *Bad Girls* and *Benidorm*. She ran her own theatre company which staged many Shakespeare productions and classical plays often with Kate acting, managing and helping put up the set! Following the tragic suicide of her son Dickon, Kate lost her battle with cancer on 30th March 2014 aged 74.
Number of Brothers episodes: 36

LIZA GODDARD (b. 1950) continues to be a busy actress on stage and in television. She is particularly remembered for the popular children's series *Woof* and as Phillipa Vale in *Bergerac* as well as a team captain in the ITV charades quiz *Give Us A Clue*. Liza has appeared extensively in theatre in productions such as *Blithe Spirit*, *The Importance Of Being Earnest*, Alan Bennett's *Single Spies* and reunited with Colin Baker in *She Stoops To Conquer*.
Number of Brothers episodes: 16

GERARD GLAISTER would go on to create and produce some of the most popular prime-time television screened by the BBC during the 1970s and 80s. His hugely successful wartime escape saga Colditz ran for two seasons. Other series he created included *Oil Strike North* centered around the team on a oil rig, *Secret Army* a series about the French Resistance in World War 2 (which was famously lampooned in *'Allo 'Allo*) and its post war sequel *Kessler*. *The Fourth Arm* returned to a wartime setting as a group of special agents attempt to destroy a Nazi missile factory. One of Glaister's biggest successes was *Howards' Way*, a glossy Sunday night serial set around the Mermaid Boatyard, which had many parallels with *The Brothers*. His final serial for the BBC was a horse racing saga *Trainer*. Gerry passed away on 5th February 2005, aged 85.

NORMAN "N.J." CRISP eventually wrote 36 episodes of *The Brothers*. As co-creator he was also responsible for much of the character development and story-lining ideas. He continued to write for television with episodes of *Spy Trap*, *Colditz*, *Oil Strike North*, *Secret Army*, *Enemy At The Door* and creating the series *A Family Affair* and *Buccaneer*, about an air freight business. Crisp penned the television movie *Sherlock Holmes And The Masks Of Death* starring Peter Cushing. He wrote several successful plays, two of which *Fighting Chance* and *Dangerous Obsession* had lengthy West End runs. He was a novelist of note too and his books include *The Odd Job Man*, *In The Long Run*, *The London Deal* and *Ninth Circle*. Norman passed away on 14th June 2005, aged 81.

ACKNOWLEDGEMENTS:

I'd like to thank the following people without whom this book simply could not have happened:

Samantha Blake at the BBC Written Archive Centre, Christine Absalom, Annette Andre-Weingarten, Robin Chadwick, Liza Goddard, Sarah Grazebrook. Margot Hayhoe, Jonathan Newth, Francoise Pascal, Hannah Page at Simply Media, Brian Peck, Meron Roberts (the Lynn to my Alan Partridge), Kate Slesinger (Hilary Tindall's daughter), Steve Ubels, Douglas Watkinson, Frances Wilson (Jennifer Wilson's daughter), the estate of Norman Crisp. A big shout out to Ian Fraser for his brilliant cover design.

Extra special thanks to Colin Baker and Jennifer Wilson for opening up their archives and answering my barrage of questions, with such good grace, about events nearly five decades ago. You are both diamonds. Have a drink on me!

The Brothers is available on DVD from Simply Media. **www.simplyhe.com**

Printed in Great Britain
by Amazon

48409904R00084